CLASSICAL GREECE AND THE POETRY

OF

CHENIER, SHELLEY, AND LEOPARDI

Classical Greece and the Poetry of Chenier, Shelley, and Leopardi

STEPHEN ROGERS

UNIVERSITY OF NOTRE DAME PRESS

NOTRE DAME   LONDON

Library of Congress Cataloging in Publication Data

Rogers, Stephen.
　Classical Greece and the poetry of Chénier, Shelley, and
Leopardi.

　Bibliography: p.
　1. Poetry, Modern—History and criticism.
2. Literature, Comparative—Greek and European.
3. Literature, Comparative—European and Greek.
4. Romanticism.　I. Title.
PN1126.R64　　　809.1　　　79-85350
ISBN 0-268-00503-6

　Manufactured in the United States of America

TO DANA

Contents

Preface

The idea that ancient Greece was itself a myth to Chénier, Shelley, and Leopardi was not a preconception which I brought to this work. That argument occurred to me only after my study of the poetry and its relation to Greek culture was mainly complete. The notion of myth as I sketch it in the introduction developed along with the writing of this book, but on different tracks. Then, while I was seeking a way to communicate the unity I felt in these studies, in fact, one evening as I tried to escape my dissatisfaction with the wearisome term "vision of Greece," two layers of thought met and suddenly recognized each other. I knew that for these poets Greece had the force and value of a myth. It behaved in their thought as myth does. It organized their poetry and endowed it with life. It shaped their conceptions of themselves, of history, of mankind, of the natural world, and of God, as myth does. I have therefore built the introduction around a notion of the symptoms which generally appear where myth is present. It has seemed unnecessary to insist on any one theory of myth or to reiterate my thesis throughout the chapters that follow. The introduction stands as a measure of the unity that runs through the whole.

Translations not assigned in notes are mine, of course. Though I might often have found better ones, I chose to risk my own because they frequently reflect my understanding of the passage in question in a way that could not be conveyed equally well otherwise.

To Irving Babbitt's *New Laokoon* I am more indebted than would appear from the notes, for it was that book which led me to the attitude I finally adopted toward Shelley's Platonism, though my view of romanticism is hardly the same as Babbitt's.

I am happy to acknowledge the abundant help I have enjoyed. I am grateful to the Danforth Foundation for support during the first year of this work. I wish also to thank many others. The late Professor Renato Poggioli planted the first seeds of this task and read Part I with generous care. Professor Dante Della Terza suggested significant revisions in the Leopardi chapters, as did Professor Craig La Driere after his reading of the whole. Professor Harry Levin has offered much kindly guidance and criticism.

But there are others whose contributions I gladly indicate here, though my thanks are all too brief. I mean volunteer readers such as Mrs. Helen Erhardt of South Bend, Indiana, and those of the Catholic Guild for All the Blind in Boston. Margaret Carroll, Mildred O'Toole, Dorothy Pedersen, Dorothea Sullivan, Mrs. Lawrence Davis, Mrs. A. Stone Freedburg, Mrs. Judith Laing, Mrs. Henry O'Bryan, and Mrs. George Putnam each read to me regularly during several years, and each one became a unique friend. Mrs. Kellogg Birdseye and Mrs. Brown Patterson helped me transcribe and decipher many pages of Greek during the first year of this project. Alma Dufour brought me cheerfully through innumerable books, especially in French; she taught me a great deal. Readings with Dr. Ruth Clark, emeritus professor of French at Wellesley, were wonderful tutorials in which she shared her great knowledge. Mrs. Margarita Willfort and Mrs. Karel Waigner got me through many hours of both French and German. The Italian readings of Lenore Padula, Teresa Gironi, Julia Gironi, and Mrs. Anna Yona began my acquaintance with that literature and especially with Leopardi. I am especially grateful for the devoted friendship of Helen Clifford, who read to me in both English and French and tirelessly hunted out information at the beginning of these researches. Nor can I fail to single out Brian Dibble and John Hamilton for special mention among my student assistants at Notre Dame.

Above all, my wife Dana has given her help in countless ways through unnumbered and difficult hours, with knowledge, skill, and good-humored patience. Her judgment of argument and style has shaken much chaff from these pages: their accuracy is mostly hers; the mistakes, entirely mine. She has made this possible. All that she has given and done is beyond my telling.

Introduction

The subject of these chapters is the poetry, mainly lyric poetry, of Chénier, Shelley, and Leopardi, who, despite their differences of language and intellect, share the common influence of classical Greece. The lives of these poets stretch throughout the time when European romanticism grew and came to its flowering. This period can be marked from André Chénier's birth in 1762 to the death of Giacomo Leopardi in 1837. Shelley's life, of course, began (1792) about two years before Chénier's execution and ended three decades later when the romantic tide was at the flood, and Leopardi was still in his early twenties. The figure that suggests itself is a large ellipse that broadens where the productive lives of Shelley and Leopardi overlap. Then the major focus falls in 1819. This was not only Shelley's *annus mirabilis* when he finished his *Prometheus Unbound* and other mature poems; not only the year when Leopardi wrote the first of his *Idilli*; it was also the year when Chénier's bucolics and elegies were first published, a quarter of a century after his death. In-

1

deed, it turns out that most of the poems discussed extensively in these studies made their public appearance less than ten years before and scarcely more than fifteen years after this pivotal date.

Though none of these poets knew the others, they all shared a multitude of collective influences. They were men of their time, and to a large extent, sons of the eighteenth century. They all read Rousseau and the *philosophes*. They all felt the pressure which Locke exerted on the mind of the Enlightenment. Each, moreover, knew the languages of the others (Chénier and Shelley both spent important time in Italy, Italy being in this age, as in the Renaissance, a principal funnel through which Greek culture passed into northern Europe). But above all, the shared experience which allows us to consider them together was classical Greece, both as an ideal and as a set of facts.

Classical Greece appeared to the men of our period as a singular union of ideal with fact. Thinkers of the eighteenth century and their romantic successors were passionately interested in letting concrete facts and artifacts communicate to them the feeling of antique value. The age that advanced, if it did not invent, the science of history had its fresh encounters with antiquity mainly through historical inquiries. These, of course, were the discoveries at Herculaneum and Pompeii, the researches into art, and the quests for the historical Homer. The unearthing of the buried cities gave undeniable stimulus to many imaginations, even if archeological results came with frustrating slowness. In France, by the 1780s, statues and murals were appearing in reproductions. Engravings by François Anne David were calling attention to Bacchic and Priapic ceremonies of the ancients, traces of which were being found on the walls of the buried cities.[1] Greek figurines were finding their way into the boudoirs, and under the Directorate, Spartan dress became the fashion.

We sense the Hellenizing mood of the 1780s when we are told that Chénier's youth was surrounded with medals and pictures, and that for a time he may have persuaded himself that he was actually Greek. His mother, having roots in Constantinople, spoke Greek. Her drawing room attracted scholars, artists, statesmen who came to her with a common yen for authentic examples of Hellenic culture; and

Mme Chénier satisfied them by dancing in Grecian attire and by singing. She sang a poem from Anacreon, as one princely traveler related, or a piece about Ariadne abandoned, which she performed so as to give one distinguished Homeric scholar "the delicious impression of a sweet melancholy."[2] In superficial things the taste for the Hellenic increased and spread. It was evident in the literary journeys of Barthélemy's Anacharsis the Younger or in the *Voyages littéraires en Grèce* by Guys, one of Mme Chénier's visitors who, incidentally, mentioned her in his book. Finally, the Greek taste showed up in decoration and architecture, where the rococo was yielding to the "Pompeian," ornateness giving way to greater simplicity of line.[3]

The fashionable interest in Hellenic things did not, of course, popularize the study of Greek language. If anything, that diminished. In Italy the monuments claimed more attention than texts. The language became the province of specialists—of scholars like the distinguished Richard Porson, who created for England an "ideal of finished and exact verbal scholarship"—or the concern of ardent amateurs like Vittorio Alfieri, who taught himself Greek at forty-six and translated the fifth-century dramatists.[4] Even the learned, who were more accustomed to reading the late Greek of the Hellenistic period, often perceived the writers of the fifth and fourth centuries B.C. through a film of Latinity. It was German philology that gave the classics as we know them a central place in European culture.[5]

But those who knew Greek, as well as those who did not, were enthralled, not only by what they made of its message, but also by a nostalgia for the antique. Pope and Boileau had reasoned of content and form. But to our three writers and many others of this time, Greece was a state of mind to be felt. Monuments of Greek poetry and art were not merely sacrosanct (they had been canonical in neoclassical taste and represented the unassailable essences of nature herself); now they were also holy things, still in this world and yet not of it. This is why Keats's *Ode to Psyche* catalogues ancient religious things, why Don Juan has a principal adventure in the isles of Greece, why the Shelleyan heroes love mystic scrolls and ruins. For the same reason Chénier was enslaved to the miniature poems of the Greek Anthology: they were relics of the pagan past. More ancient texts and mythic images produced this effect in Leopardi. Freighted with mysterious culture, antique things brought a wistful sense of a "heaven of time," to borrow a phrase from Shelley. The incense of oldness exhilarated the imagination.

A perfect example of the romantic mood in dynamic relation with neoclassical principles and views is the work of Johann Winckelmann. His love was sculpture, though he knew ancient texts and cited them to support artistic judgments. The ideal, he thought, in which art surpasses nature, must be a composite of individual excellences. Beauty, therefore, is not particular, nor is it a "metaphysical abstraction."[6] It is a concrete universal. But the parts must be related to one another and to the whole in a serene harmony. Such beauty is self-contained, complete, perfectly concentrated inward. It does not scatter itself abroad in distracting reference to the here and now by copying particular people, their actions, and their passions. It contents itself rather with the remembrance of Ajax's frenzy or with the hint of pain to come to Niobe's children. For while actions and passions lend beauty the power "to affect, to persuade, and to convince," these signs of "ethos" or individual character detract from the ideal. Beauty pure and unalloyed stands apart, neither sad nor gay, but perfect and untroubled in the mean.[7]

In the art of the ancient Greeks, the highest expression of this ideal was never-ending youth. We may divine Winckelmann's interpretive mood in his enthusiasm for the *rapprochement* of Greek art and Greek religion:

> To human notions, what attribute could be more suitable to sensual deities, and more fascinating to the imagination, than an eternal youth and spring-time of life, when the very remembrance of youth which has passed away can gladden us in later years? It was conformable to their idea of the immutability of the godlike nature; and a beautiful youthful form in their deities awakened tenderness and love, transporting the soul into that sweet dream of rapture, in which human happiness—the object and aim of all religions, whether well or ill understood—consists.[8]

Greece itself was a place of perfect happiness, and the way back to this "dream of rapture" from the eighteenth century was a sort of imaginative memory, a creative contemplation, that anamnesis which Proust called *souvenir* (the romantics had the idea first). Thus Winckelmann imagined himself in the amphitheater at Athens, watching the statues perform, as if alive, in the Olympic games. He perceived the nature of the Greek hero in works of Greek art. Consequently, he supposed that the hero's disciplined mind must allow only hints and sparks of passion to appear. Winckelmann did not notice that such inferences might arise from necessary limits in sculpture, which requires the interpreter to confer motion and story on a still image. Indeed, Winckelmann's impression of Greek life was unaware of the tragic side, as Walter Pater observed. It forgot the Aeschylean conflicts and the view of Thucydides that civilization, even in the age of Pericles, is a thin veneer which fear and lust for power strip away. Winckelmann's Greece is itself a work of art, an endowing of matter with Appolonian life, "with a soul."[9]

A sketch of Winckelmann's opinions is worth our while for his leading concerns are an outline map to topics we shall encounter in these pages. Moreover, Winckelmann's Greece was a prototype of the Greece of Schiller and Goethe. Is not Schiller's "naive" poetry the effect of direct perception, untroubled by reflection? It was the intuition of spontaneous life and unity of consciousness that roused Goethe's devotion to classical Greece, his "Grecomania."[10] Nature was good to the Greeks, all agreed. In Greece, nature benevolently established herself in the mean, Winckelmann said; therefore "her productions are marked by more regularity of shape."[11] On the people themselves she bestowed her choicest gifts, making them kindly, generous, of a genial disposition, as appears from their avoidance of Roman fierceness in their games, and humane in war, as their truces for festival prove.

In Greece, moreover, it was easy to be learned. Almost everyone believed that. But Winckelmann, like Vico, Chénier, Shelley, Leopardi, imagined that in the best days every Greek was a poet. Vico and Shelley, following Plato, called poets the true prophets and legislators of mankind. Winckelmann, citing Socrates, claimed that artists in the unique Greek world were the wisest of men. There, fostered by good government and encouraged by public attention, the artist had a chance for distinction that has never been equalled; and the superior artist was given the name "godlike."[12]

Shelley catches the spirit of these qualities in his "Discourse on the Manners of the Ancient Greeks Relative to the Subject of Love":

> The firm yet flowing proportion of their forms; the winning unreserve and facility of their manners; the eloquence of their speech, in a language which is itself music and persuasion; their gestures animated at once with the delicacy and the boldness which the perpetual habit of persuading and governing themselves and others; and the poetry of their religious rites, inspired into their whole being—rendered the youth of Greece a race of beings something widely different from that of modern Europe.[13]

Actually, Shelley's immediate purpose was to justify the Greek practice of transferring "sentimental love" to homosexual objects. He ends up with the conclusion that his beloved Greeks, being a race apart, are not subject to ordinary standards. They are, in a sense, above the law or at least above the measures and rules of the present. What is identified with value cannot be evaluated; the measuring rod cannot be measured. Thus Greece itself is different from modern Europe and its history. Greece holds a place apart. It is a sacred realm of once upon a time,[14] and is divided from the here and now as dreams are. This radical separateness, which Winckelmann senses, is what Shelley is driving at in a chorus of *Hellas*. There the fables of the Greeks are remembered as "radiant shapes of sleep," dispelled by the "killing truth" of a new consciousness, in this case Christianity. The same perception Leopardi struggled to utter through a thousand notes on the lost fantasies of the ancients. But Greece, in truth, was not a dream; it was a historical epoch. Though it might refresh the spirit as fantasies do, its remains were words and tangible stones.

This unique normative time was at once a part of history and yet "all breathing human passion far above." History and fable coincided. Man was his diviner self, and yet he was still man. One proof of this is the consensus that during the Greek flowering men walked, as it were, with the gods, as the men of the golden and the heroic age had done. "Of no other epoch in the history of our species have we records and fragments stamped so visibly with the image of the divinity in man."[15]

What Winckelmann saw through the statues and Shelley glimpsed in the manners, Leopardi discerned in the myths of the ancient Greeks. The ancients gave "human qualities to the gods," he believed, because they had loftier notions than we do of "human things" and of life here on earth. "The ancients had so grand an idea of man and the things of man, they set so small an interval between him and divinity, that they judged god and man to be capable of union in a single substance so as to form a single person" (*Zibaldone*, 3494).[16] Chénier, it is true, could be positive in his estimate of modern things. He valued the progress of reason. Like Shelley at some moments, he could distinguish advancing science from the static emotion and retrograde morals of modern life. But he sought to endow modern experience with the clear countenance of ancient forms. Like Wordsworth, he saw a large task which was to confer even on science a poetic humaneness and hence intelligibility. It is more than rhetoric; it is a strong if vague conviction that bids the Muse make Newton speak "language of the gods." Such language is poetic, filled with exalting life. And the first fire and fullest sweetness of such language were to be found with the ancients, especially the Greeks, for they were close to nature, the source of science and poetry alike. The Greek world had worn a countenance of varied divine life, and the religious vacuum, caused by the enlightened assaults upon Christianity, left the shingle of the world bare indeed. Keats was not the only one to lament that divine physiognomy had been drained from the world.

The particular nostalgia of the Hellenists often fastened on Homer. Homer received some of the sentiments which other primitivists attached to Ossian. Chénier's Homer is the primitive and pastoral bard, as we shall see in the first chapter. To Shelley, Homer was even Shakespeare's superior, perfect as he was in the union of sensuous immediacy with clarity of thought.[17] Leopardi's reflections on Homer are even more revealing. To Leopardi, Homer was a literary mystery that endlessly fascinated his speculations and supplied him

with critical standards and with examples of poetic technique. Indeed, after reading through Leopardi's notes on Homer, one feels the
justness of Nello Carini's surmise that to Leopardi Homer was a sort
of god.[18]

   In general for the writers of our period, Homer had the double
status which they gave to Greece itself. He is one example of Schiller's naive poet who, like the deity in the universe, is in his work and
yet concealed behind it: "he is *himself* his work, and his work is *himself*."[19] Thus Homer is involved in the romantic developments of
that Renaissance doctrine which says that the poet is a creator—a
doctrine which Shelley embraced and Leopardi came to adopt.[20]
And by analogy with the method of St. Paul, who found the invisible
things of God revealed in the things that are made, the Reverend
John Keble tried to discern the person of the true Homer through
the evidence of his poems.[21] For if Homer was regarded as a divinity,
he was also the object of concrete historical research, and the latter
two-thirds of the eighteenth century produced a new hypothesis
about the real author of the *Iliad* and the *Odyssey*. Friedrich August
Wolf, influenced by English writers, argued that the Homeric poems
were the fruit of a long oral tradition and were composed in an age
when writing, had it existed, would have been thought a hindrance
rather than a help to poetic invention.[22] As Coleridge summed it up
in 1830, Homer became "a mere concrete name for the rhapsodies
of the *Iliad*."[23] Or, as Vico who really originated the theory said,
"the Greek peoples were themselves Homer"; he was the personification of Greek "poetic wisdom" and "lived on the lips and in the
memories of the peoples of Greece throughout the whole period
from the Trojan War down to the time of Numa. . . ."[24]

   Leopardi was the only one of our poets who certainly knew this
theory, but the others in one way or another shared a sense that
Homer stood for an ultimate value, not only in literary excellence,
but in the conduct of life as that was represented through his poems.
Thus the greatest of Greek poets was in particular what ancient
Greece itself was at large. Both, too, were nature itself, and both
were models, not so much of form as of excellence. Indeed, as we
have been trying to suggest, Greece, being a history with a god in it,

came to have some of the characteristics we associate with myth. (According to Vico, "myth" once meant *vera narratio*.) It was a large organizing image that lent philosophic meaning to life.[25] It was an actual exemplar—a source of conscience to Diderot. To Hume, enlightened Europe in its intellectual freedom was "a copy at large, of what Greece was formerly a pattern in miniature."[26] It was also the image of political liberty, as many examples would show. But above all, it was the domain of artistic freedom, the freedom of the imagination. (This release of the imagination from the strictures of Greek form is an important index of the change from neoclassical beliefs.)

But Greece itself did not become a myth. It was rather one term in a universal mythical pattern. "In the world's childhood," Vico said, "men were by nature sublime poets"; deficiency of reasoning resulted in nobler poetry than all the art and philosophy and criticism have since produced.[27] The era of imagination came to be identified with the golden age, and the time of reason with the age of iron. Greece either was this best of human times or was closest to it in history. Through this mythic telescope our three poets and many others looked at Greek life and art and found that they were good. When they turned the telescope around they found that their own era, being actual, was mean and ugly, since it was a time of full rational consciousness rather than imaginative freedom. The elegiac contrast of youth and age will come under the sway of this pattern; so will the romantic antithesis of innocence and experience. It is the purpose of the following studies to examine the ways in which these attitudes became poetry in the works of three leading poets of the period.

ANDRE CHENIER

I

Bucolics and Elegies

It has been said that Chénier was the best poet in the age of Louis XVI. He is surely different from his contemporaries in that age when poetry was retiring from its encounter with the Enlightenment. The anthologies give us little to remember from this time of change. The poetic spirit, more and more strongly identified with sentiment, was spending its energies in prose. *La Nouvelle Heloïse,* the story of *Paul et Virginie,* and the sentimental pastorals of Florian variously captured the French imagination. Science was encroaching on verse. The wit of argument in the hands of the polemical *philosophes* sometimes swept poetry into its bag of instruments without consulting the Muses. Voltaire's versified reply to the *Contrat social,* like his other polemical poems on the earthquake or the natural law, and Condorcet's poetical sketch of the history of man outline the progress of this tendency. Didacticism and pomp were undermining the strength of the poetic spirit; poetry had sunk quite low.

Therefore, to call Chénier the best looks like a left-handed compliment. Indeed, he has become known through only a small number of his *Bucoliques,* two or three representative selections from the *Iambes,* and a passage from *L'Invention,* his poem on poetry. Only two of his poems reached the press while he lived, both of which were occasional odes with little permanent appeal. Chénier was largely known by the circumstances of his death. This was as much romanticized, in the popular sense, as his poems were. The sensitive young Frenchman, who was the last poet of talent to speak the language of ancient myth,[1] had written his last lines in the prison of Saint-Lazare—fierce lines they were, proud and stern with satire. They were his *Iambes,* which he wrote in pale ink on narrow strips of paper. Sainte-Beuve even supposed, contrary to the fact, that Chénier composed the last *iambe* on the morning he died.[2] Chénier was only thirty-one when he was beheaded on July 25, 1794, three days before the execution of Robespierre, whose death would have saved him.

André Chénier's work and his character emerged slowly after his generation had all but died out. The story of the poet got started with Chateaubriand, who read some of the Chénier manuscripts many years before they were brought out in the edition of 1819. A note in the hugely successful *Génie du christianisme* (1802) presented the unknown author to the attention of a wide public for the first time. Chateaubriand compared the *Bucoliques* with the pastoral poetry of Theocritus, and he regretted the early death of the promising young poet as one more charge against the Revolution. These two facts caught the public fancy. Chénier was both the reviver of antiquity and a political martyr. He was a poet for writers to identify themselves with and a new kind of hero for those who reflected on the wounds of the Revolution.

The fact that Chénier brought a breath from the past into the turmoil of the closing years under Louis XVI enhanced his interest for a critic like Sainte-Beuve, who had a concern for the precise meaning of "classic" and "romantic." "Une voix pure, mélodieuse et savante," Sainte-Beuve said, "un front noble et triste . . . voilà André Chénier."[3] He felt that the verses of his predecessor were "perfumed" with antiquity. He judged them the proper accompaniment on the flute or the lyre for the statues of Venus and Ganymede and Bacchus—for "tout cet art de marbre retrouvé," which was being dug from the Italian ruins.[4] Sainte-Beuve adopted Chénier as a favorite whom he frequently praised and often defended in the romantic battle of the books. He greeted Chénier as a model and "frère aîné des poètes nouveaux."[5] Chénier was, therefore, in Sainte-Beuve's terms a "classic."

On the other hand, Victor Hugo admired, not the flavor of Mimnermus or Anacreon, but Chénier's "sensibilité profonde sans laquelle il n'est point de génie."[6] Others remarked this sensibility, too. According to Nodier, Chénier was "le seul poète de ce temps dont l'âme tendre parut s'associer à l'immense tristesse de la société en deuil."[7] From at least one simile in *Néaere* Heredia experienced "un frisson religieux," as if in response to one of the finest poems in the French language. These lines were pure, simple, symbolic, he said, indicating his own predilections, and he too expressed surprise that such poetry could have been written at the end of the eighteenth century.[8]

Outlined in the shifting views of his successors, Chénier becomes a complex problem for literary judgment. The impression of the isolated spirit of poetry and the romantic exile is only one more illusion which arises from the fact that Chénier did not live long enough to make his mark on contemporary opinion or publish enough during his lifetime to mingle his influence in the evolution of the poetic spirit. Strictly speaking, Chénier did not alienate himself from his age, as Vigny, for instance, tempts us to believe. With a kind of naiveté, he recognized the crucial literary problem of his age. This problem, of course, was the dichotomy between the poetic imagination, with its beautiful fictions, and scientific reason, with its analytical power over the laws of things as they are. It is an axiom that the cleavage between the rational and aesthetic ways of apprehending and ordering experience, which was widening throughout the eighteenth century, arose from the break between *finesse* and *géométrie*.[9] Chénier's famous solution, "sur des pensers nouveaux faisons des vers antiques,"[10] seeks a reconciliation grounded in the humanistic ambition to synthesize modern feeling and thought with the forms of ancient poetry.

Chénier turned to Greece for lyrical unity and for that lyrical immediacy of experience which he could not find in the age of Louis XVI. To Latin, Italian, French, and even English literature he went for other ingredients of his work. We are reading him to feel his contact with Hellenism, which for him represented a golden age that still was real through its literature. For the most part, however, Chénier's models were not the earliest Greeks. He imitated, instead, the Hellenistic poets, Callimachus, the pastoral writers, and the writers of epigrams, both sepulchral and amatory. Of the three poets these pages will discuss, Chénier is the Alexandrian. The Greeks whom this name describes were his chief models, and their imitators among the Latin poets were his guides. Chénier is a derivative poet, who mounts from learning to inspiration. He imitates in order to create; he adapts in order to make his efforts conform with the masterpieces of a past whose poetic superiority he acknowledges. In considering Chénier's bucolics and elegies, we turn to groups of poems which draw on antiquity both for idealized feelings and for literary models.

In the *Bucoliques* Chénier simplifies the conventional machinery of the pastoral for the sake of a direct lyric appeal, with just the right emotional tone.[11] Verses rich with allusive echo evoke primitive emotion; ancient myths impose shape on the amorphousness of crude feeling. Literary echoes, borrowed images, turns of thought, even borrowed sentiments have the power to raise delicately calculable associations. Such materials are already charged with meaning in the memory.

With this evocative technique, Chénier apostrophized Bacchus, Diana and Proserpina as the deities of his pastoral. Out of a profusion of words conveying an indistinct sense of the antique, a mood emerges, for which the Bacchic procession, for example, provides an organized sequence of selected images. These images in themselves are vague to mental perception, but taken together, they are connotatively rich. The images present tones or colorings, and the effect is a kind of neoclassical local color, such as Racine achieved by using names from myth or ancient geography to introduce his audience not only into the scene but into the atmosphere of *Phèdre*.[12] Chénier, however, meant his technique to be the basis for a new species of allegory. It is not the allegory of ideas, as in some of Virgil's *Eclogues,* or the allegory which alludes to real persons, as in Theocritus' *Harvest Home* and Milton's *Lycidas;* this is the allegory of ideals, which refers to emotions and states of the mind: "L'allégorie est la langue de l'esprit. . . . Il faut encore en inventer de nouvelles." Chénier wrote in his "Essai sur les causes et les effets de la perfection et de la decadence des lettres et des arts":

> La póesie donne un corps, un visage à tous les vices, à toutes les vertus, aux passions . . . elle transporte sur le visage même qu'elle leur donne les traits, les marques, les signes par où elles se manifestent sur les visages des hommes . . . par exemple, . . . Vénus est le besoin de jouir; Apollon, les Muses désignent le penchant et le gôut de la póesie. . . .[13]

Though the examples he cites are disappointing, Chénier's *Bucoliques* exemplify his intention well enough. The passions are his subject— love and pity, fear and hatred mainly, but also any human desire that alters the countenance.

The idea of allegory seems almost unnecessary, like a superfluous critical device; yet allegory is Chénier's intention. Instead of imagining fresh details, he preferred to exercise his memory through the use of allusions. He wished to unite the levels of mental experience, not through analogy or similitude, but with obscurer emotional ties of association, which give value to memories insofar as they release pent-up feeling.

At an early age, when he could hardly have formulated these intentions, Chénier made the following translation from Sappho (frg. 164):

> "Virginité chérie, ô compagne innocente,
> Où vas-tu? Je te perds ah! tu fuis loin de moi!
> —Oui, je pars loin de toi; pour jamais je m'absente.
> Adieu. C'est pour jamais. Je ne suis plus à toi."
>
> [*Épigramme VI*]

In the Greek poem *parthenia* (maidenhood) does not answer the nymph's question, but merely says, "I will come to you no more, beloved, now I will come back no more." *Parthenia* is the projection of a fact, which emerges as a person, to utter a few words, like an echo. Whatever pathos we feel arises from the gulf which the dialogue with the personification of a thing no longer actual or even possible opens up to the mind. Chénier's "poetic" words, on the other hand, decorate the naked fact with a particular emotion—"chérie, ô compagne innocente." There is a difference between the Greek and the French versions of this experience; it is the difference between the use of an illusion to represent a fact and the use of an illusion to specify a feeling.

The poetry of allegory, according to Chénier, reembodies particular feelings in particular shapes, which have individual meaning in their own right. The bull that seduced Europa and the heifer sacrifice by Pasiphaë have received meaning from art and tradition. Bucolic poetry which imitates the ancients, and especially that which adopts the subjects and the language of the Greeks, is already allegorical by Chénier's definition. Since the passions, virtues and vices are both isolated within each individual and common to every age, the problem of expressing them with truth to nature is largely a problem of form. As ancient heroes exhibited beautiful conduct which was both natural and reasonable, so ancient writers exemplified the just recording of the beautiful life. Chénier might have said with Schiller that "as long as man dwells in a state of pure nature . . . all his being acts at once like a simple sensuous unity," and the "naked" spirit of the ancients and of the Greeks above all communed immediately with things as they were.[14]

The ancients had only to copy nature; the moderns must therefore copy them, and Chénier would have subscribed wholeheartedly to Pope's conclusion that "nature and Homer were . . . the same." He would have insisted that he imitated the Greeks and those who wrote like them because they were human paradigms both in life and in art. The use of Greek ideas through translation and the appropriation of Greek art would guarantee that aesthetic reasonableness, which Chénier and the neoclassicists like Pope regarded as adherence to nature. And since poetry endows the passions, virtues, and vices with natural traits, such as actually appear on the faces of men, it also satisfies Coleridge's romantic definition of poetry, by imitating how nature unfolds the universal in the particular.[15]

In general, just as every object, no matter how unknown or neglected, gives the artist a new image, a lively expression, a delicate allusion or an ingenious emblem, so too every passion is a fit subject for art.[16] The poet perceives the passions in himself, as he translates the impressions of nature through himself, in order to project them for all men in his art. *"Homo sum,"* Chénier wrote, *"voilà le principe, le but, l'objet de tous les arts. . . . Et lorsque des préjugés, des institutions fausses ont ecarté de la . . . , on n'a point vu les vrais rapports des choses. . . ."*[17] His aim is at once to make his work universal and intimately personal: *"il veut que chaque homme, à tout âge, dans tous les temps, dans tous les pays, dans toutes les circonstances possibles, puisse en le lisant se retrouver dans quelque endroit de ses ouvrages, s'en appliquer quelque morceau. . . ."*[18] The work is at once a monument and a vessel of human intercourse. The man who reads it can say to himself: *"Je ne suis pas seul au monde et cet auteur a pensé à moi."*[19]

For the passions are the same, Chénier argues, in every age, only the forms change. The same passions are common to the moderns and the ancients alike, and therefore, the poet who takes on the task of delineating his emotions has full liberty to scan the literature of the past for models that give form to his kindred experience. The imitated beauties establish intelligible relationships, without which new thought, new perception would be incomprehensible. Contact with the ancients prevents both artist and reader from being alone in the world. Imitation crystalizes emotional experience and myths organize it.

As Chénier realized, a mediocre genius can follow a route that has been travelled before.[20] But he did not feel that his search for Greece was following the path of slavish mediocrity. The union of French passion with Greek thought should beget the truest lyrics, because passion is a common bond, and the ancient images are the truest to nature. Even the translations from the *Odyssey* or from the twenty-seventh idyll of Theocritus and the second of Moschus square with

Chénier's meaning for allegory. They awaken contemporary feelings, which the ancient imagery expresses and controls. They touch common chords, and they organize the response. They are inspired by common sense ("le bon sens"), finding a kindred element among the ancients, which, as Chénier asserts, guides true genius into legitimate paths.

Nor is his literary standpoint fixed. The ambiance of his work, as well as many of its techniques, associates him with Theocritus, as Chateaubriand suggests. More than once, Chénier's translation of Theocritus (*Idyll XXVII*), though not so perfect as the translation by Lebrun, for example, catches the real flavor of French conversational tone: "Satyre, que fais-tu? Quoi! ta main ose encore" (*Bucolique XV*).[21] More significantly, the total impression of Chénier's conception of the interaction of man and nature justifies a comparison with the Greek poet who founded the pastoral genre. The range Chénier's mind conceives for the pastoral is broad—as it was for the Greek poet—but not without limits, which crude excess of active passion could transgress. Chénier is more concerned with shapeliness both of idea and of phrase; Theocritus offers an appearance of realistic detail, which Chénier's stylistic habits blur. Theocritus is the keener dramatist, while Chénier shows more characteristic consciousness of the exact emotion he seeks to stimulate.

But one tradition, which Theocritus established and Chénier interprets, they hold in common, namely, that the delicate nuances of pastoral feeling must never be strained to the pitch of tragedy or compete with the sister art of comedy. Love, as in the dialogues of flirtation or the daydream of seduction (*Bucolique XVI*), anger, as shown in the revenge of Odysseus, and awe, as in the poems about ancient gods—these generic causes of human behavior must be present, but they must be sung in softer modes without the admixtures of violence or satiric wit. The pathos (suffering or even more generally, experience) is uncomplicated. The pastoral emotion—whether it is external pathos, the contact between a man and a set of more or less malleable circumstances, or internal sentiment, a man's dialogue with his own feelings—achieves its purpose in a controlled isolation. But such pure emotions are neither real nor plausible without the stringent designs of art. Never, therefore, in Theocritus, and seldom in Chénier does pathos, the favorite pastoral emotion, exceed these measured limits. Flowers and streams do make their responses to human feeling; nature adapts her moods to his love and grief. Chénier's lovers seek to read their fates in the grove where they meet; in Theocritus, Pan and indeed all nature attend, a bit reluctantly, at the death of Daphnis. But in both writers, nature preserves her autonomy, even if she does not always assert her indifference to man.

But the guarantee of this similarity is a basic difference in the emotion they treat, which acknowledges the historical distance between them. The art of Theocritus lies hidden behind an ambiguity. As Professor Poggioli points out, the art of the pastoral is not "naive" but "sentimental."[22] It is self-conscious, and seeks not infrequently to reveal itself and be its own commentator, delighting in its own performance, as if art lay in exhibiting art. But though Theocritus spent some time in Alexandria and learned the ways of its poets, he seems "naive," "spontaneous," "negligent." The art of Theocritus, "however little it may tempt us to the use of the term realism," seems to record impressions from the Sicilian countryside with an attention to detail "that it is possible even now to verify from the folksongs of the south."[23] But he also showed those very qualities which Chénier admired, knowledge about letters and the human heart, and learning in nature. He had recourse to mythical allusion as if it were part, not of the landscape, but of the common information possessed by pastoral characters and pastoral readers alike. Converting the Cyclops into a buffoon whose pleas invite a faint smile and asserting in his Heracles the domestic side of the Greek hero as a "speaker of words," he stands at that half-way point in literary development where myth as an objective natural phenomenon seems to pause before it becomes myth, the decoration of artifice. But despite Chénier's repeated admiration for the Greeks' openness to the impressions of nature, such usages did not attract his imitation. Theocritus simplified nature for the sake of illusion, whereas Chénier sought plausibility through the addition of imaginative details.

Chénier had a purpose in embellishing Theocritus, however, as he also did in simplifying his borrowings from the later pastoral writers.

In one of his notes, which may sketch some unfinished plan for the *Bucoliques,* he makes this intriguing connection between some typical pastoral subjects and the "romantic" and the "picturesque"—

> Des Nymphes et des Satyres chantent dans une grotte qu'il faut peindre bien romantique, pittoresque, divine, en soupant avec des coupes ciselées, chacun le sujet représenté sur sa coupe; l'un: "Étranger, ce taureau, etc. . . .", l'autre, Pasiphaé, d'autres, d'autres."[24]

The first of these subjects, the abduction of Europa, came from Moschus, *Idyll II,* which Chénier translated in *Bucolique VI* and interpreted in *Epigramme XXIX.* In this epigram, the poet seems to be contemplating a piece of sculpture:

> L'art a rendu l'airain fluide et frémissant;
> On croit le voir flotter. Ce nageur mugissant,
> Ce taureau, c'est un Dieu; c'est Jupiter lui-même.

This is already a work of the imagination, an illusion produced by art. It does not need a prophetic dream or the precedent of Io, engraved on Europa's flower basket in Moschus' idyll, to lend credibility to the marvelous voyage of a bull over the sea. Chénier's translation (in *Bucolique VI*) concentrates on the main mythological image, the voyage itself. There, his stress falls on the change, from innocence, as it were, to experience: Europa's duty was to guard the girdle of her maidenhood in the meadow among the flowers; her fate was to become the mother of Jupiter's offspring. In the epigram, the question is, what does this image signify or recall from the story which surrounds it? And Chénier's answer is a set of reflections which interpret the traits and follow out the gestures of a statue.

The second subject, derived from Virgil's "song of Silenus" (in *Eclogue VI*) and developed by Chénier in one of the existing *Bucoliques,* is the story of Pasiphaë, which in itself is "one of the most lurid examples of Hellenistic interest in the violent and unnatural power of tragic Eros."[25] Here again, the narrative explains a mythological scene. The poem begins:

Tu gémis sur l'Ida, mourante, échevelée,
O reine, ô de Minos épouse désolée,
Heureuse si jamais, dans les riches travaux,
Cérès n'eût pour le joug élevé des troupeaux.

[*Bucolique V*]

The calm of this moment gives way to an account of the frenzy which led up to it. We have a glimpse of a heifer "addressing a soft lowing to her proud lover," and abruptly, Pasiphaë leads this rival off to the mountain to be sacrificed:

Elle-même à son front attache la guirlande,
L'entraîne, et sur l'autel prenant le fer vengeur:
"Sois belle maintenant et plais à mon vainqueur."
Elle frappe et sa haine en la flamme lustrale
Rit de voir palpiter le coeur de sa rivale.

The grotesque equations which these discordant juxtapositions suggest turn the pathos of the opening picture into a fleeting sense of horror.

Gustave Lanson's remarks about Chénier's versification might be applied equally well to the logic of these narratives. Attracted by the example of the Greeks, he substitutes harmony for symmetry, and he conceives this harmony broadly enough to include "the principle of dissonance."[26] These are not such unheard melodies as Keats discerned in his "Attic shape" with its "brede of marble men and maidens." Yet Chénier must have been familiar enough with Theocritus' use of a visual artifact in his description of the cup in *Idyll I*. In this famous passage, Theocritus describes the decorations—the ivy dusted with gold, the woman flirting with two lovers whose weariness appears in the swelling beneath their eyes, the aged fisherman with the strength of youth preparing to cast his net, and the child, a symbol perhaps of the pastoral artist, so intent upon weaving a locust cage that he pays no heed to the foxes, symbols of reality, which are plundering his vines and his breakfast. This cup, hinting at the imperfections that the poet discerns in the domain of permanence and

immutability where "beauty is truth," might be taken as the image
or faithful analogue of pastoral song. It is an image of serenity in
which the harsher facts of life, though present, are deliberately ig-
nored. At any rate, in presenting this image, Theocritus was content
to describe without comment. But for Chénier, besides recreating artifacts which have a similar value, poetry was also an interpreter.

The narrower subject matter of Chénier's first *bucolique* isolates
the technique of the picturesque, which is the key to the emotional
content of the whole collection. Poetry comes to the banquet of the
gods to sing their victory in the battle with the Titans:

> Vierge au visage blanc, la jeune Poésie,
> En silence attendue au banquet d'ambroisie,
> Vint sur un siège d'or s'asseoir avec les Dieux,
> Des fureurs des Titans enfin victorieux.

These lines assign the mythological date to the poem they introduce.
The time is the restoration of peace and the serene order of things
after the war between heaven and earth in which the mighty chthonic forces came within a hair's breadth of unthroning Zeus and the
ethereal powers that dwelt on Olympus. The passions are still; the
heavens have been established in tranquility. This is the setting for
the bucolic muse, whether she sings of great deeds or love, and this
is the moment Chénier knowingly chooses.

Neither the import of these couplets nor their stylistic peculiarity
appear, however, without a glance at the four lines from Homer
which may be an ancient parallel:

> The gods sitting next to Zeus were holding assembly on the gold-
> en floor; lady Hebe in their midst was pouring nectar as wine, and
> they pledged one another in golden cups, while looking upon the
> city of the Trojans. [*Iliad* IV, 1-4]

The descriptive value of this passage, which as Lessing says might
have been composed by an inferior Greek poet, is notably, perhaps
deliberately, vague. It gathers the gods into a place and hints at their
arrangement, by the side of Zeus with their cupbearer in their midst.
The verses are not descriptive but expository: "They contain material for a picture, but are in themselves none."[27]

These passages hold diametrically different views of the gods. The pale-faced poetry celebrates the past in a moment of tranquility, but she is not the sort of being to be absorbed in the narration of actions as if they were at hand. She is rather like Pindar's personification of music (*Pythian I*, 1-28), who is impassive, though she has power to delight the gods and to harass the giant, Typhos, pinioned beneath Aetna. Chénier and Homer stand at opposite extremes, even in the difference between the crisp strokes of the Greek lines and the suspended motion of the French which weights the noun and the verb of the main clause with lengthy qualifiers. This effect of stately pauses seems quite as deliberate as the swiftness of the Greek. The accident is that we see more in Homer, though Chénier gives more description.

The proper subject of a poem, Lessing says, is a "visible progressive action, the various parts of which follow one another in time."[28] Thus Homer "paints nothing but progressive actions."[29] On the other hand, the typical subject in painting is "a visible stationary action, the development of whose various parts takes place in space."[30] Poetry's dimension is time; its medium is sound in motion; its materials, contrary to the colors and forms which painting uses, are signs related not spatially but in sequence.[31] Moreover, as Lessing says:

> Painting, in its coexistent compositions, can use but a single moment of an action, and must therefore choose the most pregnant one, the one most suggestive of what has gone before and what is to follow.

> Poetry, in its progressive imitations, can use but a single attribute of bodies, and must choose that one which gives the most vivid picture of the body as exercised in this particular action.[32]

When poetry allows itself to be static, it loses its power to impress or engage the mind, as does Virgil's description of Aeneas' shield for example. Homer, on the other hand, describes the shield of Achilles not as finished "but in the process of creation"—

> Here again he has made use of the happy device of substituting progression for coexistence, and thus converted the tiresome description of an object into a graphic picture of an action.[33]

But Chénier's lines on poetry exclude almost every action that could be suggested in a painting:

> Et, de sa belle bouche, exhalant une voix
> Plus douce que le miel ou les baisers des Grâces,
> Elle dit des vaincus les coupables audaces,
> Et les cieux raffermis et sûrs de notre encens,
> Et sous l'ardent Etna les traîtres gémissants.

> [*Bucolique I*]

As in the opening lines, so here at the close, the words referring to tremendous action are put in the place of modifiers. The sentence structure balances the attributes of poetry with the actions of the gods, waiting and victorious, and with the deeds of the Titans. The intentionally static symmetry deliberately suppresses movement to contemplate a moment of dynamic tension. Chénier's verbal picture satisfies Lessing's conception of propriety in the visual arts, where gesture and emotion should be subordinated to the requirements of spatial unity.

Lessing's insistence that the arts be kept distinct really extended the neoclassical law of separate genres. But Chénier would dispute the German critic's precept; the orthodox neoclassicists and the romantics, with their vivid images, would dispute it too.[34] Chénier believed the metaphors from painting and sculpture with which he often described his poetic activity. The poet, he thought, is a sculptor of ideal figures. Had he been challenged with Lessing's suggestion that the poet who seeks effects of the visual arts is at a disadvantage, he might have replied that the province of poetry is not narration alone but the evocation and control of feelings, which poetry more than any other art makes intelligible. Though the shield of Aeneas might fail by the standards of Homeric narrative, Virgil's description of the frieze on Dido's temple rouses pathos which every reader shares with Aeneas. Poetic pictures, such as the flower basket of Moschus' Europa, or Theocritus' cup, give contemplative order to the emotional import of the narrative. The suggestion of passion, such as Winckelmann had seen in the aesthetic generality and formal repose of the Laocoon and the Ajax of Timomachus,[35] was also the intention of Chénier's "allegorical" imitations.

Therefore, Chénier's practice was in sympathy with the view which neoclassical critics traditionally derived from Horace—that poetry is like painting ("ut pictura poesis")—or from Simonides—that "painting is silent poetry, and poetry is painting that speaks."[36] In this view, even the lyric poem with its personal emotion was a picture, the Abbé Batteux had affirmed in 1747.[37] Thanks partly to Winckelmann and the Comte de Caylus, this view was kept fashionable in late eighteenth-century France. As Diderot observed, there had been in antiquity a continual exchange of ideas between poets and painters.[38] And the Comte de Caylus, whom Lessing criticized, went so far as to consider the number and kind of pictures which poets offer to be a sort of "touchstone" or "scale" for assaying their genius.[39] It may even be that Chénier's *Bucoliques* were formed as much by the paintings of his contemporaries as by his readings in ancient texts. The subjects of several paintings which Diderot describes in his *Salons* provide striking parallels with the *Bucoliques*.[40] At any rate, insofar as these lyrics strive toward the expression of universal emotions under the aspect of the "stillness" and "repose" which Winckelmann pronounced to be prime qualities of beauty,[41] they exemplify the Louis XVI "style," with its tendency toward the idealized serenity of the "plastic" arts.[42]

Diderot's art criticism is an eminent witness to the kind of feeling which the eighteenth century wished to arouse and to control with the visual arts, when their subjects were antique. This effect was the "poésie des ruines," by which he meant the perception of secrets and of danger, and precious memories, between two eternities.[43] Diderot referred to the painting of ruins in general with their message from the past that all things decay. The mood which these eternities of memory and annihilation generated is melancholy, in which thoughts of love and death range tranquilly together in the liberated mind. His remarks about painting are equally applicable to the fragments of statue and sketch which are Chénier's *Bucoliques*.

* * * * *

Morts et vivants, il est encor pour nous unir
Un commerce d'amour et de doux souvenir.

[Épigramme XVI]

When man does not possess beliefs that guarantee a life beyond
the grave, he may nevertheless keep up the illusion of communion
with those who have gone before him into death. The ruins of things
recall the men who fashioned them, and secure in his own life, the
man of sensibility can find pleasure in his feeling of kinship with
those who are no more. Indeed, as Walter Pater said in his essay on
Winckelmann: "This pagan sentiment measures the sadness which
fills the human mind, whenever its thoughts wander from what is
here and now."[44] In the "commerce of love and sweet memories,"
he gains temporary comfort from the illusion that, as Gray put it in
his famous *Elegy*, "ev'n in our Ashes live their wonted Fires." In
reality, his commerce with the dead is a dialogue with his own echo
as it returns from the barriers of the unknowable country which reason cannot map; and from this illusion, a reflected projection of himself, comes a delicious sentiment, shapeless thought susceptible of
any shape.

Chénier, therefore, sounds the notes of a favorite contemporary
theme when he writes:

Bergers, vous dont ici la chèvre vagabonde,
La brebis se traînant sous sa laine féconde
Au dos de la colline accompagnent les pas,
A la jeune Mnaïs rendez, rendez, hélas!
Par Cérès, par sa fille, et la terre sacrée,
Une grâce légère autant que désirée.
Ah! près de vous jadis elle avait son berceau
Et sa vingtième année a trouvé le tombeau.

[Épigramme XVI]

The situation of this young girl's epitaph is a ready-made bucolic
dialogue across the distance between the upper and lower world. As
for Gray and Young, so for Chénier, the reminders of death, more
than the fact, have power to fill the heart. This poem and the Greek

sepulchral epigrams which inspired it assume that the reader of an epitaph is already in a state of mind which makes him responsive to the elegiac mood. This poem does not call specifically for lament or eulogy. The dead girl requests the rites of memorial; her epitaph calls upon the rustics to bring flocks and garlands of flowers, and pour libations of milk upon the tomb amid the bleating of sheep and the music of the flute. Its model is a Greek sephulchral epigram by Leonidas of Tarentum.[45] Greek epitaphs are well known to reflect an almost universal pessimism with regard to any life beyond the grave. Only the famous, or those who died gloriously, are assured of immortality, and the only kind of immortality possible is to live on in the memory of posterity.[46] Hence, through the ritual piety of a small circle and the rites that "belong to the dead" and "are the favors and requitals for those who have dwindled away,"[47] the unheroic gain a brief extension to their lives.

In his sepulchral poems, Chénier faithfully follows the argument of his Greek models, though he tries to enrich the bare Greek statements with sensuous detail. *La Jeune Tarentine,* which the romantics admired, reworks an ancient epigram into a style and mood congenial with eighteenth-century taste. In the Greek by Xenocritus of Rhodes[48] the poignancy comes from a stony simplicity: a girl on the way by sea to her wedding was drowned in a storm, and her bones were washed up on the shore. Her death was a bitter woe to her father, who, conducting her to the nuptials, brought neither maid nor corpse. Chénier transforms this bare poignancy into a lacework of delicate metonymies alternately evoking sadness and expectation. Adding the poetry of rich association to the Greek sketch, Chénier aims at a definite reaction, by controlling perception and guiding the memory. The emotional intensity, being lower than that which generates metaphor, relies on things carrying rich "associative signals." Hence, the opening summons to mourn, invoking the halcyons, is balanced with the chests containing bracelets, robes, and perfumes, signs of the bridal preparations. The crude fact of the girl's drowning is elevated and softened by the chorus of sea nymphs, who at the behest of Thetis carry the dead bride to the Cape of the West Wind and celebrate her funeral in an elegiac procession representing

the sympathies of nature. In a typical elegiac apostrophe in the closing lines, the chorus recapitulates the notes of promise and disappointment:

> Hélas! chez ton amant tu n'es point ramenée.
> Tu n'as point revêtu ta robe d'hyménée.
> L'or autour de tes bras n'a point serré de noeuds.
> Les doux parfums n'ont point coulé sur tes cheveux.

> *[Bucolique IX]*

In a sea setting, Chénier has thus made a miniature pastoral elegy
by amplifying the narrative idea and situation from a minor Greek
source with the legacy of pastoral conventions.

This kind of poetry issued from a labor of composition, piecing
together fragments from the past. The rule or *modus operandi* intu-
itively may be one, but the technique is synthetic.[49] Consequently,
attitudes seem to shift. With the detachment of the literary historian,
who planned to include in "De la perfection et de la décadence des
lettres" a history of Greek literature from Homer to the decline of
letters among the late Alexandrians, Chénier wandered through the
literary pantheon, imitating Homer, the Homerides and Mimnermus,
or Theocritus and the pastoral writers, or Callimachus, the librarian
at Alexandria. Perhaps without quite knowing why, his spirit struggled over the choice between a jovial Anacreontic indifference and
the genuinely active and personally engaged passion of an Archilochus. The technique remained stable, unified and restrained, while
the spirit fidgeted, changing its postures of freedom, love, and death.

He was born for love, he says (*Élégie II*). His verses will beautify
a beloved, who of herself is but a slight thing, or they will avenge
him at her expense. When he has spent all his money and Laura
scorns him, he thanks the gods and returns to his writing; when he
has money again and another Laura comes along, he throws money
and literature to the wind (*Élégie XI*). Waiting for the "jeune ro-
maine," he anticipates the enjoyment of the feel and the smell of
her, just as Propertius had done. These gestures of inconstancy are,
in fact, the poses of the Latin elegists, Propertius, Catullus, Tibullus,

and Ovid. Their fickleness is a formal motif through Chénier's elegies. Like the bucolic permutations of love's possibilities, crystallized in mythic images, this formal strain also receives statuesque permanence from a climactic picture. When the chisel of death cuts off his days, Chénier says, copying Ovid (*Amores*, II, 10), he would wish his soul peacefully to depart as he is reclining on the breast of a beautiful woman, so that travelers who might hear of him should say: "Thus may I live and die" (*Élégie VII*).

The elegies, vessels of experience as they pretend to be, propose imaginary ideals to dream by rather than metaphysical ideals for action. The lover is free (*Élégie VI*), and he who does not know how to be poor is a slave (*Élégie I*). The life of the poor poet (with a moderate income) can be free if he does not have to put up with the whims of tyrants, priests, and magistrates, or occupy the armchair of a supercilious rimer in the French Academy (*Élégie II*).[50] This freedom is essentially negative, and its message is an unsocial solitude, which Chénier was ultimately forced by the political disorder to relinquish. If these Latin imitations do not promise the spirit of the *Iambes*, their technique is nevertheless capable of boundless variety. Like a beacon it swept the productions of the past searching for excellence, and testing the assumption that great poets must have been good men, it guided Chénier in the evolution of a conscience formed from the precipitates of aesthetic experience.

The notes foretelling Chénier's last days are struck from his stubborn isolation in the face of life and death. For just a moment, he speaks like Leopardi's saddest lyrics, though without the Italian poet's emotional power:

> Souvent, las d'être esclave et de boire la lie
> De ce calice amer que l'on nomme la vie,
> Las du mépris des sots qui suit la pauvreté,
> Je regarde la tombe, asile souhaité;
> Je souris à la mort volontaire et prochaine;
> Je me prie, en pleurant, d'oser rompre ma chaîne;
> . . . .
> Et puis mon coeur s'écoute et s'ouvre à la faiblesse;
> Mes parents, mes amis, l'avenir, ma jeunesse,

Mes écrits imparfaits; car à ses propres yeux
L'homme sait se cacher d'un voile spécieux.
A quelque noir destin qu'elle soit asservie,
D'une étreinte invincible il embrasse la vie;
Et va chercher bien loin, plutôt que de mourir,
Quelque prétexte ami de vivre et de souffrir.
Il a souffert, il souffre: aveugle d'espérance,
Il se traîne au tombeau de souffrance en souffrance;
Et la mort, de nos maux ce remède si doux,
Lui semble un nouveau mal, le plus cruel de tous.

[*Élégie XXIV*]

The Anacreontic indifference gives way to a clearer vision. The conflict resolves itself in favor of life. He is capable of breaking through the precedent of Propertius, by which he refuses the obsequies of burial (*Élégie XXV*), or of discarding the mask of Anacreon, in which he says he can forget death, like one of the trivial things women resolve in tears, and remember love, ecstasy, poetry, and a mistress (*Élégie XXII*). He can put off the frivolity he may have learned from Mimnermus—

Sans les dons de Vénus, quelle serait la vie?
Dès l'instant où Vénus me doit être ravie,
Que je meure, sans elle ici-bas rien n'est doux.[51]

[*Épitre VI*]

—and raise his melancholy to that mood in which that early elegist saw that "black destinies are ever standing by, one holding the finality of grievous old age, the other that of death" (Mimnermus, frg. 2).

This melancholy, as Chénier reveals it in the *Élégies*, is an effect of social dissatisfactions. No one can sympathize, he says; every one hides himself from his brother, and in the manner of Rousseau, he adds that we pity only ourselves; we envy anyone with the same sorrows (*Élégie XXIII*). He wishes to live in woods with his friends and practice the fine arts, free from the discontents of tyranny and riches. His model is the bee, which inhabits a natural society and works only for itself:

Il est si doux, si beau, de s'être fait soi-même,
De devoir tout à soi, tout aux beaux-arts qu'on aime;
Vraie abeille en ses dons, en ses soins, en ses moeurs,
D'avoir su se bâtir, des dépouilles des fleurs,
Sa cellule de cire, industrieux asile
Où l'on coule une vie innocente et facile.

[*Élégie I*]

In this haven for the self-indulgent artist, he would take refuge
from the press of the city and the clamorous crowd. The companions
for this second part of the pastoral ideal come not from Greece or
Rome, but from the Scriptures: he mentions Joseph seeking his
brothers in the fields of Sichem, Rachel, whom Jacob's love bought
with years of servitude, and Ruth following the grain. But the mood
is the same, whether the characters it remembers come from Arcadia
or Canaan. As Chénier says, it is melancholy, that extensive and il-
lusional emotion that haunted the eighteenth century, which he
wishes to indulge in all its expressions and forms. This craving after
melancholy looked for satisfaction in the literature of the past, in
study, in sentiment, in solitude with its unreal but magnanimous
possibilities. This is the setting for Chénier's vision of suffering, away
from the strenuous but fragmented social demands of his age. In
melancholy he conceived the possibility of suicide. In this context
the Chénier of the elegies celebrates his loves, his friendships, his
hopes, his concern over death and failure, his insistence that there be
some creed of freedom, and his aspirations toward artistic fame and
a manly rank in our memory.

Néaere gives utterance to this melancholy through a *persona* such
as belongs to the pastoral artifice and projects into an antique setting
the themes of love and death as well as a romantic mood, which we
shall have reason to notice in some of the elegies. This story of disappointed love, introduced by a comparison with the song of a dying
swan with which Ovid had begun his seventh epistle (from Dido to
Aeneas), is a monologue. Néaere's last energies draw all the strands
of her life into one final utterance. Against imminent oblivion, she
projects her memory back into nature. This vague figure takes on
the pastoral struggle of art against the natural course, to inject the

traces of her mournful personality into the activities of nature, as Theocritus had done for Daphnis, Bion for Adonis, and Moschus for Bion. Néaere laments herself, however. Her appeals to the woods and mountains and nymphs to remind the beloved of his dying love are condensed acknowledgments of familiar conventions elaborated by the ancients. Even the repetition of words and verbal patterns belongs to the stock of devices by which the pastoral elegy expresses its peculiar pathos. Néaere's speech presupposes a state of lowered consciousness and suggestibility:

> "O! soit que l'astre pur des deux frères d'Hélène
> Calme sous ton vaisseau la vague ionienne;
> Soit qu'aux bords de Poestum, sous ta soigneuse main,
> Les roses deux fois l'an couronnent ton jardin,
> Au coucher du soleil, si ton âme attendrie
> Tombe en une muette et molle rêverie,
> Alors, mon Clinias, appelle, appelle-moi.
> Je viendrai, Clinias, je volerai vers toi.
> Mon âme vagabonde à travers le feuillage
> Frémira. Sur les vents ou sur quelque nuage
> Tu la verras descendre, ou du sein de la mer,
> S'élevant comme un songe, étinceler dans l'air;
> Et ma voix, toujours tendre et doucement plaintive,
> Caresser en fuyant ton oreille attentive."

> [*Bucolique VIII*]

The poet who wrote these lines knew that the mode of perception is in the perceiver; or, as Condillac said, "En effet, il semble que nous ne devrions voir que notre âme modifiée différemment."[52] Indeed, the mood which Néaere's words suggest recalls the reveries of Rousseau and even the *Souvenirs* of Lamartine. In *Néaere* we may find on a deeper level than in many of the *Bucoliques* and *Élégies* this fusion of ancient and modern which Chénier was seeking through much of his poetic work.

But Chénier's melancholy, though often presented in antique guise and fostered by the poetry of the ancients rather than by the "genius" of the North, was essentially in accord with the emotional ethos of his own age. It is true that he sometimes imitated the ancients, especially Propertius, to express his sense that pleasure is fleeting and death inevitable.[53] His elegies are not suffused with what Henri Potez called "la mélancolie, la tristesse sans cause déterminée, harmonieuse et vague, la lamentation sonore et sans fin du XIX'*e* siècle."[54] Chénier only anticipates the full romantic orchestrations of the pathos of the self. His self-transformations through reverie are rare:

> Ainsi, bruyante abeille, au retour du matin
> Je vais changer en miel les délices du thym.
> Rose, un sein palpitant est ma tombe divine.
> Frêle atome d'oiseau, de leur molle étamine
> Je vais sous d'autres cieux dépouiller d'autres fleurs.
> Le papillon plus grand offre moins de couleurs;
> Et l'Orénoque impur, la Floride fertile
> Admirent qu'un oiseau si tendre, si débile,
> Mêle tant d'or, de pourpre, en ses riches habits,
> Et pensent dans les airs voir nager des rubis.
> Sur un fleuve souvent l'éclat de mon plumage
> Fait à quelque Léda souhaiter mon hommage.
> Souvent, fleuve moi-même, en mes humides bras
> Je presse mollement des membres délicats,
> Mille fraîches beautés que partout j'environne;
> Je les tiens, les soulève, et murmure et bouillonne.[55]

[*Les Amours, Lycoris*, 3]

Nevertheless, Chénier was familiar with the "insensible et charmante langueur" which for the "ami des champs" in the eighteenth century was a basis of imaginative inspiration. Alone, safe from the ennui of the city where the crowd shouts down the voice of the Muses, the poet indulges in the spiritual inertia which was the condition of Rousseau's communion with nature:

> Quand le soir approchait, je descendais des cimes de l'île, et j'allais volontiers m'asseoir au bord du lac, sur la grève, dans quelque asile caché; là, le bruit des vagues et l'agitation de l'eau, fixant mes sens et chassant de mon âme toute autre agitation, la plon-

geaient dans une rêverie délicieuse, où la nuit me surprenait souvent sans que je m'en fusse aperçu. Le flux et le reflux de cette eau, son bruit continu, mais renflé par intervalles, frappant sans relâche mon oreille et mes yeux, suppléaient aux mouvements internes que la rêverie éteignait en moi, et suffisaient pour me faire sentir avec plaisir mon existence, sans prendre la peine de penser.[56]

In a passage where he speaks like another *promeneur solitaire* Chénier concludes:

> Il regarde à ses pieds, dans le liquide azur
> Du fleuve qui s'étend comme lui calme et pur,
> Se peindre les coteaux, les toits et les feuillages,
> Et la pourpre en festons couronnant les nuages.

> *[Élégie II]*

He is reporting the images he saw in the surface of the water. But the state of mindless indolence, which seems to be an effortless route back to contact with the things of nature as they are, is really a form of self-absorption, in which nature mirrors the purest sensations of the self. Chénier knows this force: its name is "mélancolie," and this sluggish psychic spring from which the streams of pathos flow he identifies with the "Déesse tutélaire" of his caves and forests. Chénier, resisting the theories of doubt, the outlook of reason, cultivates the deceits of that "aimable mensongère," his pastoral goddess.

> Il revoit près de lui, tout à coup animés,
> Ces fantômes si beaux à nos pleurs tant aimés. . . .

> *[Élégie II]*

Thanks to melancholy these phantoms emerge out of a more or less accurate imagery of perception. It imposes on the natural scene an acknowledged fiction. These "aimable chimères" are far from Greek. They have apparently little in common with the nymphs and genii the ancients saw in their streams.[57] They are bookish beings, whom it is rationally difficult, but emotionally pleasing to believe in. Memory, like an Aeolian harp, contains the forms, and under the right conditions becomes the poetic instrument:

Je suis de ma mémoire absolu possesseur;
Je lui prête une voix, puissante magicienne
Comme aux brises du soir, une harpe éolienne. . . .

[*Élégie XXII*]

And melancholy breathes life into these forms. They are the shapes of Odysseus or Julie, Néaere, "la jeune Tarentine," or Bacchus, Proserpina, and Diana, or figures drawn from the pastoral life of the Old Testament patriarchs and the book of Ruth. Both recent and antique ideals, from novels, myths, and Scriptures alike, are brought before the poet's eyes by the pleasing deceptions of the melancholy heart. Under the influence of this power events as well as persons, things as well as scenes issue from the memory; they are chiefly the fruits of other imaginations which the poet of recollection has gathered.

As Chénier's simile of the Aeolian harp (*Élégie XXII*) reminds us, memory was to become an important lyric instrument in the service of romantic melancholy. Chénier's melancholy would be replaced in Wordsworth's definition of poetry by "emotion recollected in tranquility." In poets of larger vision, such as Ugo Foscolo, the nostalgic reminiscence of antiquity and the sense that "even from the tomb the voice of nature cries" could create a morally and socially useful illusion with which poetry could replace a worn-out religion:

Vero è ben, Pindemonte! Anche la Speme,
ultima Dea, fugge i sepolcri: e involve
tutte cose l'obblìo nella sua notte;
e una forza operosa le affatica
di moto in moto; e l'uomo e le sue tombe
e l'estreme sembianze e le reliquie
della terra e del ciel traveste il tempo.

Ma perché pria del tempo a sé il mortale
invidierà l'illusion che spento
pur lo sofferma al limitar di Dite?
Non vive ei forse anche sotterra, quando
gli sarà muta l'armonia del giorno,
se può destarla con soavi cure

nella mente de' suoi? Celeste è questa
corrispondenza d'amorosi sensi. . . .

[*Dei sepolcri*, 16-30]

In Foscolo's conception the poet is enjoined with a sacred duty to
transmit the hallowed past. A wish of ancient poets too, the plea for
future memory, is on the lips of Homer in the *Hymn to Apollo*:

> In aftertimes you will remember me, when some much-enduring
> stranger, coming here from men upon the earth, shall ask: "O
> maidens, what man walked here, the sweetest of minstrels to you,
> and in whom did you take delight above all?"

But the memory of the "voluptueux penseur," in the *Élégies* and
in the *Bucoliques*, served, for the most part, the inclinations of his
own heart, though he tried to see them as universal. Chénier's memory translated regrets, disappointments, unsatisfactory relationships
into correlatives drawn from a past powerful to provoke tears. In
his treatment of Homer (*Bucolique XXVI*) we see how his literary
memory enters the service of sentimentality. By accident, "l'aveugle"
arrives in a pastoral scene, where three shepherd children find him
and listen to his story—how cruel sailors abandoned him on an unknown shore, hungry and alone. Looking like a god ("dieu protec-
teur de la Grèce"), the patriarchal figure of Homer is completely pastoral, with his rude lyre hanging from his rustic belt, as he is led into
the village where an appreciative audience extends a welcome. Homer has come to a place of rest and security. The pastoral is more
poignant, as Professor Poggioli suggests, when it seems to provide a
fleeting resting-place, or when, as under the conditions of Diderot's
"poetic of ruins," one is safe in the contemplation of danger or misfortune.[58] Like *Le Mendiant* (*Bucolique XXV*), which unites two
friends after the reversals of fortune, and *Le Malade* (*Bucolique
XXIV*), in which a mother wins a match for her son who is dying of
love, *L'Aveugle* seems to exemplify the sentimental axiom of wish-
fulfillments, namely, that life is hard as if to prepare us for its happy
endings.

We can find in this *bucolique* illustrations of many techniques and intentions already noted throughout the portion of Chénier's poetry which we have been examining. This story, reflecting Chénier's acquaintance with the Homeric hymn to Apollo[59] and the well-known legend of the poet Arion, is, in reality, an extended pastoral frame, which furnishes a setting and an atmosphere for Homer's song. The song itself is a typically Hellenistic catalogue of subjects.[60] We read the first half of his song as if it was a tour through a gallery of ancient pictures, and we feel that Chénier might have been paging through the *Iliad* and the *Odyssey*, recording a sequence of impressions. The song as a whole stirs in the reader's mind imprecise literary memories and produces a sequence of bright and somber feelings. We may conclude that though Chénier had a vision of the free and noble Greek spirit, his re-creations of that vision often took the form of a Hellenistic facade. Despite his reaching back to antiquity through association, through memory, and through allusion and myth, the Homer the romantics read in his verses was shrouded in a curtain of nostalgic melancholy.

II

L'Inventeur

In resorting to antiquity, Chénier sought patterns and images sufficiently typical, with power sufficiently acknowledged, to gain a hearing in the community of human experience for the wordless stirrings of unsocial melancholy. He assumed a broad analogy between moderns and ancients and, beneath that, insisted on an emotional identity common to all men. But his apparent belief that the motives of late eighteenth-century thought and action must be allegorized in the glories of the past in order to elevate the emotions indicates a profound pessimism. A pastoral escape from the age that professed the infinite perfectibility of man cannot but be skeptical: any retreat of learning into the past during such an age casts doubt on the value of advancing knowledge. Already in 1782 he formulated the wish to form, together with Lebrun and Brazais, a society of friends to rekindle ancient virtue in France and reanimate the fine arts, revealing thus how soon dissatisfaction with the moral state of contemporary France disquieted him. On the other hand, Chénier's intention to popularize the discoveries of scientific reason adds to the dialectic of memory and melancholy a thesis of apparent optimism in favor of the modern mind. Thus when he asserts the glory of enlightened science, he is caught in the acute dilemma of eighteenth-century thought: science has advanced to deeper insight into natural mysteries; yet men were better, nobler, freer, happier, and generally more perfect in virtue and art when they were primitively close to nature or even identified with it, as Homer was thought to be.

The plan for a poetic synopsis of the science of nature and man is *Hermès*, "ma plus belle espérance, / . . . l'objet le plus cher des veilles de dix ans,"[1] a didactic poem projected during the years when the elegies and bucolics were being written.[2]

> Il faut que le sage magicien qui sera un des héros de ce bizarre poème ait passé par plusieurs métempsycoses propres à montrer allégoriquement l'histoire de l'espèce humaine. . . .[3]

In the first song, the migrant soul of Chénier's poet in search of heroes and subjects would narrate the origin of the earth, the formation of animals, and the coming to be of man. An allegorical capsule abbreviating Lucretius' etiology for the mythic personification of Cybele (*De Rerum Natura*, II) would represent the earth under the metaphorical emblem of a great animal. There were to be new heroes from among the figures in the forefront of contemporary thought, Newton, Buffon, Condillac, Rousseau, whose works Chénier read or reexamined in 1785-86. *Hermès* is not only a concession to the modern mind, but a working effort to fit enlightened accomplishments into the context of the past:

> Là je vais mon sein méditant à loisir
> Des chants à faire entendre aux siècles à venir;
> Là, dans la nuit des cœurs qu'osa sonder Homère,
> Cet aveugle divin et me guide et m'éclaire.
> Souvent mon vol, armé des ailes de Buffon,
> Franchit avec Lucrèce, au flambeau de Newton,
> La ceinture d'azur sur le globe étendue.[4]

Pleasing or not, the fact is that modern knowledge is more believable than the fables of ancient Muses. However reluctantly, we must face the conclusions of Newton, Montesquieu, Condillac, that science, custom, and law have changed their content. To ignore these men and their discoveries would be to disallow all hope for the present. The solution,' therefore, is to synthesize: while banishing error from Apollo's court, let Urania make Newton speak the language of the gods—"sur des pensers nouveaux faisons des vers antiques."[5] There would seem to be no difference more radical than that between the epics of Homer or even Virgil and Montesquieu's laws and the science of Buffon. Yet Homer exemplifies how a poet can preserve the customs of a society. Virgil, whose literary technique suggests "a larger significance by combining traits from various sources into a new unity,"[6] gives Chénier a still more important precedent. Virgil was postscientific too, Chénier thought, inasmuch as the Greek philosophers had given him their veiled insights into nature's secrets. The new thinkers, "plus doctes, plus heureux dans leurs puissants efforts,"[7] have revealed a treasure of new fables and laws for new Virgils, for André Chénier. The scientists are the modern Argonauts, whose adventures remain to be sung:

> Aux yeux de nos Jasons sortis du sein des mers:
> Quel amas de tableaux, de sublimes images,
> Naît de ces grands objets réservés à nos âges![8]

A metaphor which thus blurs the difference between science and myth illustrates Chénier's reluctance to separate imaginative and rationalistic thought.

When, in *L'Invention,* he raises the question of such a separation, he speaks in terms that recall the battle of the books. Against the claim that poetry can enter the fields of science, it is objected that the workings of science are too abstruse, its findings too recondite for popular understanding; and, far from being "what oft was thought," they are even hard for common sense to accept. Chénier admits that modern inquiries in the natural sciences have the advantage of greater truthfulness. He acknowledges that ancient fables are merely a brilliant system of artifice that went under the name of nature:

> Mais enfin, dites-moi, si d'une oeuvre immortelle
> La nature est en nous la source et le modèle,
> Pouvez-vous le penser que tout cet univers,
> Et cet ordre éternel, ces mouvements divers,
> L'immense vérité, la nature elle-même,
> Soit moins grande en effet que ce brillant système
> Qu'ils nommaient la nature, et dont d'heureux efforts
> Disposaient avec art les fragiles ressorts?[9]

He recognizes how the domains of knowledge have been enlarged.

It is certainly difficult to see how nature can be at once the source of ancient falsehood and the originator of modern truth. Chénier's solution is to suppose that while the processes of thought remain fundamentally the same[10] (the human mind, as well as the heart, is universal), the content of thought may change from age to age; and whereas the value of life has declined since antiquity, the power of insight has increased. Chénier holds to the optimistic if unclear position that the poetic and scientific intellects can collaborate. In fact, under the general category of art he includes both science and poetry:

> Tous les arts sont unis: les sciences humaines
> N'ont pu de leur empire étendre les domaines,
> Sans agrandir aussi la carrière des vers.[11]

The artistic intelligence, in this general sense, resembles in its operations the partitioning and harmonizing activities of order-giving nature herself. Chénier would have accepted the idea that in every age "art," as d'Holbach said, "is nothing but nature giving help to the instruments which she herself has made."[12] The "inventor" is a kind of architect who, having been nourished by the ancients, takes his turn and adds a new column in man's unfinished temple to nature.

New myths, created along traditional lines, ought to be as effective as the ancient models had been in representing contemporary "truths." With such a view in mind, Chénier's notes for an epic, *L'Amérique*, tried to adapt ancient legend to the traditionless vacuum of the American wilderness. He wanted to imitate the end of the *Oedipus Rex*, so he imagined an American Oedipus, a disinherited wanderer who accidentally murders his father and at the end of his life, in the presence of his children, curses and finally kills himself. An American Philoctetes is called back from exile, and it is presumably the same character of whom Chénier says: "Il salue tendrement à l'antique la cabane qui l'a conservé."[13] There is a Spaniard in America like the Heracles of the *Alcestis,* an American Job somehow to be brought into the Homeric picture of Priam asking Helen for the names of the Greek heroes at Troy, and an American woman who laments her dead child with a sentimentally primitive ceremony that resembles Hellenic sepulchral rites. There would also be an imitation of the *Persae* to be applied to the story of Pizarro and an American Coriolanus taken from Plutarch.

Chénier's attitude toward all these sources is that "les histoires anciennes écrites par des hommes si éloquents fourmillent de peintures grandes et pathétiques et que l'on peut transporter a d'autres personnages."[14] Had Chénier made greater advances in his reading of Milton, whom he also intended to imitate,[15] he might have discovered a method for integrating the strands of diverse cultural sources. As it was, however, his inspiration usually came from specific texts rather than from some unifying plan.

However much he appropriated of the Homeric techniques, Chénier's compilation of his literary gleanings would not have produced that unity of design and intention which made Homer's whole heroic world "a metaphor."[16] The invention of something in the "taste" of the shields from the classical epics, to represent the history of the empires being born and destroyed from their origins in the North down to Roman times, would lack relevance in Chénier's poem to a coherent symbolic scheme. Chénier's epic images are not credible vehicles for expressing the objective interplay between the individual and the universe. They are not the offspring of "the sort of memory possessed by the early archaic mind, which refabricates all experience into myth."[17] Nor are they, as the classical myths were for Milton, the pagan analogues for a system of spiritual truths. They remain, in *L'Amérique* as in the *Bucoliques*, the "echoes" of great souls, to borrow the language of Longinus,[18] capable of stirring the poet's emotion, but lacking the capacity to organize his experience of historical

and scientific fact. *L'Amérique* tends to justify the belief that new
subject matter, whether of science or sentiment, is incompatible
with the prefabricated myths and verbal pictures which in their own
right were the outgrowth of a coherent cosmic view.[19]

At least in working on his epic, therefore, Chénier neglected
Young's advice for the judicious use of ancient masters: "When we
read, let our imagination kindle at their charms; when we write, let
our judgement shut them out of our thoughts."[20] Nevertheless, Chénier's theoretical opinions in one sense constitute an expanded, if
ambivalent, neoclassicism. Though he reacted against the thesis that
there is a sacred corpus of poetic objects, he insisted with Boileau
that the genres of poetry had been set forth once and for all by the
Greeks. He believed that art is the imitator of nature and that it
forms "ce qu'elle n'a point fait, mais ce qu'elle a pu faire," in order
to create beauty itself from the selected traits of many beautiful
objects.[21] His emphasis on "vers antiques" affirms a loyalty to the
notion of a kind of poetic diction, though that notion is never precisely defined:

> Changeons en notre miel leurs plus antiques fleurs;
> Pour peindre notre idée, empruntons leurs couleurs;
> Allumons nos flambeaux à leurs feux poétiques. . . .[22]

Plainly he intends more than diction, however: he adopts the metaphors of "sweetness" and "light."

Chénier means, in fact, through metaphors of both enlightenment
and passion, to assert the value of poetry, if not its intellectual superiority:

> Elle seule connaît ces extases choisies,
> D'un esprit tout de feu mobiles fantaisies,
> Ces rêves d'un moment, belles illusions,
> D'un monde imaginaire aimables visions,
> Qui ne frappent jamais, trop subtile lumière,
> Des terrestres esprits l'oeil épais et vulgaire.[23]

Surely we are not to take his dreams and visions for what we might
nowadays call the myths of science. Rather, we must understand
that as he develops his idea of the poetry that would illuminate

scientific mysteries, he glides, perhaps unwittingly, away from the difficulties of rational thought. We may exemplify the "inventor's" treatment of subjects in nature with the lines describing the poet-hero of *L'Amérique*, despite Chénier's protest that this poet is not he:

> Ses vers ont revêtu, prompts et légers protées,
> Les formes tour à tour à ses yeux présentées.[24]

These Protean verses, like figments of the Shelleyan imagination that from the perceptions of nature could create "forms more real than living man" (*Prometheus Unbound*, I, 748), have a power over the winds and the sea:

> Puis, d'une aile glacée assemblant les nuages,
> Ils volent, troublent l'onde et soufflent les naufrages,
> . . . .
> Puis, d'un oeil doux et pur souriant à la terre,
> Ils la couvrent de fleurs; ils rassérènent l'air.
> Le calme suit leurs pas et s'étend sur la mer.[25]

The inventor makes contact with facts and phenomena in the manner of the "silencieux rêveur."[26] Indeed, if in the famous "artifice dialectique"[27] we substitute *passions*, *épreuves*, or *fantômes* for the word "pensers," "inventor" is another name for the writer of the *Bucoliques* and *Élégies*. With the fresh and striking image of the amber bit which traps and preserves an insect in its flight, Chénier sums up the characteristics of his poetry:

> Seule, de mots heureux, faciles, transparents,
> Elle [poetry] sait revêtir ces fantômes errants:
> Ainsi des hauts sapins de la Finlande humide,
> De l'ambre, enfant du ciel, distille l'or fluide,
> Et sa chute souvent rencontre dans les airs
> Quelque insecte volant qu'il porte au fond des mers.[28]

This intriguing simile gracefully combines elements of the picturesque, the remote, the recherché, and, at the same time, the natural, which Chénier sought in his "vers antique," but it sheds little light on the techniques with which the would-be poet of science and natural history would work.

Neither does it prepare us for the account of the "inventor's" enthusiasm. There are classical statements on inspired transport, of course, such as Virgil's lines on Cybele or Plato's ironic theory in the *Ion*. Chénier compares his conception of this solemn fury with the torments of Io:

> Sous l'insecte vengeur envoyé par Junon,
> Telle Io tourmentée, en l'ardente saison,
> Traverse en vain les bois et la longue campagne
> Et le fleuve bruyant qui presse la montagne;
> Tel le bouillant poète, en ses transports brûlants,
> Le front échevelé, les yeux étincelants,
> S'agite, se débat, cherche en d'épais bocages
> S'il pourra de sa tête apaiser les orages,
> Et secouer le Dieu qui fatigue son sein.[29]

To understand how this apparent excess is compatible with the restraint of the Hellenistic miniaturist, we may perhaps resort to Longinus:

> . . . from the great natures of the men of old there are borne in upon the souls of those who emulate them (as from sacred caves) what we may describe as *effluences*, so that even those who seem little likely to be possessed are thereby inspired and succumb to the spell of the others' greatness.[30]

At the center of *L'Invention* Chénier granted the fundamental validity of the neoclassical reverence for the achievements of ancient writers. The freedom and noble daring of thought fascinated his imagination and filled him with a sense of grandeur: ". . . libre, sans détour, / Chaque homme ose être un homme et penser au grand jour."[31] Working back from the example of Cicero in Rome, he thought of Demosthenes, and the voice of Pericles, "de tous les coeurs maîtresse," then the objects of poetry in Pindar's odes, and finally the Dionysiac festival, the setting for the tragedies and "d'une sainte folie un peuple furieux."[32] Chénier wished above all to carry the spirit of this Greek harmony of virtue and eloquence into his own verses:

> Puis, ivres des transports qui nous viennent surprendre,

Parmi nous, dans nos vers, revenons les répandre.[33]

To judge from a lyrical experiment in *L'Amérique*, the power of inspiration might also have been extended to include the "enthousiasme errant" of the preromantic fancy. It is "fils de la belle nuit," the intuition of Nature herself by the poetic genius. This enthusiasm, recalling passages from Thomson and Young,[34] is the logical extension of the recourse which the elegiac poet, disciple of Rousseau, has to phenomenal nature as the source of imaginative stimulation. But it is noteworthy that this excerpt from *L'Amérique* transfers to the *philosophe* the reverence which Chénier and Longinus bestowed on the great writers of antiquity.

We are not disappointed to find that *Hermès* and *L'Amérique* were abandoned during the years of the Revolution. Probably they could never have been finished. The expressions, myths, and poetic conventions of antiquity might be regarded as the native language of the imagination, which they filled with aspirations. But they are inadequate to reveal the technical thought of the eighteenth century.

Chénier's enthusiasm in only a pale herald of the romantic quest for participation in "the eternal, the infinite, the one."[35] His flight beyond the stars to the eternal springs of nature where the soul feels its divinity is not really typical of his poetic work. Instead, as the poetry of the last period shows, his intention to write as the ancients would have done had they lived at the end of the eighteenth century —that intention which failed in its literal application—found partial fulfillment during the French Revolution in ways more consistent with Chénier's temperament and his aspirations as an artist.

During this period, the number of direct quotations from the Greek or definite allusions to Greek thought and poetry diminishes. Life in revolutionary France gains a pathos and an intensity proper to itself, and Chénier seems to put aside his texts, while the authors sometimes come alive in his memory.[36] Thus, in the fourth ode, for example, where Chénier carefully imitates Pindar's strophic form both by the construction of his stanzas and the movement of thought, the language borrowed from Pindar serves a distinctly new purpose. Pindar's arrows "that speak to the wise" in the second *Olympian* (83-85) become the weapons of a poet who has assumed the role of critic and public conscience.

> O mon esprit, au sein des cieux,
> Loin de tes noirs chagrins, une ardente allégresse
> Te transporte au banquet des Dieux,
> Lorsque ta haine vengeresse,
> Rallumée à l'aspect et du meurtre et du sang,
> Ouvre de ton carquois l'inépuisable flanc.
> De là vole aux méchants ta flèche redoutée,
> D'un fiel vertueux humectée.

[*Ode IV*]

This passage indicates that poetry is still a moral power able to teach and to record noble actions. Chénier is partly recalling Pindar's conception that in the paths of virtue the poet is the equal and companion to the heroes and rulers for whom he writes.

The conviction that literature guides and determines moral action partly motivated Chénier's numerous prose articles. In these he counseled the people and criticized the revolutionary government, speaking out against parties and factions, and attacking with special indignation the Jacobins, who having appropriated the role of the people to a small clique, satisfied their self-interest by the spilling of innocent blood in the name of the constitution.[37] As Jean Fabre has pointed out, Chénier supposed that writers and philosophers gave both life and direction to the Revolution: ". . . tout ce qui se fait de bien ou de mal dans cette révolution est du à des écrits." But at the same time, as Fabre has observed, "Ce poète humilié, hanté par un idéal de grandeur qui le fuit, rend naturellement responsable de son échec un monde où la poésie dépérit."[38]

It is in this spirit, as the poet who remains dignified and proud though defeated by the state of society around him, that Chénier took up his satirical stance and adopted the "pieds inégaux" of his *Iambes*.[39] He looked on the atrocities of the Terror as an outrage against his own personal dignity. "Gallus de Byzance," the name with which he had represented the elegiac poet, gave up his solitary pursuits to become, as he said, the son of Archilochus:

> Fils d'Archiloque, fier André,

Ne détends point ton arc, fléau de l'imposture.
    Que des passants pleins de tes vers,
Les siècles, l'avenir, que toute la nature
    Crie à l'aspect de ces pervers:
Hou, les vils scélérats! les monstres! les infâmes!
    De vol, de massacres nourris,
Noirs ivrognes de sang, lâches bourreaux des femmes
    Qui n'égorgent point leurs maris;
Du fils tendre et pieux; et du malheureux père
    Pleurant son fils assassiné;
Du frère qui n'a point laissé dans la misère
    Périr son frère abandonné.

                                   [Iambe IV]

Chénier did not imitate Archilochus as he had imitated Virgil or Theocritus or the writers of the Greek Anthology. The satire in the *Iambes* is concerned with the Marats and the Barères who caused such inhuman cruelties. Chénier rarely uses the language of Archilochus, though we may here and there suppose we have found some remote parallels. Chénier distinguishes his verses from the personal vindictiveness found in the fragments that remain from the Greek poet: "mes fureurs servent les lois" (*Iambe I*). If Archilochus shaped "his own personality by clothing it in the heroic costume of epic phraseology,"[40] Chénier, associating his poetic voice with the memory of Archilochus, recalls that tradition in which the Greek elegiac and iambic poets conceived of themselves as "the general voice of the country."[41]

In this respect, then, the *Iambes* exemplify the doctrine of *L'Invention*, according to which the modern poet receives moral and spiritual inspiration from his imaginative self-involvement in the traditions of Greece. His wrath and his sacrifices acquire dignity from such association. But if we turn back to the illustration of this doctrine in *Ode IV*, we realize that the optimism with which it had been enunciated is gone.

PERCY BYSSHE SHELLEY

III

To Discover a Myth
of Innocence

Shelley's literary studies and his search for the materials of poetry touched a wider surface of Greek culture and his insight was deeper than Chénier's. His need for what he felt the Greeks could supply was at once keener and more explicit. Even more decidedly than Chénier, Shelley was split by a play of opposite tendencies. On the one hand, he longed for such a deep and careless union with nature that man would be governed by necessity, and therefore irresponsible. On the other hand, he wanted autonomy for the person, with freedom of thought, stability of will, and such dignity as could restore man to the center of the universe. Gradually, to reconcile these opposites, he turned to the Greeks for their understanding of both nature and man.

Shelley began with *Queen Mab* at the point where Chénier's quest for unity broke down in an undigested mélange of Greek poetry and eighteenth-century science. The Shelley of *Queen Mab* is still to a large extent a man of the Enlightenment. He was still trying to practice its "religion of philanthropy," believe in its "generalized self-love," and pretend that public activity generalized personal feelings and that "virtue produces pleasure." He preached the "benevolent passions," and asserted that "the more thought there is in the world the more happiness and liberty will there be."[1] But how to bring thought and feeling together was the question that drove him in search of peace, to snatch at whatever doctrine offered itself.

> At a triumphant pitch, he cries:
>   'Spirit of Nature! thou
> Life of interminable multitudes;
>   Soul of those mighty spheres
> Whose changeless paths through Heaven's deep silence lie;
>   Soul of that smallest being,
>   The dwelling of whose life
>   Is one faint April sun-gleam; —
>   Man, like these passive things,
> Thy will unconsciously fulfilleth:
>   Like theirs, his age of endless peace,
>   Which time is fast maturing,
>   Will swiftly, surely come. . . .'

[*Queen Mab*, III, 226-37]

The fact that the Nature Queen bears off Ianthe's soul to commune with the spirit of the world indicates that such intercourse is possible for human powers.[2] As early as 1811, Shelley had "long been convinced of the eventual omnipotence of mind over matter," and the realization of this "golden age," he thought, would "be the task of human powers."[3] But this escape into the realm of principle and spirit did not disguise the poet's sense of real isolation:

> . . . The universe
> In Nature's silent eloquence, declares
> That all fulfil the works of love and joy, —
> All but the outcast, Man. . . .

[*Queen Mab*, III, 196-99]

Shelley's moral and metaphysical loneliness during the months after his expulsion from Oxford on account of his atheism illustrates the lasting effect in his person of those adolescent inquiries into God, man, and the universe, which were so dissonant in *Queen Mab*. His zest for social reform at this time indicates the force with which his energies overflowed. In offering the edification of a godless philanthropy to his friends and to the poor of Ireland, his intention was not a Byronic defiance, though it came from the camp of rebellion. Shelley did not, to suit his own convenience, merely shift his allegiance from God to the devil. Indeed, by the time he wrote the preface to *Prometheus Unbound*, he recognized the "casuistry" of excusing Satan's sins because of the great punishment they drew.[4]

Shelley's difficulty was that he could not make up his mind about God or the devil. His early novels treat diabolic characters with an ambivalent sense of admiration and fear. The doubts and failures of his early life joined this attitude to action without certainty. The "Necessity of Atheism" argues that we cannot know any such reality or Creator behind the world as religion makes the resting place of belief. Though he did take the "sacrament" a few months after the pamphlet on atheism, the religion of compliance with a cult was unacceptable because it was the agent of restraint. Shelley asserted that its forms were the wreckage of a dead past, its cruel history a contradiction of the feelings it claimed to foster. Had it sustained itself "by the mere force of reasoning and persuasion," he wrote in 1813, its resemblance to other tyrannical institutions that have decayed "would be inadmissible"—

> We should never speculate on the future obsoleteness of a system perfectly conformable to nature and reason; it would endure so long as they endured; it would be a truth as indisputable as the light of the sun, . . . and other facts whose evidence, depending on our organization and relative situations, must remain acknowledged as satisfactory, so long as man is man. [Note on *Queen Mab*, VII, 135]

As these reminiscences of Paine and Hume reveal,[5] Shelley sometimes believed that reason, interpreting or speaking for nature, should be the final judge of institutions. This belief appealed to the scientific side of Shelley's personality. This rationalist Shelley cherished the view, derived from Hume and Godwin,[6] that

> Motive is to voluntary action in the human mind what cause is to effect in the material universe. The word liberty as applied to mind is analogous to the word chance as applied to matter. . . .
> [Note on *Queen Mab*, VI, 198]

But where "Necessity" is "mother of the world," there is no chance, either outside or within the mind. Therefore, there is no responsibility. Man conforms to the indifferent will of a world soul, if we may express the anomaly thus. He is a "puppet," to borrow Plato's phrase from the *Laws* (644-45), his actions, loves, hates having been planned for him.

Shelley wished to approach the problem of good and evil like an astronomer, with the sort of law that would apply equally to the stars and to the souls of men. In "his flight from the intensely human to the intensely cosmic," he thought, as Joseph Barrell points out, that he could achieve an "unanthropomorphic spirituality."[7] From the sky palace of Queen Mab, the earth seemed a tiny, far-off point of light; the petty concerns of men seemed to have been subsumed under the universal laws that rule the stars. Precisely at this state, where the coupling of natural and moral science gave the illusion of success, Shelley's adoption of the science and philosophy of his time disposed him to receive the definitive influence of Plato.

We have only to imagine a kind of reversibility in the progress of history in order to suppose that some of the materialists of the eighteenth century might have been converted to Platonism by the aid of "pure reason."[8] Nor is it so strange that Shelley should assert the beliefs and sentiments of his time and yet become "vehemently excited" by Plato's "reveries" and by that doctrine especially "which teaches that all our knowledge consists of reminiscences of what we had learned in a former existence."[9] Indeed, though the term "reverie" was inaccurate as the *philosophes* used it to disparage Plato's reasonings toward a higher consciousness,[10] it serves well enough to describe not only Rousseau's unreflective absorption in his own existence, but also the romantic habit of dissolving consciousness for the sake of disembodied feeling. Shaftsbury, after all, as well as Milton, had been a Platonist. Not only cosmic order but the claims of emotion could be symbolized in Platonic terms. Stressing Plato's intuitive myths, to the exclusion of his logic, Wordsworth had adapted the doctrine of recollection to fit the sentimental paradox of the philosopher-child. Shelley, who was to carry the Platonizing of emotion further than any of his contemporaries, was to seek Plato's help in the solution of his intellectual problems as well. Man or nature or some inscrutable and supreme power—which one was the measure and therefore the judge of all things? Wordsworth's God in the woods and streams was too low a standard for "those thoughts that wander through eternity."

Is the life of mind compatible with the life of feeling? Somewhat softening the extreme of pleasure, which Plato's Philebus and Calicles had espoused, Rousseau taught that mind and feeling are not compatible, and elected feeling, with what nature forbids as the main stricture. Was love good then, or evil? Again, Shelley's contemporaries gave him no standard. By convention and law, it was restricted, but Godwin had repealed such rules in his *Political Justice*. By experience, love's consequences were painful, as Shelley's adventures had proved. But Plato had touched the question of love in the *Symposium* and the *Phaedrus*, and had sorted the ways in which love was an urgent necessity, a celestial hope, or an earthly blight. And finally, is knowledge virtue, as eighteenth-century optimists such as Condorcet had implied, with quite a different meaning from Socrates' intention? Does it come from sensation alone, as Locke believed? Is it perception of the mind of God, as Berkeley said, and no guarantee of the external world? Is it good, or is it guiltily associated with the corruptions and oppressions of European society, as Rousseau claimed? Plato had grouped such questions around what man is and ought to be, his baseness or his dignity. He had realized that the proposition "man is the measure of all things" is not an axiom of ethical judgment, but an axis on which the constellation of human problems might be rotated in review.

Shelley, of course, had no such succinct understanding of contemporary affinities with Greece when he wrote *Queen Mab*. If he had read Plato's *Timaeus* for himself, he did not appreciate the consistency with which the astronomer-moralist applied his probabilities to man, with the result that excessive passion could be blamed on too much seed around the spine, a defect for which man's natural constitution was responsible (*Timaeus,* 86). But the point at which he failed to give himself over to Plato in *Queen Mab* is also the point at which the eighteenth century failed him.

Having reached a climactic detachment among the stars, Shelley turns, in *Queen Mab,* from the ecstasies of paradise to attack the central evil, the tyranny of religion, oppressing men on earth. This oppression drew his rage as it had provoked the ironic pathos in Blake's songs. Shelley's attack shows that his reference point was also the "human heart divine." Though he should flee to the end of the universe, his heart could not forget its intimacy with good and evil.[11] The church, the law, the selfishness and customs of men entangled in the nets of order and restraint were only signs of "pride and avarice," the familiars of the human heart. The ultimate triumph, as Shelley conceived it, would not be indifferent law but man-made benevolence, which could abrogate all law. The age of gold must depend on a gigantic wish that could transform nature to suit the will of man.[12] This must be a will powerful enough to raise islands from the sea and stabilize the seasons by straightening the earth's axis. We must remember, if we are inclined to sneer, that Shelley was carrying the revolutionary dream of "infinite perfectibility" across the boundary to infinite perfection; his paradise is a dream as ancient as mankind and as common as childhood. Rousseau too, conceiving power as human will, had clothed the nakedness of his wishes in discourses of reason.

Shelley was discovering that the solitary poet could not drink in peace from nature's eternal springs. He was learning—as the waning of his interest in radical action suggests—that the poet's first task would be to reconstitute the cracked vessel of the poet's self. The letters and conduct of the early period reveal how Shelley felt, in his own person, the cleft he saw in man: a slave but yet capable of freedom, a tyrant but oppressed, a victim of his own ignorance though desirous of virtue by his very makeup, he was racked on the machinery of his own constitution. This "feeble, wavering, feverish being,"[13] fed on the metaphysical and epistemological doubt of his age, was cut off from the substance of the world and the Divinity behind it. Like a Pico without the guarantee of permanence, Shelley was capable of everything yet nothing, an "elemental god" or the "insect that sports in a transient sunbeam, which the next cloud shall obscure for ever."[14] In 1811, aware of his condition, though ignorant of its cause, he told Hogg how his moods veered between self-love (or *filautia* as he called it) and the absence of self-love (*afilautia*):

> What a strange being I am; how inconsistent in spite of all my boasted hatred of self: this moment thinking I could so far overcome Nature's law, as to exist in complete seclusion, the next starting from a moment of solitude—starting from my own company, as if it were that of a fiend—seeking anything rather than a continued communion with *self.* [Letter to Thomas Hogg, May 8, 1811]

Shelley was wrestling with the Socratic riddle of self-knowledge even before he closely studied that dialogue (*Phaedrus,* 230) in which Socrates asked: ". . . am I a monster more complicated and swollen with passion than the serpent Typho, or a creature of a gentler and simpler sort, to whom Nature has given a diviner and lowlier destiny?"[15] Like Plato, Shelley realized with increasing certainty that the question "What am I?" is inseparable from the question "What should I be?" In literature and philosophy the Greeks had wrestled with the problems of man's nature and his fate up to the time of Plato's synthetic formulations. This tension which the Greeks felt between the inner, free, and human world, and the outer world of rule, obligation, and hardship was at bottom ethical. Similarly, speculation about reason, sentiment, and nature forced Shelley to ask what was fundamentally a question of values.

The radical question of values, that floating pair of unstable correlatives—what is and what must be—had become a problem in Shelley's thinking during the Eton and Oxford days, while he was avidly reading Gothic romances and turning out some of his own. This was also the question which his major heroes tried to resolve. Increasingly for Shelley, this basic question became one of human relationships, as it had been for Plato: man's relation to nature, to society and to the feelings and consciences of other men, to law (both human and extra-human), and above all, the relationship of man to himself.

In *Queen Mab* Shelley had reached a contradiction because he had been too ambitious, without a scheme or building plan. In *Alastor* (1815) he simplified his problem to a bare minimum, concentrating on the simplest relations of all, those of a solitary human being to nature and himself. Thus amid the intellectual and moral alternatives, toward which he was reaching for stability, his return to narrative poetry rephrased the Socratic question as a central concern in romantic literature. Though Shelley could not at the time have calculated all the deep affinities, the plot of *Alastor*, which is the typical nucleus of his stories, brought Platonic thought into startling rapport with key points of romantic interest. *Alastor*, as a rich though clouded parable, shows how the pressures of contemporary thought and the torments in his soul pushed Shelley to raise these dialectical issues with Plato's help.

* * * * *

I

Whether or not Shelley had read the *Phaedrus* carefully by 1815, it is clear from *Alastor* that he too had seen through the illusion of natural sympathy for man, even though he would never entirely abandon the language of that theory. In fact, *Alastor* combines the theme of solitude with another formula which makes this poem a paradigm of sentimental love. The hero of *Alastor* spent his life in solitary sympathy with nature, untouched by the "heartless things . . . of the world" and the blandishments of women, until a dream shatters his peace and

> The spirit of sweet human love has sent
> A vision to the sleep of him who spurned

Her choicest gifts. . . .

[*Alastor*, 203-05]

In his dream, this hero beholds that "veiléd maid," whose figure floats through romantic poems in various guises. Spectral luminousness, which invests this heroine and eventually becomes the raiment of Asia's transfiguration in *Prometheus Unbound,* is Shelley's literary remembrance of Luxima's appearance, which Miss Owenson's missionary also saw in the vale of Cashmere.[16] But she behaves like that "damsel with a dulcimer," whose "singing of Mount Abora" captivated Coleridge in his dream of Xanadu. She is, in fact, solitude's answer to the poet-hero's need for sympathy with something more than "trees and the country." She bears to her poet-hero the same relationship which the poet of *Kubla Khan* intended when he said that if he could only remember his damsel's song, he could rebuild his vision and become again that youth who looked on paradise within an enchanted circle.

Perhaps the root of this relationship of power and subject is the relationship of the soul to itself in love. Thus the dream, it seems, has begotten from nature, not merely a companion, but the Shelleyan hero's feminine alter ego. She is "herself a poet":

Her voice was like the voice of his own soul
Heard in the calm of thought; its music long,
Like woven sounds of streams and breezes, held
His inmost sense suspended in its web
Of many-coloured woof and shifting hues.

[*Alastor*, 153-57]

Shelley seems to be confronting us with that romantic combination of reverie and nature which we have noticed before in Chénier's twenty-second elegy. But in Shelley's scattered accounts of the search for a wholly satisfying beloved we notice a clearer sense of the ideal.

"This object or its archetype forever exists in the mind," Shelley says:

> . . . the mind which selects among those who resemble it that
> which most resembles it and instinctively fills up the interstices
> of the imperfect image in the same manner as the imagination
> moulds and completes the shapes in clouds, or in the fire, into
> the resemblances of whatever form, . . . happens to be present
> to it.[17]

This creation of the mind is far more intimate with the poet's secret
imaginings. Hero and heroine are as one being, "whose nerves, like
the chords of two exquisite lyres, strung to the accompaniment of
one delightful voice, vibrate with the vibrations" of the poet's own
nerves.[18] The narrator of *Alastor*, like an Aeolian harp awaiting the
breath of nature, has projected this image of himself onto both the
dreaming hero and the visionary maid. The hero too is "a fragile lute,
on whose harmonious strings / The breath of heaven did wander"
(667-68). His consort's hands sweep "from some strange harp strange
symphony," and clothed in the same "sinuous wind," her fame is also the instrument for her music. Here the dream is a real dream, not
merely a conscious reverie. The two-in-one relationship of dreamer
and ideal stresses unity, and nature's role reflects that epistemological uncertainty which troubled the young Shelley: whether nature
is really sensation or a projection of thought.

But the "nympholeptic" vision of *Alastor* conforms to Shelley's
early theory of love so as to make us believe that he had already
resolved this doubt effectively in poetry, even if his speculations remained always uncertain.[19] The "Essay on Love" describes the mental archetype in a passage which is worth quoting at length:

> We dimly see within our intellectual nature a miniature as it were
> of our entire self, yet deprived of all that we condemn or despise,
> the ideal prototype of every thing excellent or lovely that we are
> capable of conceiving as belonging to the nature of man.. . . a
> mirror whose surface reflects only the forms of purity and bright-
> ness; a soul within our soul that describes a circle around its
> proper paradise which pain, and sorrow, and evil dare not over-
> leap.[20]

This model is visible to the mind alone, in which it has always existed. The mind may test sensation in this mirror, but the external world can only color, qualify, or quicken this inner center of the soul, through the mediation of the mind. The apparently spiritual "wind of heaven" and the apparently physical breath of nature are equally metaphorical stimulants; we still do not know whence they come. But we shall see these elements assume more distinct roles in *Prometheus Unbound* and in the famous lyrics.

For now, we need only mark that the difference between prototype and fact can be extreme. As Alcibiades said in Plato's *Symposium,* one has only to break the statue in half to find the golden images of the gods within. Shelley has, indeed, changed the quality of the prototype. The internal gods have become the figure of a dominant woman. The "veiléd maid" will mature into the powerful Cythna and finally into the nearly omnipotent Asia of *Prometheus Unbound.* She will be glimpsed for a moment in the flesh-and-blood person of Amelia, in *Epipsychidion.* But the Platonic relationship holds. The ideal self is, as it were, the goddess within the perfect and beautiful other self. Or, as Plato argued in the *Phaedrus,* the human object of love is the image of the god within the soul of the lover, and beauty, though it is felt subjectively, is the keenest sensuous manifestation of objective, absolute truth.

The "fulfillment and rounding out of the self" is the meaning of Shelleyan "nympholepsy," as Carlos Baker has suggested.[21] The dream of discovered personality contains the hero's hope that the myth which Aristophanes tells in the *Symposium* is both plausible and true. To the search for the other half of our divided nature, Shelley also makes the Socratic qualification: it is the quest for the better half, in fact, for the good itself. Although, as we shall see, there are wide differences between Shelley's theory of love and Plato's, Shelley had an uncanny instinct for finding what he wanted in his reading,[22] and he saw in Plato that subjective strain, which he interpreted for his own purposes.

Even as late as the translation of the *Symposium* and the composition of the discourse on the practices of love in Greece, Shelley attributed to the Greeks what he called "sentimental love." Both ancient Greece and modern Europe "had arrived at that epoch of

refinement, when sentimental love becomes an imperious want of
the heart and of the mind."[23] Though "deprived of its legitimate
object," owing to the enslaved condition of their women, the Greeks
were nevertheless capable of this love, since the living person was at
best its occasion, not its object:

> If we consider the facility with which certain phenomena con-
> nected with sleep, at the age of puberty, associate themselves
> with those images which are the objects of our waking desires;
> and even that in some persons of an exalted state of sensibility
> that a similar process may take place in reverie, it will not be
> difficult to conceive the almost involuntary consequences of a
> state of abandonment in the society of a person of surpassing
> attraction, when the sexual connection cannot exist.[24]

Shelley is interpreting that passage in the *Phaedrus,* where Plato describes the lovers' meetings:

> . . . in gymnastic exercises and at other times of meeting, then
> the fountain of that stream, which Zeus when he was in love with
> Ganymede named Desire, overflows upon the lover, and some
> enters into his soul, and some when he is filled flows out again;
> and as a breeze or an echo rebounds from the smooth rocks and
> returns whence it came, so does the stream of beauty, passing
> through the eyes which are the windows of the soul, come back
> to the beautiful one; . . . [the beloved] loves, but he knows not
> what; he does not understand and cannot explain his own state;
> . . . the lover is his mirror in whom he is beholding himself, but he
> is not aware of this. When he is with the lover, both cease from
> their pain, but when he is away then he longs as he is longed for,
> and has love's image, love for love (Anteros) lodging in his breast,
> which he calls and believes to be not love but friendship only.
> [*Phaedrus,* 255]

Read by itself, the subjectivity of this passage agrees with the
withdrawal from nature and for a time from society too for the sake
of self-discovery: the beauty proposed here is reached through communion with a higher self. Shelley's coupling of romantic sensibility
and Platonic love makes it likely that had he ventured in 1818 to

interpret *Alastor,* he would have said that his poem crystalizes the Platonic theory of love in its simplest form. The "sparkling rivulet" beside which the poet-hero "stretched his languid limbs," the mirroring well in which he saw himself near death, those yellow flowers sympathetically gazing on their image in the water do remind us that "the poet in Shelley's poem is merely another Narcissus given a new and more elaborate myth."[25] But in the light of Shelley's maturing thought, this myth is a Platonic parable, refined for the needs of the spirit: "sentimental love," it teaches, desires the echo of the transcendent self. The "veiléd maid" is not just an erotic companion. Her name is "knowledge and truth and virtue . . . / And lofty hopes of divine liberty" (*Alastor,* 158-59). At least the words that describe her beauty resemble that interior wisdom and virtue, that nobler self, which the scapegrace Alcibiades beheld within the satyr Socrates.

If we break this fiction into its parts, we can trace them, as many critics have done, in the works of Shelley's contemporaries. The context of music and eros, the dream that passion makes more real than life, the question of solitude or society all appeared in Keats's *Endymion,* where the dawn of the transcendent personality is also told with the Narcissus legend. Keats was not only answering Shelley's *Alastor;* Keats was exploring this set of contemporary problems for himself, and it is unlikely that he had any direct contact with Plato. A strain of traditional Platonism runs through even such Continental novels of the time as *Werther,* for example, and Constant's *Adolphe,* or Foscolo's *Ortis,* in which the beloved of the youthful hero is both perfectly ideal (Ortis would replace God with his Teresa) and ideally inaccessible. That gap between the mind and the real world which we have already seen in eighteenth-century thought was extended into the romantic love story. The perennial tension between fantasy and fact (a conflict which classical stories resolved in maintaining plausibility) was increased by those doubts about the mind which Shelley also felt. Fantasy commonly got the upper hand, because the desire that the romantic imagination served felt frustrated in the presence of facts.

"A moment's thought is passion's passing bell," Keats observed in

Lamia, and he meant thought of the outside world. Marriage, duty, honor, conscience, modesty, prejudice, or the "cold eye of philosophy" would destroy all charms of the imagination which created the romantic beloved. Or, as Constant's Adolphe discovers, the possession of the mistress spoils the ideal she occasioned. The poet-hero's loss, in *Alastor,* of "that beautiful shape" forever "in the pathless desert of dim sleep" stresses the point which many such novels and poems of the period adumbrate, that the beloved in these stories is a figment of the lover's mind. The fruitless search through nature and society for a counterpart to the vision underscores with heavy pathos the view that the world is inadequate to the needs of heightened sensibility.

Such love is Platonic, of course, only in the popular sense, as love which cannot find fulfillment in a world of disappointing appearances. What Keats called the "calm'd twilight of Platonic shades" (*Lamia*) describes the romantic mood rather than Socratic contemplation. Though Plato frequently compares the dawn of knowledge with the dream, though Socrates' knowledge is "as disputable as if it were a dream" (*Symposium,* 175d-e), the discovery of love, in that reverie which was the matrix of romantic inspiration, is a concession to fantasy which Plato did not make. For Plato, the dream was an image or analogue which expressed one feature of the mind's experience in knowing, and love was another such image. On the other hand, though the romantics were concerned with that "fellowship of essence" whose hierarchy Keats described in *Endymion,* they mingled the volatile emotional essence, which is fleeting, with the stable permanence of intellectual essence. Sometimes, as in *Alastor,* it is difficult to distinguish image from meaning, or to separate, as Plato always did, mind and emotion. The romantic imagination is synthetic, as Shelley and Coleridge realized. This faculty achieved its meaning through a combining or adding up of symbolic materials already steeped in associative value. Its motivation in desire deprived this faculty of that clear double vision by which Plato and the Greek poets held idea and allegory in harmony yet distinct. Shelley's borrowings, therefore, from the Platonic opus often refract the nuances toward an anti-Platonic point of view.[26]

When just before the moment of embrace the visionary maiden of *Alastor* rises, "as if her heart impatiently endured / Its bursting burthen" (173-74), the context of eros and knowledge almost persuades us that this language has been lifted from the *Symposium.* It is the kind of language Plato also uses to reveal one of the most important situations of the mind: "to one pregnant, and, as it were, already bursting with the load of his desire, the impulse towards that which is beautiful is intense, on account of the great pain of retaining that which he had conceived."[27]

This analogy of "conception in the beautiful according to the body and according to the soul" is a favorite Platonic figure. In the *Theaetetus* it is intellectualized to include the detached midwifery of Socratic teaching and the bringing to birth of ideas. It elevates the begetting of ideas above the generations of the body, and keeps thought rigorous and love sensuous, without the loss of figurative force. This imagery refers to a critical moment in Platonic thought: "The bodies and souls of all human beings are alike pregnant with their future progeny, and when we arrive at a certain age, our nature impells us to bring forth and propagate."[28]

The soul, Plato says in the *Phaedrus,* can rise to the verge of essential being or fall, as a result of this moment, and be a fool in the world below. The instant is rich with metaphysical and moral possibility. Plato had used the sensations of love as a lowly analogue for the philosopher's birth into the realms of thought. In Shelley's use, the language of Platonic love refers to the birth of passion. The metaphysical connotations are now refracted and set the passion forth in a purifying light. The things of the mind which that language had expressed—thought and the ways of thought—become emblematical of the concrete fact, the moment of puberty as it were, to which the romantics traced the emergence of the self. Moreover, although this moment poses the problem over which the hero of *Alastor* perishes, the use of Platonic language opens the way to Shelley's partial solution of that problem.

* * * * *

II

Love, whether of mortal beauty or of immortal wisdom, assaults the enchanted circle of the dreaming ego. In order to be reunited with their ideal, men have to leave or be driven from the paradise of solitary self and pass through time and imperfection to attain what is yearned for as a higher bliss. If love has the capacity to confer immortality, as Diotima argues in the *Symposium,* it comes, nevertheless, as a destructive force. The awakened hero of *Alastor* is "as an eagle grasped / In the folds of a green serpent" (227-28). Shelley repeats this language in *The Revolt of Islam* and uses it again in *Prometheus Unbound.* But we remember also Alcibiades in the *Symposium* who was "bitten by something more keen and vehement than the keenest of all things by which any one ever was bitten, wounded in my very heart and soul, . . . by the words of philosophy which pierce more sharply than a viper's tooth, when they seize on a fresh and not ungenerous spirit."[29]

Having glimpsed the ideal, the hero of *Alastor* is impelled to love the vision during a period of trial and probation, so that he may be lifted to reunion with his ideal on a plane of new equality. The true and lasting union requires the casting off or purging of mortality. This is the reason why death as well as suffering is the correlative to love in so many of the parallels we have cited in connection with *Alastor.*

Alastor represents the first stage in this typically romantic plot. But this narrative, which makes an allegory out of the coming of love, points to a Greek formula which lies at the center of Plato's dialectical concern. Man is a dying god, this story says, an incompatible mixture of body and soul, mortality and immortality, passion and mind, forced to persevere between the world of "permanence" and the world of change, participating in both. Love is, in Plato's phrase, a genius or *daimon,* belonging to the interstice between God and man. Like virtue, which unites mind and passion, love, for Shelley as for Plato, is a spiritual essence whose middle state is aptly symbolized by the mating of poverty and plenty (*Symposium,* 203). But as Empedocles said, explaining how the presence of the *daimon* in mortality was associated with unhappiness and guilt:

> There is an oracle of Necessity, an ordinance of the gods, ancient, eternal, and sealed by broad oaths, that whenever one of the *daimones,* whose portion is length of days, has sinfully stained his hands with blood or followed strife or forsworn himself, he shall be banished from the abodes of the blessed for thrice ten thousand seasons, being born throughout the time in all manner of mortal shapes, exchanging one toilsome path for another. . . . One of these am I now, an exile and a wanderer from the gods, because I put my trust in insensate strife.

> Alas, unhappy race of men, bitterly unblest, such are the groans and struggles from which ye have been born!

> But at the last they appear among mankind as prophets, poets, physicians and princes; and thence they arise as gods, exalted in honor, sharing with the other gods a common hearth and table, free from the miseries of mortality, without part therein, untroubled.[30]

The golden age may seem like Eden; in the beginning things may have been the same for gods and for mortals, as Hesiod said (*Works and Days,* 110-120); but the Greeks found it difficult to conceive of the human compound as possessing an innocence proper to itself. Whether souls were sown from the stars, as Plato tells (*Timaeus,* 41-42), or wakened into consciousness by the fire of mind, which Prometheus stole from heaven, there is a strong inevitability in their constitutional evil. "God made man such as he is, and then damned him for being so," Shelley said in 1813, showing how his early thought had predisposed him to the Greek view.

Conceiving the coming of love as a necessary moment in the life of every man, Shelley thought of his allegory as universal. This dawning of self-consciousness "dooms to a slow and poisonous decay those meaner spirits that dare to abjure its dominion," and the moment of this mixture in stronger proportion—like "that Power which strikes the luminaries of the world with sudden darkness and extinction, by awakening them to too exquisite a perception of its influences" (Preface to *Alastor*)—is more swiftly fatal in more gifted natures. In other words, the coming of love activates the power of intelligence already present in the hero. It bends the heightened intellect inward in search of the ideal. Of itself, the passion is both necessary and innocent. The variable is intelligence. But the combination of passion and intelligence is not only destructive, it is also guilty.

Athanase, the Shelleyan hero at the middle stage in this romantic trilogy, suffers from a sense of an unknown guilt buried deep in his soul, as if this being with the name of immortality had been damned from eternity for a forgotten reason. The sense of imperfection in *Alastor* is identified as a brooding remorse in *Prince Athanase.* Friends bring explanations of his disorder from the four corners of knowledge: they ascribe it in turn to madness, to the recollection of a past life which makes a hell of this one, to a divine punishment for steadfast love, or to the shadow of a dream forgotten within the gulf of the soul. The "adamantine veil" which separates the mind and the heart of this hero denotes the same barrier between the world of consciousness and the paradise of sleep which troubled the hero of *Alastor*. In a deeper sense it is true of Athanase that unless the world of conscious thought and the world of feeling can be made compatible, there is no living at all. In *Prince Athanase,* the epistemological problem of *Alastor* is given the dimensions of a moral problem as well, and in a surprising way the Platonic problem of knowledge and virtue takes its place in the romantic narrative.

The nearly successful love story of Laon and Cythna strengthens this argument by giving a partial solution to the several problems that haunted the hero of *Alastor* and Athanase. Laon's dream parallels his real relationship with Cythna. Fantasy and fact agree. Both his personal and his sexual relations can stand the test of social conflict. Society can inflict punishment, and in turn, its victims can reform society. With the help of human sympathies and magical powers of speech, the hero and his real "second self" can overcome the cleavage between feeling and consciousness, between desire and restraint, and bring this cyclic tale to an end.

Of course, this story of "soul making," with its dense imagery and unreal atmosphere, bears little superficial resemblance to the Greek drama with which it ultimately became associated in *Prometheus Un-*

bound. But the identification of mortal man as a dying god is also the climactic point toward which Greek tragedy reaches through its tightly plotted action. The plague, the prohibition, the banishment, or any animosity which the world displays toward the tragic hero is real and obstinate. But though guilt projects itself into the world, it sustains itself on the vitals of an Oedipus or an Orestes. It is the inner conflict that sets edict and taboo at odds. The incandescent passion for self-assertion in the Greek hero is sterner stuff than the self-gratifying desire of the romantic professional sufferer, but the two have the same basic relationships. The boundless desire for selfhood or absolute autonomy radically opposes the limiting discoveries of intelligence. The knowledge in which Oedipus put his confidence finds him guilty although, as he says in *Oedipus at Colonus,* he has done no conscious wrong. The action that entails guilt in the irrational world of Sophocles is the act of knowing, as Professor Whitman has skillfully demonstrated.[31] As we examine Shelley's reconstruction of the Prometheus myth, we shall see how he adapted the treatments which Aeschylus and Hesiod gave this myth to suit his Platonic allegory of the soul, and how the wish to believe that guilt is proportionate not to passion, but to intelligence, found support in a reading of this Greek tragedy.

* * * * *

III

In Aeschylus' Io, exiled for her dream of union in love with a god, Shelley might have found a more or less convincing likeness for the hero of *Alastor* and an apt illustration of the sufferings that come with the birth of desire. But by the time he wrote his *Prometheus Unbound* he was concerned with a more general "type of the highest perfection of moral and intellectual nature, impelled by the purest and the truest motives to the best and noblest ends."[32] The Aeschylean Prometheus is an etiological personification of intelligence, a complexly symbolic everyman, a pre-Socratic hero who exorcises passion and implants a kind of self-knowledge. For Aristotle, a century and a quarter later, the possession of speech, the *logos* (often translated as the rational principle), was seen to distinguish men from the brutes (*Politics*, 1253A 10-16; 1332B 5-6). But Prometheus also knew that words are physicians if applied at the critical moment (*Prometheus Bound*, 377-80), and by means of words he controls his suffering and instills in the chorus of timid sea nymphs a share of his own courage and sympathetic love. His gift of fire to men brought the civilizing arts which enabled creatures of a day to form and order their experience, to direct their actions, and to discover dignity in their existence. But if the willful theft of this symbolic fire from heaven was an error disturbing the order of nature, then that transgression is a sin (*Prometheus Bound*, 266).[33] If the Promethean gift is sinful, then the human compound, which received that gift and which contains the same mixture of heaven and earth as the Titan, is a guilty mixture. Prometheus, in his chains, his anguish, his indignation, and his intelligence, is the divine expression of the human condition.

To outline the first act of Shelley's play is to show his debt to Aeschylus for the characters and the plot that shaped his myth of innocence regained. But while in one sense Shelley rewrote the Aeschylean poem, in another sense he re-created it. After a piece of exposition, in which the Titan soliloquizes on the lesson of love which he has learned through three thousand years of suffering on the "eagle-baffling" rock, the four movements of this act, each with its recollection of the past, its present experience, and its glimpse into the future, deepen the lesson and draw its consequences.[34] Each of these episodes introduces a new encounter between Prometheus and some force, friendly or hostile. The shade of Jupiter, suggested perhaps by the Zeus of the underworld in the *Suppliant Maidens* (230-31), repeats the curse against the actual ruler of the universe, though Shelley's Prometheus has repented of his cursing. Mercury, a composite of the sympathetic Hephaistos and the proud Hermes of Aeschylus' play, tries to extract the secret that a future marriage with Thetis will bring about Jupiter's overthrow. The Furies, agents of an archaic and inadequate but tormenting conscience, as in the *Oresteia*, afflict Shelley's Titan with visions of horror drawn for the most part from human history. And finally, in the fourth encounter, the spirits of thought, sent by the Earth, recalling those benevolent chthonic powers who, according to Hesiod, have lingered since the golden age befriending men, prophesy the Promethean triumph over his enemies, tyranny, necessity, and evil. Shelley has reversed the Aeschylean pattern of alternating statements of sympathy and pain so that the result will be positive.

But Shelley was more sensitive to the large outlines and to the striking details of image than he was to the careful art or dialectical design which combined them. The natural imagery of the Greek play had impressed him strongly. "Like that described in the *Prometheus* of Aeschylus," the Alpine scenery which he saw in 1818 was "vast rifts and caverns in granite precipices . . . walls of toppling rock only to be scaled, as he described, by the winged chariot of the ocean nymphs."[35] Shelley's mountain, "black, wintry, dead, unmeasured; without herb / Insect, or beast, or shape or sound of life" (*Prometheus Unbound*, I, 21-22), might as well be Mont Blanc as Aeschylus' impassable wilderness in a remote region of the earth. The "bright chains" which "eat with their burning cold into my bones," the "earthquake-fiends," the "genii of the storm" are not entirely inconsistent with the Aeschylean theme, but the details of personal emotion are too minutely pictured: ". . . icy Springs, stagnant with wrinkling frost, / . . . vibrated to hear me, and then crept / Shuddering through India" (*Prometheus Unbound*, I, 62-64). The infinite extension of the Promethean feeling into nature is cut short in the very attempt to make it explicit.

The Aeschylean use of nature imagery, and the highly organized world view, both mythical and philosophical, on which it depends, is confidently anthropomorphic. The Greek poet did not hesitate to orchestrate his meanings with natural effects, because the life of man is seen to be inseparable from the larger, dominating patterns of nature. There is no shortage of sympathies in the Greek play. The Promethean suffering rings through the universe to the inmost recesses of the ocean caves:

> Now all the land has cried in desolation. . . . As many mortals as dwell in holy Asia, their neighboring home, groan for your race and honor, suffer in your endless woe. [406-14]

With a shout, the sea wave clashing, the deep groans; black
Hades rumbles in the hollow earth; the springs of purest rivers
groan for piteous woe. [431-35]

The chorus of sea maidens who utter these lines are, as befits their
character, all turned to tears. But they have entered into the sufferings of Prometheus by reasoned inquiry into his guilt. Aeschylus did
not avoid the personification of nature. He endowed the elements,
not only with immense feeling, but also with the traits of fully drawn
character.

The tearful qualities of the scene are present in Shelley, of course.
Pity, in fact, is the basis of contact between his Prometheus and the
powers that console him. The "misery" of his crucifixion is stamped
on the elements, which remember, each in turn, the details of their reaction as the whole creation groaned under the first shock of his en-
chainment. The rigors of the scene are softened, however; the strenuous demands of intelligent compassion are eased. The elements are
vague voices without shape: they are metaphors for thoughts and
sensations, and they lack mythical objectivity. The wonderful *hubris*
with which the Greek Titan invoked the natural witnesses to the anguish of the human condition is untuned. Displaying a petulant
egoism, Shelley's Prometheus moans:

> . . . Mother, thy sons and thou
> Scorn him, without whose all-enduring will
> Beneath the fierce omnipotence of Jove,
> Both they and thou had vanished, like thin mist
> Unrolled on the morning wind. . . .

> [*Prometheus Unbound,* I, 113-17]

Hubris, with its cosmic implications of real and paradigmatic
struggle, has collapsed. The drama has been transferred from the
world of experience to the domain of thought. Shelley's Prometheus
hears a voice:

> . . . an awful whisper rises up!
> 'Tis scarce like sound: it tingles through the frame
> As lightning tingles, hovering ere it strike.

> [I, 132-34]

This lightning comes apparently from the "cloud of mind," but the experience of thought and nature is scarcely separated:

> Obscurely through my brain, like shadows dim,
> Sweep awful thoughts, rapid and thick. . . .

[I, 146-47]

The "spirit" or "melancholy voice" announces herself to be the Earth. Her coming causes the Titan to feel "faint, like one mingled in entwining love"; she is an intermediary through whom Prometheus can reach back into the past. She enables the immortal to commune with the world of the dead. Allegorically, she is the earthly side of the "offspring of heaven and earth," and brings immortal consciousness into contact with the perishable or mortal memory.

Consciousness is usually opposed to dreaming. For the early Greeks it was rooted in experience, tested by reality, characterized by the recollection of hardship, and symbolized in the Promethean sufferings. It was the way, the means, the road to wisdom; as Aeschylus says through the symbolism of Prometheus, it was the teacher, the physician of the human race. Shelley tended, on the contrary, to identify consciousness in the Aeschylean sense with guilt. In the *Prometheus Unbound,* the Furies, who might well be taken as the cause of "woe-remembering distress," resemble their Aeschylean type inasmuch as they are ". . . dread thought beneath thy brain, / And foul desire round thine astonished heart" (I, 488-89). But they also review the woes that have befallen mankind throughout history, climaxing their revelation with the vision of the crucified Christ. The afflictions which haunted the heroes of *Alastor* and *Prince Athanase* are included in a more general list by the Furies that torture Shelley's Prometheus:

> Leave the self-contempt implanted
> In young spirits, sense-enchanted,
> > Misery's yet unkindled fuel:
> Leave Hell's secrets half unchanted
> > To the maniac dreamer. . . .

[I, 510-14]

They are spirits of hell and hounds of Jupiter, agents of consciousness expressing itself as conscience. From the view of things which they embody, the Promethean gifts have the same results as the coming together of passion and intelligence in the hero of *Alastor:*

> Dost thou boast the clear knowledge thou waken'dst for man?
> Then was kindled within him a thirst which outran
> Those perishing waters; a thirst of fierce fever,
> Hope, love, doubt, desire, which consume him for ever.
>
> > [*Prometheus Unbound,* I, 542-45]

These are the effects of the Promethean gifts in a world where "all best things are thus confused to ill" (I, 628). Christ is only an "emblem" of the fact which Prometheus must accept and apply to himself:

> . . . those who do endure
> Deep wrongs for man, and scorn, and chains, but heap
> Thousandfold torment on themselves and him.
>
> > [I, 594-96]

The effects of consciousness, which we have already noted, are identified with conscience through the mythical persons of the Furies, and these effects are generalized:

> In each human heart terror survives
> The ravin it has gorged: the loftiest fear
> All that they would disdain to think were true:
> Hypocrisy and custom make their minds
> The fanes of many a worship, now outworn.
> . . . .
> The good want power, but to weep barren tears.
> The powerful goodness want: worse need for them.
> The wise want love; and those who love want wisdom.
>
> > [*Prometheus Unbound,* I, 618-27]

The Shelleyan consciousness, then, is the life of the mind in a world of "sundered power," to borrow Lattimore's translation of a phrase from Pindar.[36] The world in which men live is a domain of separations. Not only does an impassable gulf divide desire from fulfillment, but ideal and fact, value and ability are also estranged. Love is the highest value, the sovereign gift of Prometheus, which binds "the disunited tendrils" of the human heart. Yet in the real world love is shadowed forth in the form of ruin, the Greek Ate, the Homeric goddess of calamity.[37] But according to the Greek view which Carl Kerenyi has traced to Hesiod, this divided power or separated existence occurred in Mekone, Hesiod's mythical field of poppies, when "gods and men disputed" in the sense that they differentiated or distinguished themselves, and men left behind the life of the gods, which is spent in everlasting ease.[38] For the pious Hesiod, the story of the decline from the age of gold, when men received the bounties of nature in harmony with justice, was simply another way of telling the consequences of the Promethean theft. To Hesiod, the coming of the age of iron proved that men became too clever for their own good. Thus Shelley's romantic and modern conception of the fall from innocent, if deluded, harmony with nature is aligned with the almost canonical Greek account of the separation of gods and men, according to which the two planes of myth and experience were said to have been established. From Asia's dialogue with Demogorgon (*Prometheus Unbound,* II, iv) it is clear that the stages of spiritual development are paralleled by the Hesiodic account of the generations of gods and men.

Shelley has adapted his Greek sources with careful attention to the shades of his own doubts and certainties and with meticulous fidelity to his own sentiments. "Who reigns?" Asia asks, seeking a name for the persona behind which the cause of evil lurks, and her answer is a Shelleyan synthesis of Greek cosmogonic myths (II, iv, 43 ff.). But she is also remembering how the Prometheus of Aeschylus enumerated his gifts to gods and men and uttered his contempt for the state of mindless innocence:

> Who else but I gave these new gods their honors? . . . But hear instead the sufferings of men, how, when they were fools, I made them intelligent, and they gained the use of their senses. [*Prometheus Bound,* 439-44]

Aeschylus is posing the riddle of intelligence itself: as the artificer of

cosmic order it appears to be a ruthless necessity, while in the soul of
man it is a suffering rebel. In the character of rulers, according to the
mythic presentations, the Promethean ingredient inspires tyranny.
To the will of Jupiter are due all the evils that beset men in the age
of iron, not only the inclemencies of external nature, but the ruin of
the human heart as well. Shelley extends the idea of necessity from
man's environment to his motives, "from the links of the great chain
to things, / To every thought within the mind of man" (II, iv, 20-21).
The Aeschylean *ananke* merges with Godwin's "necessity." The result is that Shelley's position comes to resemble Plato's assertion, developed in the *Laws* (679 ff.), that circumstances and hardship drive
men from pastoral simplicity toward strife and civilized corruption.

The Aeschylean *Prometheus* provided only a statement of Shelley's poetic problem and a symbolic frame. Shelley superimposed on
this frame a half-philosophic, half-lyrical myth of the invisible world.
He recognized that this invisible world is the domain of Platonic
mind; but he converted the philosophic conception into fantasy:

> Dreams and the light imaginings of men,
> And all that faith creates or love desires,
> Terrible, strange, sublime and beauteous shapes.
> There thou art, and dost hang, a writhing shade,
> 'Mid whirlwind-peopled mountains; all the gods
> Are there, and all the powers of nameless worlds,
> Vast, sceptred phantoms; heroes, men, and beasts;
> And Demogorgon, a tremendous gloom;
> And he, the supreme Tyrant, on his throne
> Of burning gold. Son, one of these shall utter
> The curse which all remember. . . .[39]

The "sufferer's curse" must be recalled to be buried once and for
all in repentance and oblivion. But beyond its dramatic value, the
process of recollection is allegorically important. If Prometheus can
introduce himself into that inner world where the mind is sovereign,
he can entirely overcome the Jovian tyranny, the necessities and exigencies of consciousness. The whole rhythm of the play is a series of
movements between consciousness, in our narrow sense, and the invisible imaginings of the inner life. Shelley is not chiefly concerned

with the Promethean conversion from hate to love: the Promethean
love is taken for granted; it is the very pith of the hero's character
and his most important gift to men. If the play is the "biography of
an hour," as Carlos Baker has said,[40] it is the hour when love prevails because desire is freed from restraint and hope is unalloyed with
disappointment. The lyrical development of this Shelleyan dialectic
will be the subject for our next chapter.

For now, suffice it to say that by the time he wrote *Prometheus
Unbound*, Shelley had realized that if the Platonic philosopher could
enter before death into a world of real power and real being, the poet
could do the same:

> Nor seeks nor finds he mortal blisses,
> But feeds on the aëreal kisses
> Of shapes that haunt thought's wildernesses.
>
> ⟨   [*Prometheus Unbound*, I, 740-42]

To put the matter very simply, the poet can dream while he is awake.
He can look on nature without yielding to consciousness:

> He will watch from dawn to gloom
> The lake-reflected sun illume
> The yellow bees in the ivy-bloom,
> Nor heed nor see, what things they be;
> But from these create he can
> Forms more real than living man,
> Nurslings of immortality!
>
>   [*Prometheus Unbound*, I, 743-49]

And if, as Shelley did, we take the Platonic argument without the
Platonic reference or the proper philosophical content, these forms,
conceived in the setting of Rousseau's reveries but stripped of natural
contingency, are "more real" because they belong exclusively to
thought.[41]

Even in *Alastor*, the strangely metamorphosed stream in which
the dying poet contemplated his reflection had its "type" in the be-
holder:

... "O stream!
. . . .
Thou imagest my life. Thy darksome stillness,
Thy dazzling waves, thy loud and hollow gulfs,
Thy searchless fountain, and invisible course
Have each their type in me. . . ."

[*Alastor*, 502-08]

But then, the "type" was still largely unknown: entangled in his uncertainties, Shelley had not yet clearly chosen the ways of the mind.
But the *Prometheus* extends this relationship, so that the mind dominates nature through art. Prometheus is the giver of all arts, including
sculpture as well as speech which "created thought." The gift of "all-
prophetic song" freed the spirit from mortal care (II, iv, 72-79). Prometheus has, in Shelley's view, provided the great "way" or "means"
to the good life, which Aeschylus did not conceive. By means of the
fine arts and their power to transform reality or their power to bring
the mind into contact with its own operations, Prometheus opens the
route to the millennium, to which he finally retreats with his cortege
of feminine disciples. This work of Love, whom Plato's Agathon calls
the supreme poet and the cause of poetry in others, is the Shelleyan
artifact *par excellence.*

Although we anticipate the next stage in our argument, it is important to point out here that, for Plato, the key to virtue is knowledge; for Shelley, "the great secret of morals is love" ("A Defence
of Poetry"). For Plato, the way to knowledge is dialectic or rational
discourse; for Shelley, the great instrument of love is the imagination. At the center of Shelley's developing Hellenism is the increasing
effort to unite these parallel lines, which in Plato's view never meet.
But the Shelleyan metaphysics is a lyrical effect, not a philosophical
system, and having established its basic character, we can go on now
to examine it more closely in the hymns and odes of the middle
period.

IV

Shelley's Poetic Inspiration and the Forms of *Arete* in the Middle Lyrics

With the promise of his release we must leave Prometheus briefly, and with him the treatment of the Shelleyan story, and shift our attention to four main lyrics which Shelley wrote (1816-19) after *Alastor* and before the completion of *Prometheus Unbound*. In examining the *Ode to the West Wind* and its forerunners, the *Hymns of 1816* and *Lines Written among the Euganean Hills,* we discover the lyrical form of that hope which Shelley opposed to the strictures of necessity, consciousness, and restraint. With the help of these discoveries, we will be able to complete our interpretation of *Prometheus Unbound*.

We find, in fact, that the content of this lyrical aspiration reduces to the equation: love is *areté*, *areté* is love.[1] This chapter must try to elucidate gradually through the interpretation of his poems in the light of their Greek sources how Shelley understood the Greek word *areté* and what he meant by love. If we can demonstrate that his conceptions of power and virtue—his equivalents for the Greek word[2]—

signified those configurations in which the Greeks conceived this pattern and standard of their culture, then we shall see once again how the lyric passion of a modern poet formed itself and beheld its dignity and salvation in terms of a Greek ideal.

From his indebtedness to Plato and Aeschylus, we might already infer that though the Alexandrian pastoral was to attract Shelley by its mood and pathos, he devoted his studies and his imitation mainly to the authors of the period from the birth of Pericles to the death of Aristotle (ca. 499-322 B.C.).[3] To that period he gave his unqualified admiration. In the genius of its legislators, poets, and other artists, he recognized the highest civilizing force, which was most nearly perfect because most nearly primitive,[4] and he condemned the political life or measured the poetic capacities of men in his own day by the standard of Greek achievement in the fourth and fifth centuries.[5] Like Chénier, he believed that the men of this age were gifted by nature with a spontaneous eloquence which the sublimity of their language reflects,[6] and in 1817, before he learned the hardships of composition from his labors to write his *Prometheus*, he thought that the spontaneous outpourings of a mind filled with "nature and the most celebrated productions of the human mind" could not help but succeed as poetry.[7]

Although such a remark is typical of Shelley's unfamiliarity with the disciplined side of Greek poetry (legend has it that Euripides finished as few as three lines in as many days), we have less reason to think he was deceived about his acquaintance with Greek thought. Besides the traces of Plato and Plutarch and allusions to Homer in the text and notes of *Queen Mab*, we know that Shelley translated from Aristotle's *Nichomachean Ethics* in 1813 and that from this time onward he came more and more under the Hellenizing influence of his friend Thomas Love Peacock, who may have introduced him to Pindar. We need not doubt Shelley's early encounters with the ideals of his favorite period in Greek literature, even if, before 1817, he read Plato in translation and mainly for content rather than style.[8] We should not be misled by Shelley's wavering taste, which sometimes followed the bent in his current readings so far as to rank a speech in one of Godwin's novels with Agathon's speech in the *Symposium.*

Shelley did have to outgrow his literary and philosophical uncertainties. The propensity toward the Greeks of the so-called classical age, with Plato at their center, was present from the start of his creative years.

Let us examine the emotion that underwent the Hellenizing change in the middle lyrics, in order to grasp its relation to the forms of *areté* in which it is clothed. Significantly, this emotion is often represented as an echo of antiquity. Not only Greek words but ancient relics are its occasion. The imaginary towers of Babylon and Baalbek create feelings of sublimity. "Broken tombs and columns riven" seem to confer charismatic power, which is signified in scrolls of mortal mystery. "Too long, too long, / Sons of the glorious dead, have ye lain bound / In darkness and in ruin!" the hero cries in his transport, "Justice and Truth their wingéd child have found" (*The Revolt of Islam,* II, 775-78). Laon's response to the remains of Byzantium is typical. It is an inspiration to lofty thought, reborn through meditation on the grave and the monuments which recall mortality. In Shelley, this moral regeneration through rebirth of the past is the dominant event, whether lyrical or narrative.

As early as *Queen Mab,* but more decidedly in *Alastor,* Shelley shows us a relationship between the contemplation of the dead and the vision of transcendence. In the first poem, Ianthe has to fall into a state which is hardly distinguishable from death in order to make her educational trip to the realm of the Fairy Queen. But in *Alastor,* Shelley tells us how his personal experience and his poetic method prepare for the narrative of the hero's dream. The experience comes from that time, probably at Eton, when the schoolboy, in the mood of a Gothic villain conjuring with magical conundrums, called some ghost whom he wished to question about life and death:

> Like an inspired and desperate alchymist
> Staking his very life on some dark hope,
> Have I mixed awful talk and asking looks
> With my most innocent love. . . .

> [*Alastor,* 31-34]

And though he got no answer, his recollection of this incident put him in a frame of mind in which he could receive or create the vision of the "veiléd maid." But this experience which we have already explored in one of its results, was capable of almost endless possibility and variation.

In fact, this is the moment which Shelley reinterpreted in the fifth stanza of the *Hymn to Intellectual Beauty*:

> While yet a boy I sought for ghosts, and sped
>> Through many a listening chamber, cave and ruin,
>> And starlight wood, with fearful steps pursuing
> Hopes of high talk with the departed dead.

He repudiates the "poisonous names," apparently "Demon, Ghost and Heaven," fossils of Christianity, and addresses the spirit of beauty:

> When musing deeply on the lot
> Of life, at that sweet time when winds are wooing
>> All vital things that wake to bring
>> News of birds and blossoming,—
>> Sudden, thy shadow fell on me;
> I shrieked, and clasped my hands in ecstasy!

> I vowed that I would dedicate my powers
>> To thee and thine. . . .

[55-62]

A similar sense of failure and balked desire occasions the prayer to the West Wind. And the opening stanzas of *Lines Written Among the Euganean Hills* luxuriate in the melancholy of life's voyage to the grave and the macabre spectacle of death on a barren seashore. There, the prospect of personal mortality is the source of gloom, whereas, in the *Ode to the West Wind,* the cause of melancholy is specified as a failing to recapture the youthful emotion with its poetic potentialities. The handling of this emotional pattern varies from poem to poem with the imagery and coloring their subjects require. But each of the poems we are considering finds its exultant vision in the heart of doubt, despair, mutability, or fear. The contemplation of death, whether one's own or the general fate of men and things in a world of dissolution, seems to produce the brief illusion that the mind which has such thoughts must be enduring. It is as if the sense of self-negation must pass into self-esteem and despair become hope by some unexplained transformation, as though the feeling of loveless-ness turned into a comfortable cloak for the wounded ego.

A linear conception would call this contrast the distance between desire and the ideal fulfillment which it craves. Before the summit of vision or transport can be reached, it is necessary for the "very spirit" to fail or fade from a hostile reality, "driven like a homeless cloud from steep to steep / That vanishes among the viewless gales" (*Mont Blanc,* III, 58-59). The tendency is really toward a comfortable in-animateness, rather than toward mortality. To be lifted by the West Wind, the poet must become "as a wave, a leaf, a cloud." And before the beauty of the Euganean Hills supplants the mood of "wide ago-ny," "a solitary heap, / One white skull and seven dry bones" must become "like a sunless vapour, dim" (*Lines Written Among the Eu-ganean Hills,* 48-49, 63).

This musing on annihilation is the prelude to what Keats called "the melancholy fit." Shelley did not make precisely Keats's psycho-logical distinction, but he did personify the atmosphere of his inspir-ation in the fine later lyric *To Night.* He makes death the brother and sleep the child of Night, whom he invokes "out of the misty eastern cave, / Where, all the long and lone daylight, / Thou wovest dreams of joy and fear" (3-5). This figure of Night, almost like Keats's Au-tumn, is a refined synthesis of mood, both experienced and read.

Laon's conversion to Hellenic virtue occurred in a scene sugges-tive of nocturnal melancholy, and the teacher of the lovesick and guilty Athanase reminded his pupil how

> ". . . Plato's words of light in thee and me
> Lingered like moonlight in the moonless east,
> . . . .
> And Agathon and Diotima seemed
> From death and dark forgetfulness released."
>
> [*Prince Athanase,* II, 224-29]

The image of Shelley's Greece appears often through the diaphanous melancholy that he had prepared for ghosts. This is the medium through which *areté* and Platonic beauty filtered into the romantic ethos. And if, as Professor Bush has pointed out,[9] it was the desire for liberty that motivated Shelley's increasing study of the Greeks, the reason is that liberty is *areté* triumphant, Promethean art and passionate wisdom as well as freedom in our narrow sense. The Athens of the *Ode to Liberty* is the emblem of liberty's "all-creative skill." It is the "image" of a Platonic form, which lies "immovably unquiet" in the "surface of Time's fleeting river," reproducing its ideal forever in the feelings of those men who aspire to Shelleyan liberty. Contact with this picture of Athens renews *areté* in history, as it ratified Shelley's early confidence in man's "hidden virtue" and the "eventual omnipotence of mind over matter"[10]:

> . . . one Spirit vast
> With life and love makes chaos ever new,
> As Athens doth the world with thy delight renew.

> [*Ode to Liberty*, 88-90]

This comparison between liberty and the source of life and love in nature points to the underlying equation in the Shelleyan lyrics. The Shelleyan One, the Good, the principle from which excellence, power, and virtue take their being, is a kind of generalized eros. This principle "which wields the world with never-wearied love, / Sustains it from beneath, and kindles it above" (*Adonais,* 377-78) manifests itself in many forms and on several levels. But in particular, Greece and its achievements are an image which this principle created, and through which it shines upon the contemplating mind. The moment toward which Shelley's lyrics strive is the organization of the emotional response to this principle according to patterns which gather it within aesthetic limits. By analogy with the Platonic scheme, which Shelley had in mind, these patterns of aesthetic perception are the forms. They are, as we shall see, the types of *areté*, which, free from the world of flux, but related to it, are the ideals of emotional experience.

* * * * *

I

If Shelley agreed with Coleridge that the work of a "genius in the fine arts" is to make "nature thought and thought nature," he seems equally aware of a need to distinguish the "moral" from the physical universe.[11] Though the distinction is sometimes blurred in practice, the lyrics depend on a separation of physical from psychological realities. Thus the power which Shelley called "intellectual beauty" is only "like the truth of nature." The ecstasy which this power fitfully brings is a substitute for the answers about death and immortality, which nature refuses.

> Thou messenger of sympathies,
> That wax and wane in lovers' eyes—
> Thou—that to human thought art nourishment,
>
> [*Hymn to Intellectual Beauty,* 42-44]

—these are beauty's proper names, and as they echo at a great distance Plato's account of the lover's traits in the *Phaedrus,* they are attributes, not of Pan, but of a human divinity.

Shelley's eclecticism is at work, fashioning his modern sentiment in accord with a tension, which he must have recognized between Greek poetry and Platonic thought. Just as Plato's thought emerges out of a synthesis of the statements of previous Greek thinkers, both philosophical and poetic, so Shelley recombines those ingredients, pressing Plato's language into the service of feeling. The "memory of music fled" does not lead reason to the forms. The summer breeze, the moonlight behind a "piny mountain," sunbows in a mountain stream and starlit clouds reflect the fluctuations of mood. But these images do not follow the degrees of thought along an upward line which leads from dim sense to intellectual radiance. They are accommodations of sense to sentiment, in which half-lights and shadows and harmonies are nuances of mood. Metaphysical suggestion elevates emotional experience to an ethereal dignity. The imagery of thought, whether from Aeschylus or Plato, rarifies the value of feeling, and lifts it above the earth in a way which Mimnermus and Archilocus might have despised. But nature, despite the vestiges of civilized refinement, remains a vast simile for the diversity of feeling, for its tone, color and intensity, for man's "scope," as Shelley said, "for love and hate, despondency and hope" (*Hymn to Intellectual Beauty*, 23-24). Nature is permitted to teach the "averting mind" only in this way, when it is emblematical of mood.

The fundamental antipathy between nature and reason had driven Shelley to dignify a feeling with the abstract name "intellectual beauty," and to re-embody the abstraction in congenial fantasies of sense. The treatment of Mont Blanc follows a similar course. The mountain is an abstraction, a personality, a symbol to which the emotions can react. The poet can vituperate against it or strive with it "in prayer," as with the West Wind. The mountain can stand for the "secret Strength of things / Which governs thought, and to the infinite dome / Of Heaven is as a law" (*Mont Blanc*, 139-41). The roaring waters of the Arve, which alternately increase the mind's splendor or reflect its gloom, are the river of perception, through which the Platonic soul, by means of sense and "true opinion," makes contact with the dimension of time.[12] This is the stream of nutriment and sensation, in which the soul is immersed at birth,[13] and as it flows from eternal being into the timeless ocean of pure space—as the Platonists would say—the Arve is an emblem for the world of becoming, which is "always generated, or advancing towards being; and therefore never truly is."[14] Because it is an image of the human spirit, the Arve comes down in the likeness of "power." In this respect rivers "imitate the mind, which wanders at will over pathless deserts, and flows through nature's loveliest recesses" (Letter to Peacock, July 17, 1816).

Wherever Shelley's major poems start, whether with the Promethean suffering or with the poet's personal depression, their goal is that plane where "mind becomes that which it contemplates" (*Prince Athanase*, 138), or where spirit and nature intersect. Shelley believed that Greek poets as well as Plato led him to this meeting place, where nature seemed to imitate mind. Reflecting on Sophocles' line, "having come by many ways in the wanderings of careful thought," he wrote:

What a picture does this line suggest of the mind as a wilderness of

intricate paths, wide as the universe, which is here made its symbol; a world within a world which he who seeks some knowledge
with respect to what he ought to do searches throughout, as he
would search the external universe for some loved thing which
was hidden from him upon its surface.[15]

The purpose of *Mont Blanc* is summed up in the question addressed
to the thought-controlling power which the mountain symbolizes:

> . . . The secret Strength of things
> Which governs thought, and to the infinite dome
> Of Heaven is as a law, inhabits thee!
> And what were thou, and earth, and stars, and sea,
> If to the human mind's imaginings
> Silence and solitude were vacancy?
>
> [139-43]

The second stanza supports this challenge by conceiving the scene as
a map for the human mind. Therefore, when Shelley perceives reality
in this way, he seems "as in a trance sublime and strange / To muse
on my own separate fantasy" (35-36). Of things "relating to the true
and waking reality of nature," we have only a "dream-like sense," as
Plato said, "and we are unable to cast off sleep and determine the
truth about them" (*Timaeus,* 52). In "The Essay on Life" Shelley
described reverie as follows:

> Those who are subject to the state called reverie feel as if their na-
> ture were dissolved into the surrounding universe, or as if the sur-
> rounding universe were absorbed into their being. They are con-
> scious of no distinction. And these are states which precede, or
> accompany, or follow an unusually intense and vivid apprehension
> of life.[16]

In the vale of Chamouni, Shelley speculated:

> Some say that gleams of a remoter world
> Visit the soul in sleep,—that death is slumber,
> And that its shapes the busy thoughts outnumber
> Of those who wake and live. . . .
>
> [*Mont Blanc,* 49-52]

The reverie ambiguously simulates either sleep or death:

> . . . I look on high;
> Has some unknown omnipotence unfurled
> The veil of life and death? or do I lie
> In dream, and does the mightier world of sleep
> Spread far around and inaccessibly
> Its circles? . . .

[52-57]

These queries are like Keats's question "Do I wake or sleep?" after the vision of the nightingale has fled. Shelley's rhetorical questions prepare a state of mind; he would have the spirit recognize its own image in the towering peak of Mont Blanc. The reverie should grant the mind a momentary omnipotence over conscious experience. Whether Mont Blanc betokens material force or a "mind so powerfully bright as to cast a shade of falsehood on the records that are called reality,"[17] its form should bring it into identity with the soul of man, which "like unextinguished fire, / Yet burns towards heaven with fierce reproach, and doubt, / And lamentation, and reluctant prayer" (III, i, 5-7). This quotation from *Prometheus Unbound* indicates how Shelley might have treated Mont Blanc three years later. In the poem as it stands, however, the vision is incomplete. It is interrupted by the possibility that the mountain's majesty is a sign of indifferent material force. The final question, which seems to imply that the whole material universe exists because of the human mind, expresses a hope rather than an aesthetically justified conclusion.

But in *Lines Written Among the Euganean Hills,* similar poetic processes show the development of thought and technique which enable Shelley to complete his vision with a version of Pindar's isles of the blest. In this poem, the attempt to discover the poetic spirit is realized through the contemplation of a landscape. The moral gloom with which the poet at first confronts the pleasant scene is brightened by the natural beauty before him. But because of the Platonic assumption that appearances reveal realities with opposite values, the poet recollects the moral degradation in the Italian cities which are subject to foreign tyranny. Then, applying the same assumption, he finds the poetic soul to be the only spiritual light in the midst of this moral darkness, and as he traces the course of the natural sun, making it a symbol of the poetic spirit, he feels in himself the power to imagine the dissipation of these moral clouds. Conceiving the destruction of tyranny and the rebirth of liberty, he is filled with moral optimism.

Then the enthusiasm which Shelley always feels at the prospect of liberty revived lifts him above temporal concerns. The elements of both the scene and the poet's previous reflections are "interpenetrated" by the outpouring of a curiously optimistic melancholy:

> Noon descends around me now:
> 'Tis the noon of autumn's glow,
> When a soft and purple mist
> Like a vaporous amethyst,
> Or an air-dissolvéd star
> Mingling light and fragrance, far
> From the curved horizon's bound
> To the point of Heaven's profound,
> Fills the overflowing sky.

[*Euganean Hills,* 285-93]

Whether it is

> . . . love, light, harmony,
> Odour, or the soul of all
> Which from Heaven like dew doth fall,
> Or the mind which feeds this verse
> Peopling the lone universe. . . .

[315-19]

—this emotion is "intellectual beauty." It gives the poet the illusion that his vision is true and that his spirit is omnipotent, though this illusion depends on almost deliberate self-deception. Given this illusion and the metaphorical premise that life is a voyage over a sea of agony, the concluding wish for a life in the island of the blest gains some aesthetic plausibility.

In the *Euganean Hills,* the blighted spirit comes by degrees from
the northern wastes "to some calm and blooming cove," as if to find
a congenial haven for the everlasting poet. The dream of desolation
and the grave, turned inside out, discloses a land,

> Where for me, and those I love,
> May a windless bower be built,
> Far from passion, pain, and guilt,
> In a dell mid lawny hills,
> Which the wild sea-murmur fills,
> And soft sunshine, and the sound
> Of old forests echoing round,
> And the light and smell divine
> Of all flowers that breathe and shine.

[343-51]

Pindar's second *Olympian* promised such a land to those spirits
who, like Achilles, make good their escape from the Orphic wheel of
fortune:

> As many as have the strength to keep their soul wholly from injus-
> tices, while they remain three times on both sides (of the grave),
> finish Zeus's path beside the tower of Kronos. There, ocean
> breezes blow around an island of the blessed; a kind of golden
> flower glistens, some growing from trees above the land, while
> others feed on water. With garlands of these they twine their
> hands and fashion crowns, according to the righteous plans of
> Rhadamanthos whom the great father, Rhea's husband, whose
> throne is highest of all, keeps as his ready colleague.

It would be difficult to count how many times, in the course of his
compositions, Shelley resorted to this Pindaric picture of happiness.
Surely, Laon and Cythna are piloted there when they are dead. This
is only the "imortal land" of their childhood revisited, where "earth
and ocean meet, / . . . Where boughs of incense droop over the emer-
ald wells" (*The Revolt of Islam,* II, 887-91). Or as they come to the
Golden City in triumph,

> A thousand flower-inwoven crowns were shed,
>   The token flowers of truth and freedom fair,

And fairest hands bound them on many a head,
Those angels of love's heaven, that over all was spread.

[V, 1860-63]

According to his habit, Shelley embellished this picture in proportion as he entered enthusiastically into the imagination of it. It is the
"paradise of vaulted bowers," in which Asia finds a Promethean people, and the locale, presumably of that cave "all overgrown with trail-
ing odorous plants," in which Prometheus plans to dwell with his
feminine consorts in pathos. It is, in *Epipsychidion*, "a far Eden of
the purple East" or "an isle 'twixt Heaven, Air, Earth, and Sea, /
Cradled, and hung in clear tranquillity" (457-58), like Plato's upper
earth in the *Phaedo* (108d ff.): the precise geography hardly mat-
ters. At any rate, Shelley comes with Emilia, his "soul's sister," to a
"pleasure-house" which Kronos or "some wise and tender Ocean-
King" built and consecrated to "his sister and his spouse."

* * * * *

II

Asia's famous lyric, which concludes the second act of *Prometheus Unbound,* perfectly illustrates how Shelley synthesized his borrowings from Plato and Pindar. For Asia, making the typical journey
from pain to the sea-girt bowers of bliss, the sequence of life and
time itself are turned around. Age precedes manhood and youth;
youth comes before infancy; death is the gateway to a divine rebirth:

We have passed Age's icy caves,
And Manhood's dark and tossing waves,
And Youth's smooth ocean, smiling to betray:
Beyond the glassy gulfs we flee
Of shadow-peopled Infancy,
Through Death and Birth, to a diviner day.

[II, v, 98-103]

The spouse and "soul's sister" of Prometheus is implicated in the
moment or "great year" of eternal return, when the revolutions of

the heavens pause and reverse their course. Then, after ages of decline, the world grows young, regaining its poise in the hands of its tutelary god. Kronos rules; peace prevails; men spring up like plants out of a friendly earth, and nature is kind to them in a golden age (*Statesman*, 269 ff.).[18]

For Plato in the *Statesman*, as for Pindar in *Olympian VII*, the world and its appearances, its times, its motions, and its moods but manifest the thoughts of a god. Being is the gift of memory.[19] Insofar as *areté*, like being, is power, this too comes with the light of the divine recollection. Bringing *areté*, the changes of fortune ultimately express the divine memory, which bestows being or nothingness on all things. That same law, which in *Olympian VII* raised Pindar's island to the light of day, rules Plato's living universe. Just as the Pindaric poet shares symbolically in the psychology of the gods, the Platonic philosopher, who reads his own soul, discovers how the cosmos fails or thrives, depending on its power to remember. Thus Shelley would find no inconsistency between Pindar's myth of immortality (*Olympian II*) and his remarks that song alone will keep a man alive when he has gone to the world below (*Olympian X*). To be remembered is to exist, and the act of recollection, from the mortal point of view, makes contact with being itself. In Shelley's view, the myth of cosmic renewal enunciated the profound principle that the world is as we think it is. The mind may become "like what it contemplates," but memory controls attitudes and experience, gives meaning to thought, and interprets those very cycles and vicissitudes which are the seasons and the ages of human life.

For the Greeks, the human mind was the image of the world. For Shelley, or rather for Shelley's Prometheus—the immortal man—the world is but an image of the mind. The spring of the Promethean rebirth of man has come to Asia as suddenly

> . . . as the memory of a dream,
> Which now is sad because it hath been sweet;
> Like genius, or like joy which riseth up
> As from the earth, clothing with golden clouds
> The desert of our life.

> [*Prometheus Unbound*, II, i, 8-12]

Asia seems to be privy to those cloud-like spirits of good thought, indigenous to the atmosphere of the human mind, which carry the types of human goodness, self-sacrifice, wisdom, poetry, and love, "from unremembered ages" (I, 672). If we rightly read the language about Panthea, who is the "sense with which love talks" and the "shadow" of both Asia and Prometheus, it is clear that Asia is the feminine counterpart or "second self" of Prometheus.[20] Asia is the feminine principle of life, the *anima* answering to the Promethean *animus*. She is by extension from the Promethean mind a kind of *anima mundi,* the feminine aspect of the universe, an archetype, if you will. The images which represent her as the wife of Prometheus, as the planet Venus, as veiled light, and later as the Earth itself have a symbolic logic and coherence of their own. She is that quality in all of these things which Shelley called love. She is the excellence which things possessed in their beginnings, and toward which "some good change / Is working in the elements" (II, v, 18-19). Her return to Prometheus is symbolized as a voyage backward through the waters of time to that mythic moment when, as Shelley learned from Hesiod, the goddess of love was born:

> . . . on the day when the clear hyaline
> Was cloven at thine uprise, . . .
> . . . .
> . . . love, like the atmosphere
> Of the sun's fire filling the living world,
> Burst from thee, and illumined earth and heaven
> And the deep ocean and the sunless caves
> And all that dwells within them.

[II, v, 21-30]

This "beauty" is a "radiance," not seen, but only felt, as it transforms the "grief" which "cast eclipse upon the soul." Asia tends to be the image of a feeling deeper than thought, a power of unresisted "weakness," which releases passion from the bonds of consciousness and makes the Promethean spirit "dizzy, lost, yet unbewailing," while she resembles "one in slumber bound." Asia personifies that spiritual joy which Shelley called "intellectual beauty," because of its power to convince the soul of its omnipotence and immortality.

With the help of that rhetorical device which takes cause for effect and effect for cause, the universe itself becomes, not a likeness only, but a metaphor for the dream soul, as Mont Blanc had done within the cave of poetry.

Asia's lyric reply to the spirit voice of Prometheus[21] illustrates how Shelley's synthetic borrowings gave mythic value to the principle that "the great secret of morals" and, one might add, of existence itself, "is love."[22] Her "soul is an enchanted boat," a vessel of desire, fashioned from many classical hints: it is the shell of Botticelli's Venus, which an epigrammatist in the Greek Anthology preserved from a lost painting of Apelles; it is Pindar's bark of song or Homer's Phaeaecian ship as swift as thought.[23] But the history of this detail only points once again to the central lyrical intention of Shelley's poems. This intention, as we have said, is a withdrawal from the road of Zeus, from the life of pain and guilt, which Jupiter, the mask of consciousness, inflicts. The goal is the tower of Kronos and that god's domain, the heart and haven of the inner man, "which everlasting spring has made its own," the island of spirit and "soul within a soul," where man begins and whither he returns, after the winter of life, as to an "antenatal dream."[24] Such renewal or regeneration, Plato says, is the work of memory, whether in man or in the universe at large. It is the "begetting in beauty" (*Symposium*, 206b), through which the mind attains to immortality of thought like that survival of the flesh through physical love. By this ultimate begetting, the mind brings forth realities, not images; its children are immortal *areté*, instead of perishable men. With this argument, from Diotima's speech in the *Symposium*, the rejuvenation of the world of man through the reunion of Asia and Prometheus is explained. The Promethean reunion with Asia represents the sovereignty of eros on three planes simultaneously: it is the rediscovery of the human spirit; it is a re-engendering of the integral self; it is a renewal of the whole universe of man, which is said to be born again in the figure of that mysterious "winged child" that floats as a messenger of innocence through Shelley's poems, until in *Hellas* it becomes an emblem of ancient Greece.[25]

It was Pindar who inspired the mood of Asia's song, and Pindar's surge of song which suggested the "silver waves of . . . singing" (*Paean VI*).[26] Though Plato called love a pilot, Pindar provided the boat of Asia's desire with its ship-captaining guide in *Paean VI*, where he said to the nymph and island of Aegina: "you will put into port harkening to a surging song, whence you have taken the ship-captaining genius and the guiding skill." Plato describes love as having been born among flowers; yet when Shelley came to tell of love's "vaulted bowers, / Lit by downward-gazing flowers" (*Prometheus Unbound*, II, v, 104-05), he had in mind Pindar's description of how Iamos was born of Euadne to Apollo, his delicate body steeped in the purple and yellow rays of a boundless grove of arrowy rushes.[27]

It was however from the speech of Agathon, the tragic poet in the *Symposium,* that Shelley drew the virtues of the inner and Promethean man. When, in the short rhymed periods of his peroration, Agathon called love the "most excellent of pilots," he expressed that character of universal rule, which Asia assigns amid similar cadences[28] to the spirit of Prometheus, "most beautiful of pilots." Agathon names Eros the god that rules the world, the source of virtue, and the guide of life:"Is it not evident that Love was the author of all the arts of life with which we are acquainted, and that he whose teacher has been Love, becomes eminent and illustrious, whilst he who knows not Love, remains forever unregarded and obscure?" (*Symposium*, 197a).[29]

Love is just, since it neither inflicts nor receives any injury. The power of love overcame even the god of war, and because it subdues all other passions, love, the greatest of passions, is most temperate (*Symposium*, 196b-d). Plato, of course, repudiates this sophistry in *Symposium,* as in the *Phaedrus* he had turned it to the service of philosophy. In neither of his dialogues of love does Plato admit the possibility of a perfect repose in eros as the highest good. Plato invariably insists that love is imperfect, that it is a *daimon,* not a god, and that it is an unsatisfied desire, which shares but does not possess the tranquility of the divine nature. For Plato, love is an enthusiastic but unquiet longing which drives us toward beauty and toward truth, where alone we can satisfy our souls. Love is not a having, but a desire to have and to keep the good and beautiful things that attract it. And whereas Platonic recollection, motivated by love, leads higher than art to an ultimate and ecstatic science, the Promethean rebirth or reawakening weds memory to poetry, as Pindar had done, and trims the Platonic language to fit a belief, which Plato sternly challenged and parodied, that eros was the godhead representing one of the forms of *areté*.

Shelley's Platonism stands dynamically in tension with his romantic faith in lyrical mood. Agathon's love is therefore Shelley's spirit of Prometheus. The equation is almost inevitable: Prometheus too, who re-created mankind by bestowing all arts, is a poet and maker of poets, in that general Platonic sense in which legislators and men of letters as well are said to be poets.[30] Though Shelley wished to be a Platonist, he held the same views which excluded Agathon from those ranks and led Socrates to point out that Agathon did not really understand what love is. Shelley refused to make Plato's fundamental distinctions. He failed to separate eros from *areté*. He took love to be excellence rather than the impulse toward virtue. In fact, he compressed the Platonic analogies until, losing their clarity and ceasing to be philosophically accurate, they became Shelleyan identities. The Platonic dialogues serve as a kind of echo-chamber, where Shelley could disguise a fleeting mood as "intellectual beauty," deepen his awareness of the Pindaric soul, and find cosmic symbols for the lyrical dream of emotional renascence.

Though we may have difficulty, therefore, in formulating our argument with absolute accuracy, its general drift is clear enough. Shelley was not a Platonist, but a poet. Looking back beyond Plato, whom he consulted for doctrine and an expanded myth, he nourished his imagination on the works of the fifth-century Greek poets, and in their lines found the shapes and patterns to express and perhaps to redeem his modern melancholy. The *Ode to the West Wind* recapitulates our major themes.

* * * * *

III

In this most famous of Shelley's lyrics the melancholy "breath of autumn's being" is transformed into a spirit of life, and the wish for death leads by degrees to a rebirth in poetry. The autumnal wind, "destroyer and preserver," is the image of melancholy. It is moreover, a personality, a genius or mythical *daimon*. The wind is the spirit of the seasons, the cosmic personification of mood. All sense of sadness in this poem is turned to transport. Melancholy, which here fills the sky "from the dim verge / Of the horizon to the zenith's height," as it did in the *Euganean Hills,* is instantly suffused with vitality, as if the West Wind was the perfect agent in the lyric ritual of transforming despondency into pleasure. The storm is both an ecstatic Maenad and the vault of a vast sepulchre.

By successive shifts in metaphor, the prayer to the West Wind carries the mind back through heavily charged associations, and revives Shelley's paradigmatic transport, his youthful ecstasy. "Let thy power, which like the truth / Of nature on my passive youth / Descended, to my onward life supply / Its calm" (78-81), he had said, asking for the continuance of "intellectual beauty." But here, despite the chains of time and the "thorns of life," at the climax of his prayer to the West Wind, he cries in a more confident tone:

> Make me thy lyre, even as the forest is:
> . . . .
> The tumult of thy mighty harmonies
>
> Will take from both a deep, autumnal tone,
> . . . Be thou, Spirit fierce,
> My spirit! Be thou me, impetuous one!
>
> [57-62]

Here, in his capacity as poet, he is being carried into communion, not with some natural *daimon,* but with the deity of his own spirit for whom nature provides a convenient symbolic parallel.

Shelley wrote in an essay of uncertain date:

> There is a power by which we are surrounded, like the atmosphere in which some motionless lyre is suspended, which visits with its breath our silent chords at will. This power is God. And those who have seen God, have, in the period of their purer and more perfect nature, been harmonized by their own will to so exquisite a consentaneity of powers as to give forth divinest melody when the breath of universal being sweeps over their frame.[31]

This familiar image, recalling Coleridge's *Aeolian Harp*, was, as M. H. Abrams has shown, a favorite romantic "analogy for the poetic mind." In the *Ode to the West Wind* the poet's passive mind is an analogue for the "universe of things." In Shelley's "Defence of Poetry," "the Aeolian lyre is the poet, and the poem is the chord of music which results from the reciprocation of external and internal elements, of both the changing wind and the constitution and tension of the strings."[32]

But Shelley may have been remembering other than romantic precedents. The lyre is an image for the body: Plato introduced it on the lips of his Theban-Pythagorean in the *Phaedo,* though he rejected the argument that the soul is a harmony. We may reasonably conjecture that Shelley associated the lyre image with Plato's pun which says that the body is a tomb.[33] Such an association ties the lyre, emotionally, to the vast sepulchre of time. The logical connection appears under the tangle of partial analogies. The forest, the wind, the sky, the sea are all humanized. The lyre, on the other hand, is an image of the poet, who is himself a wave, a leaf, a cloud, and chained to time. The lyre is explicitly compared with the forest; it is implicitly comparable with the dying world through which the Maenad storm is to pass. But in the first Pythian ode Pindar had made the lyre, not only an emblem for poetic art, but a symbol of civilization and Zeus's instrument which affirms the order of nature over destructive force.[34] Even more to the point are the lines in the fourth *Olympian* where Pindar describes the seasons that are "whirling to the sound of the harp with its shifting textures of song" (1-3). The poet's harp (*poikilophorminx*) is many-colored, like Plato's image of the sky.[35] With its changes in emotional tone the lyre imitates the cosmic pattern of strife and sadness and joy. This is the idea which Shelley partially captured in *Mont Blanc* as he passed to the cave of poetry through the "many-coloured, many-voicéd vale," in whose giant brood of pines the winds hear an "old and solemn harmony." As early as 1815 Shelley had incorporated such imagery into his picture of the "veiléd maid" of *Alastor.* Her veil was the sublimated image for the texture of nature poetically conceived.

Neville Rogers has shown that Shelley thought of his striving with the West Wind as a contest of *areté*: "By my power (*areté*), I, a mortal, vanquish you, a great god," he noted, translating from Euripides.[36] In the *Hymn to Intellectual Beauty* Shelley produced lines which closely resemble Pindar's argument that man's life is but the "dream of a shadow," except when it is ennobled by the "god-given gleam" of *areté*.[37] And in the lines addressed to "intellectual beauty" Shelley also associates nature and the Aeolian harp with this divine spiritual light:

> Thy light alone—like mist o'er mountains driven,
>   Or music by the night-wind sent
>   Through strings of some still instrument,
>
> . . . .
> Gives grace and truth to life's unquiet dream.

[32-36]

V

Forms of the Imagination:
Shelley's Art of the *Logos*

I

By the power of memory the Pindaric poet participates in the
areté of nature and in the mental life of the gods.[1] Through the return to *areté* in the dawning of love, Shelley gains power over himself
and the world. The lyric poet's harp gives utterance to the rhythms
of the inner man, which for Shelley are the types of the rhythmic
patterns of cosmic nature. But several questions remain. What is the
nature of the Promethean conversion? How do we come to that paradise which is the invariable goal of Shelley's lyrics? How is man freed
and absolved of that guilt which comes to be with consciousness in
the formation of the human person? The lyrical processes, which we
have examined, and Shelley's theory of poetic truth give answers to
these questions, especially after we have considered the "Defence of
Poetry" and *Adonais*.

Shelley arrived at his belief in the truth of the imagination largely with the help of Greek attitudes toward truth, as these were reflected in Plato's controversy with the poets. Before Aristotle, the Greeks did not divide the mind into faculties, and up to Plato's time, poets and even historians drew no clear distinctions between the literally true and the merely plausible, between the history, in our sense, of what really happened and the reasonable account of what ought to have happened. Fables taught moral truths. Myths exemplified the interlocking actions of gods and men. Even the history of the careful Thucydides included what statesmen ought to have said.

Plato indicted the imitations of painters and poets as a sort of conscious dream; they were usually false and often immoral, since they were three times removed from reality.[2] But one thing there was, which the ancient storytellers and poets shared with the Platonic dialectician. Their arts, however diverse they might seem, were all, in various ways, arts of the *logos*.[3] Simonides' tale of virtue enshrined on a height of rock is *tis logos,* but so also are Socrates' arguments in the *Phaedo*.[4] The *logos* meant the speech in Homer and Thucydides, the story in Herodotus, the legend in Hesiod; and the *eikos logos* or "likely story" of the *Timaeus* refers to the mathematical account of the structure of the universe (*Timaeus,* 48d). The *logos* is discourse, both mental and spoken. It is the vehicle of communication, but it is also the pattern of thought. It is a form for perceiving things and ordering events according to relationships which thought can manipulate and express.[5] This is the conception of language which Shelley presupposes when, in the "Defence of Poetry," he declares that primitive language is poetry; that all primitive authors are poets; that they are institutors of laws and founders of civil society, and finally, that they are called legislators and even prophets because their command of language gives them insight into the "spirit of events":

> . . . to be a poet is to apprehend the true and the beautiful—in a word, the good which exists in the relationship subsisting, first between existence and perception and secondly between perception and expression.

Or again:

> All the authors of revolutions in opinion are not only necessarily

poets as they are inventors, nor even as their words unveil the permanent analogy of things by images which participate in the life of truth but as their periods are harmonious and rhythmical and contain in themselves the elements of verse being the echo of the eternal music.[6]

Nor was this doctrine at its root a rhetorical fancy conceived in the desire to refute Peacock's argument that poetry, which originated to supply the demands of ignorance and barbarism, had run its course and been replaced by rational truth.[7] Simonides, after all, had said that "the word (*logos*) is an image of things."[8] The Pindaric harp, itself an image of the divine instrument of creative order, was one model for the persistent idea that man is a lyre and his imagination the principle which harmonizes the external and internal impressions to which he is subject. What the poets said, their plausible and compelling language, had a sort of truth because it made reality clearer to perception. The patterns of wisdom, prudence, justice, courage, and endurance, drawn by Homer and the tragedians, produced a "heart-ravishing knowledge,"[9] through which these poets were the early educators of Greece. With his "Defence of Poetry" Shelley wished to convince Peacock and to persuade himself, that Shakespeare, Milton, and the "great writers of the present age," like the Greeks, were "companions and forerunners" of social and intellectual revolution.[10]

"Poetry is a mimetic art," Shelley said in the preface to *Prometheus Unbound,* and his words have a neoclassical flavor which reminds us of Chénier, Boileau, and Pascal, as he continues:

> It creates, but it creates by combination and representation. Poetical abstractions are beautiful and new, not because the portions of which they are composed had no previous existence in the mind of man or in nature, but because the whole produced by their combination has some intelligible and beautiful analogy with those sources of emotion and thought, and with the contemporary condition of them: one great poet is a masterpiece of nature which another not only ought to study but must study.
>
> The mass of capabilities remains at every period materially the same. . . .

There is a commonwealth of mind to which all genius belongs. Through literary study and imitation, especially of the Greeks, the poet makes contact not only with nature, but with the *logos,* containing the forms of experience and human nature, which he adapts to the understanding of his contemporaries. That faculty, the imagination, which interprets the relationships in the *logos,* is "the storehouse of axioms common to all knowledge." The "similitudes or relations" which the *logos* elucidates are the "footsteps of nature impressed upon the various subjects of the world."[11] The poet's mind is the image of all other minds. The poem, "the creation of actions according to the unchangeable forms of human nature, as existing in the mind of the creator," is "the very image of life, expressed in its eternal truth."[12] Behind the Baconian phrases, we can detect the Platonizing drift of Shelley's thought. The forms of the imagination are the prototypical sources of emotion and thought, the configurations of perfect desire and triumphant human power, such as were veiled in the reunion of Asia and Prometheus or projected as possibilities in the fleeting paradise of the *Euganean Hills.* They are the intuitions of beauty, justice, and that passive temperance, the ideals of Shelleyan *areté.* They are the true, the beautiful, the good, which ancient poets claimed to carry back with them from the realms of the Muses, to instruct and edify their contemporaries. In his translation of the *Ion,* Shelley alters the wording just enough to make it appear that Plato also agreed with the view that poets are bearers of truth[13]:

> . . . the souls of the poets, as poets tell us, have this peculiar ministration in the world. They tell us that these souls, flying like bees from flower to flower and wandering over the gardens and the meadows and the honey-flowing fountain of the Muses, return to us laden with the sweetness of melody; and arrayed as they are in the plumes of rapid imagination they speak truth. [*Ion,* 534a]

Plato ironically feigned a half-serious reverence for ancient aphorisms and tales. He could and did extract fanciful hints from dubious etymologies. He took fables, allegories, quasi-historical myths, poetic aphorisms and philosophical *dicta* as the starting points for his dialectic. He used the great mythic "pictures" of the soul's "fortunes and destiny" to summarize dialectical results, to enforce their moral message or to connect them with tradition, demonstrating how myths could be rewritten to serve truth if poets were philosophers.[14] But he insisted that these were fictions, which must submit to a test of truth higher than themselves. To discourse as to the world at large he applied the rigorous distinction of phenomena from intelligence, which he outlined in the figure of the divided line (*Republic*, VI, 509d ff.). Understanding, he insisted, begins with mathematical reasoning which reaches downward to nature, through image and hypothesis, in order that the things of appearance might be considered in the realm of thought. The pictures of the poets were the shadows of shadows, he believed, and if myth was to provide a sort of poetic parable, suited to the sphere of "true opinion," its images must be authenticated and bound to an imageless truth by the chains of science (*Meno*, 97).

Carl Grabo, therefore, offers a useful formulation of Shelley's hybrid poetic theory when he says that in the role of Plato's "understanding" Shelley substitutes the Neoplatonic "imagination."[15] Plato's "understanding," the mental sphere of hypothesis not wholly free of reliance on images, introduced the discipline of reason through which the philosopher must pass in his journey upward from the cave of sentient consciousness. The Shelleyan imagination likewise lifts the poet and his hearers "beyond and above consciousness,"[16] away from the confusion and the conflicts of the strife-ridden earth to the forms or ideals of human perfection. We may not be able to satisfy our reason as to the nature of these forms. Shelley's knowledge of the good, the true, and the beautiful comes with a wind or a mysterious fire of intuition. But Shelley assures us that these transcendentals are the "divinity of man" which stamped itself most visibly on the art of fifth-century Greece.[17] Thus Shelley is not merely answering Peacock. He is replying also to Plato's attack upon the poets. In place of Plato's rational disciplines, such as mathematics, which prepare the philosopher for his moral inquiries, Shelley insisted that poetry, by enlarging the imagination, "strengthens that faculty which is the organ of the moral nature of man."[18]

But it was the Neoplatonists rather than Plato himself who taught the poets that their idealisms might be identified with the images of eternal beauty.[19] As Plotinus said:

> Still the arts are not to be slighted on the ground that they create by imitation of natural objects; for, to begin with, these natural objects are themselves imitations; then, we must recognise that they give no bare reproduction of the thing seen but go back to the Ideas [*logous*] from which Nature itself derives, and, further-more, that much of their work is all their own; they are holders of beauty and add where nature is lacking.[20]

Though there is no record of Shelley's having read Plotinus,[21] Thomas Taylor's notes in his translation of Plato's works exercised an influence on Shelley's thought and acquainted him with the Neo-platonic attitude toward poetry.[22] According to Taylor, Plato "calls by the name of idea, the reason or productive principle which sub-sists in the dianoëtic power of the artificer: and this reason, he says, is the offspring of deity, because he is of opinion, that this very arti-ficial principle itself is imparted to souls from divinity."[23] But intel-lectual beauty, "the sum of all true imagination," is the "foun-tain,"[24] to which the individual imagination returns.

From 1819 onward, Shelley's writings stress the doctrine that there is an analogy between poetic creativity and the process that fashions and controls the universe. In *Orpheus* poetry is imaged in the works of nature (87-102), and the tone implies that fancy is na-ture's rival. *The Witch of Atlas,* which has been called "a sort of Ho-meric hymn, of Shelleyan spirituality, subtlety, and color,"[25] cele-brates a preternatural power of imagination residing in a mythical world outside of time and human misery. This developed picture of the "witch Poesy" is the Shelleyan goddess of wisdom and is also identified with love, as proved by her resemblances to Asia.[26] Her thoughts clothe themselves in the elements, as if each act of mind is a created fact (210-16). The witch's veil, a "shadow for the splen-dour of her love" (152), resembles "the one life or nature of the uni-verse which the goddess (Minerva) weaves by those intellectual vital powers which she contains."[27] On the other hand, the witch's scrolls, "the works of some Saturnian Archimage" (186), contain the secrets by which imagination would restore men to innocence in a golden age

Although Shelley's somewhat obscure speculations on the imagination did not crystallize until 1821, they did follow his earlier poetic experiments, enhanced by an ever-increasing study of the Greeks. We should be surprised if the *Prometheus,* with its concern for exploiting the operations of the mind, contained no representative of the imagination among its many allegorical spirits. Our guess is not disappointed. "That imperial faculty whose throne is curtained within the invisible nature of man" does have its representative in the "veiled form" occupying the "ebon throne" of some mysterious power, like an "atmosphere" into which all the other allegorical spirits of the *Prometheus* "are gathered."[28] Demogorgon, "this allegorical divinity," says W. G. Hort in his *New Pantheon* (1854), "was the genius of the earth," regarded by "philosophers" as "the spirit of heat, the life and support of plants," and supposed by the popular imagination to have "fixed the limits of the earth" and to have "created the heavens" and the sun.[29] A fragment of 1822 shows Shelley's familiarity with such a figure:

> Within the silent centre of the earth
> My mansion is; where I have lived insphered
> From the beginning, and around my sleep
> Have woven all the woundrous imagery
> Of this dim spot, which mortals call the world;
> . . . .
> And as a veil in which I walk through Heaven
> I have wrought mountains, seas, and waves, and clouds,
> And lastly light, whose interfusion dawns
> In the dark space of interstellar air.[30]

Whether or not the Greek *demiourgos* was vulgarized as the "dread name of Demogorgon,"[31] there seems to be some kinship between this denizen of the cave of poetry and that world artificer who, according to Plato, forced on "necessity" the patterns of eternal mind. But Shelley's oracle of truth and of the heart's intuitions evinces a challenging duplicity. The impression of "light from the meridian sun.

—Ungazed upon and shapeless" (*Prometheus Unbound,* II, iv, 4-5) recalls Plato's "child of the good," except for the "rays of gloom" which "dart around."[32] We are tempted to dismiss this personified mixture of light and darkness with Plato's description of the "image-making" sophist, "an imitator of experience," who belongs "to the conscious or dissembling section of the art of causing self-contradiction" (*Sophist,* 266c-d). We cannot be sure whether Shelley's representative of the imagination is this sophist who "runs away into the darkness of non-being . . . and cannot be discovered because of the darkness of the place," or the philosopher who "always holding converse through reason with the idea of being, is also dark from excessive light" (*Sophist,* 254a-b).[33]

As Professor Bush has observed, Demogorgon "stands for the mysterious reality, the eternal order, behind and above the temporal world, and he is something like Greek fate, with a strong coloring of Shelleyan 'necessity'."[34] The dark side of Demogorgon and of the imagination is a necessary though awkward feature in Shelley's allegorical plot. Coming in the guise of "eternity," Demogorgon carries off the tyrant of the world into the dark abyss of non-being. The unlikely fact that Demogorgon is the offspring of this tyrant is a Shelleyan adaptation of Aeschylus. Shelley's Jupiter *is* consciousness— that consciousness which is associated with guilt. His Thetis may be the ominous, black-haired goddess of Pindar's sixth *Paean,* who is the unhappy symbolic opposite to the lovely nymph of Aegina. Allegorically, Demogorgon, like imagination itself, is born of earthly consciousness and earthly love, and is therefore a destroyer. The Platonic allegory describing the birth of love from plenty and poverty in the *Symposium* is ample precedent for Demogorgon's parentage.

But Shelley's conception of human nature has grown since the writing of *Alastor.* Demogorgon, like the West Wind, is both destroyer and preserver. The magnetic enchantment of his "law" does not merely annihilate the consciousness of evil; this "law" marks out the stages of anesthesia, through which Asia passes, "without a course, without a star," to a primeval but creative darkness, filled with instinctive music, which in turn conducts to a wilderness of "shapes too bright to see" (*Prometheus Unbound,* II, v, 108). If we treat Asia's descent, her interview with Demogorgon, and her voyage with the Promethean spirit as parts of one journey, Demogorgon is then seen to occupy the point of metamorphosis, at which the tendency toward annihilation and toward a negative, subterranean gloom, becomes a positive tendency toward the fruitful darkness where poetry is made. For a poet, Shelley says,

> is a nightingale, who sits in darkness and sings to cheer its own solitude with sweet sounds; his auditors are as men entranced by the melody of an unseen musician, who feel that they are moved and softened, yet know not whence or why.[35]

But we may offer a philosophic model for the process of Asia's transformation and in general for the psychological metamorphosis which Shelley's lyrics reproduce. We may compare this metamorphic instant with the event which Plato called the "moment." In the Platonic scheme, the conception of the "moment" became necessary to explain how things in the world of flux could participate in the eternal ideas. The "moment" is a cut in the continuum of time and space, through which the unity of true existence flashes among the phenomenal events.[36] Marking a gap in the flow of history, the "moment" is an indeterminate state of suspension, through which the oneness or identity of any being must pass on its way from one condition (smallness, injustice, non-being) to some other (greatness, justice, being).[37] Just as the glacier in *Mont Blanc* is motionless and yet simultaneous with the motion of the river that flows from it, the "moment" is simultaneous with the flux of phenomena. All things that change pass through the "moment," where they preserve that unity or self-identity, without which it would be impossible to step twice into the same river or to claim that the same person could perform any two actions for which he would be responsible.

In Shelley's lyrical transformations, which have roughly paralleled the conversion of the Platonic philosopher and his spiritual discipline of "dying into life," the "moment" would seem to account for the change by which a simulated death carries the poet to a heightened vision, brings him into contact with a feeling of eternal reality, liberates him from the chains of time and consciousness. This is the in-

stant when reverie is flooded with shapes of a remoter world, when
the gleam of "intellectual beauty" comes, when Asia is seen to be an
archetype belonging to the world of pristine innocence. This is the
instant when the evils seen from the Euganean Hills are forgotten or
suffused with melancholy, and the limits of the visible world within
the horizon are referred to the eternal spirit, symbolized in the infinite depth of the sky. In general, this is the instant when the lyric
gap is being closed. Plato reached the state higher than consciousness
by means of the philosophical *logos*. For Shelley, this state is a melancholy illusion, achieved by means of the various lyrical pictures
which we have already examined. The characterization of Demogorgon as the agent of metamorphosis strengthens the conjecture that
the imagination, for which Demogorgon stands, is the Shelleyan substitute for the Platonic understanding. The imagination ranges over
the three worlds. It is the keeper of eternal chaos, the offspring of
experience, the imitator of the eternal forms or paradigms of virtue
and law. It is sophist, statesman and philosopher.[38] At the heart of
this power lies the capability of passing, not merely into the eternity
of non-existence, but also into an absolutely creative dimension of
time. This is the capacity for the irrational leap by which the philosopher transcends hypotheses and the poet transforms his consciousness.

This is the moment that enables the poet to shift his point of
view, to pass safely beyond the "veil and the bar / Of things that live
and are." Let us consider Prometheus in this extra-temporal dimension of time, as he is released from his chains (Act III, ii). Prometheus
is the "form" animated by the Shelleyan virtues, "wisdom, courage,
and long-suffering love." Being freed from the allegorical chains, the
strictures of temporal life, he anticipates the life in the Shelleyan
paradise, into which he later disappears. This is at once the isle of the
blessed and the grove of the immortal child, Pindar's Iamus, but it is
above all the cave of poetry. There Prometheus and his feminine fol-
lowers will be "like lutes / Touched by the skill of the enamoured
wind." They will "make / Strange combinations out of common
things." Indeed, most of the classical hypotheses on which Shelley
drew to picture his ideal world of virtue, pleasure or poetry are
woven together in this one speech of Prometheus (III, iii). In addi-

tion to the Pindaric borrowings which we have already mentioned, the passage illustrates how Plato (*Ion,* 534a) contributed the language with which Shelley expressed the relationship between the Promethean paradise and the mortal world:

> And hither come, sped on the charméd winds,
> Which meet from all the points of heaven, as bees
> From every flower aëreal Enna feeds,
> At their known island-homes in Himera,
> The echoes of the human world.

These echoes

> And lovely apparitions,—dim at first,
> Then radiant, as the mind, arising bright
> From the embrace of beauty (whence the forms
> Of which these are the phantoms) casts on them
> The gathered rays which are reality. . . .

are music and the other fine arts which will both improve and reflect the virtues of man when he has been perfected by Promethean love. This passage is an example of a point we have already made, namely, that Shelley tended to combine his gleanings from Platonic philosophy with the more primitive images of the Greek poets. But the more important point now is that this Shelleyan synthesis of fragments selected from the various stages in the development of the *logos* creates the impression that the romantic chamber of the mind not only satisfies the heart's desires but governs and reforms the everyday world. Like Plato's philosopher in the *Republic,* Shelley's Prometheus is a painter and sculptor of ideal images, and these "Praxitelean shapes" are "the mediators / Of that best worship love" (*Prometheus Unbound,* III, iii, 58-59). Shelley implies that the Promethean change of heart, which is so variously mirrored in the *logos* representing the beings that surround him, restored the integrity of his hero and brought him into unity with the cosmic agencies. It would also seem that Demogorgon, the representative of the imagination, provided the basic means for this aspect of the Promethean conversion.

* * * * *

II

> Death is the veil which those who live call life:
> They sleep, and it is lifted. . . .

With this enigma which is intended to remind us of Socrates' insistence that the life we know is like death while the death of the philosopher leads to everlasting life, the Earth distracts Asia from her questions about the real fate of men. But these words of the Earth contradict the general impression that in reality man cannot be saved from mutability, and that, as the Earth herself has said, "death shall be the last embrace of her / Who takes the life she gave, even as a mother / Folding her child, says, 'Leave me not again.'" (*Prometheus Unbound,* II, iii, 105-7). Shelley was, to say the least, ambivalent in dealing with the question of immortality. Unless he was deliberately equivocating, he had not made up his mind when he wrote the *Prometheus.* In a note to *Hellas,* which may stand for his maturest view of this "riddle," it is the desire for immortality, rather than Plato's eternal objects of thought, which "must remain the strongest and the only presumption that eternity is the inheritance of every thinking being."[39] In *Adonais,* where Shelley directly confronts the problem of immortality, imagination conducts him to a cogent though illusory satisfaction of this desire.

To the crucial preoccupations of Shelley's major poetry—the meaning of man's life, the relation between his powers of mind and heart and the powers of nature, as well as the question of the soul's existence beyond the grave, and above all, the enigma of death—*Adonais* brings the widest variety of literary and philosophical materials at Shelley's command. The myth of Adonis came to Shelley rich with symbolic possibilities. To the ancients, Adonis was one of the half-mortal vegetation deities, whose life was bound to the cycle of flowering nature, so that for a time he flourished, like the plants themselves or like the "year-king" of another tradition, only to be killed by a wild boar or some other implacable enemy in the hunt. He was the masculine principle of vegetable nature, loved and then mourned by Aphrodite herself, who seems sometimes to have had the character even of "mother nature."[40] His name probably means "lord," and some of the ancient writers knew of his identification with Egyptian and Oriental deities of the sun, whose annual motion accompanies the growth and decay of plants. Finally, he seems to have been associated with Dionysus, who was also subject to repeated death and rebirth, and with the poet Orpheus. Orpheus' journey into the underworld to find Eurydice has not only been interpreted as an allegorical account of the journey of the sun,[41] but might also be seen as analogous to the legend that Adonis was obliged to spend one third of the year in Hades with Proserpina, who loved him for his beauty.[42]

It is important to repeat the simple but basic fact that the myth is only part of the *logos*. The myth is only the idealizing example, a link of tradition connecting the particular argument to a higher reality. The *logos* is the broad category of verbalized reality which includes argument and hypothesis as well as myth. In *Adonais* Shelley exploited all these verbal forms. His obvious sources were Bion's *Lament for Adonis* and the *Lament for Bion*, usually attributed to Moschus. He must have had these texts under his eyes as he wrote, translating from them whole passages and amplifying brief suggestions until they fit his Spenserian stanzas and his more than pastoral conception of the meaning of death and grief. Of course, he knew the joyful side of the Adonis myth from the song for the marriage festival in the fifteenth *Idyll* of Theocritus, and he was certainly familiar with *Lycidas* and with Virgil's tenth *Eclogue*. Shelley's careful work over these sources accounts so well for the real poetic virtues of *Adonais* that we might be persuaded with Matthew Arnold that "his original poetry is less satisfactory than his translations."[43]

Though *Adonais* is probably, as Shelley himself observed, the "least imperfect" of his compositions, this is not to say that it is without blemishes, which are no less distracting than the hand-clasping ecstasy of *Intellectual Beauty* or the swoon upon the "thorns of life" in the *Ode to the West Wind*. We may well object to what one critic has called the "semiprivate symbolism"[44] with which Shelley presents his languishing spirit in the procession of Keats's living mourners. Or we may find something less than poetry in the rages against the anonymous reviewer, the boar of the original myth, who by his criticisms of *Endymion,* "could crown / Life's early cup with such a draught of woe . . . yet could escape, the magic tone / Whose prelude held all envy, hate, and wrong, / . . . Silent with expectation of the song" (317-23). These are perhaps the best lines from either of the tirades against the reviewer, and they are based on a gracious compliment paid to Bion in the elegy on his death.[45] We may distinguish Shelley's unredeemed lines from those that were written under the influence of the Greeks. Wherever that influence is strong, Shelley's cogency and self-restraint usually increase. It may be said that Shelley's allegorical masks are too thin and not natural enough, or that the emotions they stir in Keats's behalf are like the seed which was sown upon the rocks and quickly withered. But the charge that *Adonais* is insincere, since it obviously could not spring from the sorrow over the loss of a close friend, would be a misunderstanding of Shelley's fundamental poetic feelings and of the ancient techniques of language and poetic design through which he handled them. The conventions of the pastoral elegy provide the means for the poet to work upon a fact, which by itself would cause a raw and unrefined suffering, until that fact is fitted into a world, as it were, of the "vague specific," where it can be treated with detachment and control. The classical lament performs its function through such detachment, within which the particular person and the particular event of his death can be gathered up into general and traditional categories of human experience. Like Milton mourning for Edward King, like all the writers of pastoral laments, Shelley, grieving for Keats, a mere acquaintance—he had wanted to care for Keats and teach him Greek —saw his own lot, and "in another's fate now wept his own." His feelings were as much engaged as they had been by the sufferings and triumph of his Prometheus.

The dynamic movement, the whole incantatory, even spell-binding effort of the pastoral lament is concentrated in a crescendo of invocations, through which the indifferent phenomena of nature, summoned in personal form, are made to share in the poet's supposed grief and to bring him consolation. The refrains—"I weep for Adonais —he is dead!"—and the catalogues of fabulous events and the processions of allegorical personages are all features of the pastoral lament, pieces of its stylized equipment. In general, of course, such conventions tend to solidify until little room remains for improvement and they are finally exhausted. In this last phase poetry is barren and abstract. It repeats without re-creating its language and its devices. The poet's "words," as Shelley observed, "become, through time, signs for portions or classes of thoughts . . . and then, if no new poets should arise to create afresh the associations which have been thus disorganized, language will be dead to all the nobler purposes of human intercourse."[46]

Shelley's inventiveness in this poem is to be seen in the way he enriched the pastoral conventions and infused into them his own Platonism, through a "poetic mode" of "progressive revelation."[47] This dialectical probing of meanings for Keats's death gradually unfolds, as Wasserman points out, through three successive and closely related hypotheses. Each of these hypotheses, giving shape to the event and to the poet's emotional responses, is stated and explored through traditional patterns of poetic and philosophical thought.

The first hypothesis (Stanzas I through XVII) is familiar to us from that attitude of wistful grace in which Chénier pictured the Greeks strewing flowers and laughing in the face of death. This is the attitude of the early elegists, Mimnermus, for example. It represents the view of life ascribed to Anacreon, though not articulated by him in the fragments we possess. It is stated in the famous elegiac comparison of the sixth book of the *Iliad* between the race of man and the generations of the leaves. In this hypothesis nature is a beautiful cloak of semblances. Death is the underlying principle of nature: the life of man is subject to the overpowering nothingness from which all things arise and into which they all return forever. "Every beautiful thing is hastening down toward you [Persephone]," Bions says, and "the goddess of Hades does not let him go."[48] Or in Shelley's lines, which are based on this:

> For he is gone, where all things wise and fair
> Descend;—oh, dream not that the amorous Deep
> Will yet restore him to the vital air;
> Death feeds on his mute voice, and laughs at our despair.

> [*Adonais,* 24-27]

Stressing man's confinement to the phenomenal world, Shelley
has fitted the ritual elements from the lament for the mythic Adonis
together with the techniques for mourning the human poet Bion.
Keats's death, in the spring of 1821, appears in the perspective
through which ancient poetry saw the bereavement of nature for a
tutelary god or a pastoral writer. With the pastoral poet as with the
mythic Adonis dies the "holy form" (*hieron eidos*),[49] the agreeable
shape or pleasing cast of nature's countenance, which seemed generous, benevolent, and full of life answering to the life of men. This
is the aspect of nature at its best, as Wordsworth said. For the ancients, it was nature peopled with nymphs and satyrs and gods, who
welcome the shepherd-poet and cause his flocks to prosper. The assumption behind this convention is that poetry, and especially pastoral song, confers upon cruel nature a humanizing, though all too
perishable, illusion of congeniality with man. When the poet is gone,
when Bion, for example, is "shrouded in silence within the hollow
earth,"[50] the unlovely singing of the frogs is all that the nymphs can
expect to hear. Nature ceases to flourish; the flocks and herds go un-
tended; the honey is left ungathered in the honeycomb. Nature is no
longer humane, no longer accommodating to man, since the pleasing
illusion is totally dependent on poetry or, in a sense, on the power of
the *logos*.

Shelley's treatment of the conventional procession emphasizes this
dependence. The vague figures who come to mourn for Keats and, as
it were, to annoint his corpse, are not companions or flocks but the
dead poet's thoughts, fancies, and poetic creations. They are

> . . . the quick Dreams,
> The passion-wingéd Ministers of thought,
> . . . whom near the living streams
> Of his young spirit he fed, and whom he taught
> The love which was its music. . . .

> [*Adonais*, 73-77]

In short, they are the mind's experience of nature and itself "all he
had loved, and moulded into thought, / From shape, and hue, and
odour, and sweet sound" (118-19). A mythic expression for the decline of vegetable nature is the strewing of flowers over the body of

Adonis. Shelley reiterates this formula in the picture of the poet's activity. Keats's poems are "fading melodies, / With which, like flowers that mock the corse beneath, / He had adorned and hid the coming bulk of Death" (16-18). Shelley acknowledges openly what the pastoral usually implies, namely, that the things of nature correspond to an emotional or spiritual terrain. Moschus' pathos is converted into melancholy in an atmosphere rather of the Promethean cave than of the Sicilian countryside. This fact underscores the character of Shelley's first hypothesis: it suggests nothing higher in the poetic mind than the combination of feeling with the perceptible surfaces of nature. Being only superficial expressions of the poet's mind peopling his world, the metaphors of flocks and flowers reaffirm the spirit's confinement to the phenomenal sphere.

But the suppositions that man and nature are coextensive and that nature sympathizes with man's griefs break down almost as soon as they are formed. A fundamental antagonism divides nature and mind. The pastoral metaphors of flowers and flocks are neither adequate nor emotionally satisfying. Even the myths of nature's seasonal return accent the brevity of human life. This poignant tension, at the heart of the pastoral elegy, leads Shelley to the subsequent hypotheses, where representatives from each grouping of image and convention are taken up again in a more ample metaphysical domain. The amplification comes at first from the Greek pastoral sources, with the admissions that nature seems not to continue to mourn or remember, that the griefs of Echo or the nightingale are fables only, and that personages, such as Spring that ceremoniously halts the course of the year, evaporate in the relentless motion of time. Shelley's notice that "Winter is come and gone, / But grief returns with the revolving year" does not announce that another year has passed; it brings into play the motif in the song of Theocritus at the Adonis festival:

> . . . how in the twelfth month, the seasons with soft feet have led Adonis from Acheron that flows forever—the seasons, dear to the blessed gods, but longed for by all mortals, to whom they come bringing something. [*Idyll* XV]

Moschus, stressing the frailty of the pastoral illusions, put this hint more boldly:

. . . the mallows, when they perish in the garden, and green parsley and the dill thick with blooms have life again in future time and are brought forth for another season; but deaf in the hollow earth, once we are dead, we great and strong wise men sleep very well a vast and endless sleep that knows no waking. [III]

The fables, creations of the mind, do not match the semblances of nature; the flowers are renewed, but men are not. "As long as skies are blue, and fields are green," Shelley says, "Evening must usher night, night urge the morrow, / Month follow month with woe, and year wake year to sorrow. / *He* will awake no more, oh, never more!" (*Adonais,* 187-90). And Shelley emphasizes that death is the real principle, from which for a time life is borrowed.

This opposition between man's fleeting life and the endless return of nature, as Wasserman points out, forms a framework for the twenty middle stanzas (XVIII through XXXVII) of *Adonais,* where the argument is founded in the "world of living men." In the Greek laments, the separation of men from the mythic demigods provides a way back into present reality. Even the ancient heroes, says Theocritus, do not make the repeated journey of Adonis back and forth between Acheron and earth. Moschus, with a last ironical tribute to the power of song, thinks of Orpheus and Eurydice; but he implies that he is no Orpheus and Bion will not really return to the mountains.

Shelley, however, does not content himself with the stern but simple futility which lies beneath the pastoral prettiness. He does not break the thread of the *logos*, but rationalizes its tension with reality by a synthesis of pastoral convention, habitual imagery, and further philosophical suggestion, weaving a new veil over the real world. He augments both sides of his basic antithesis. A simple picture of renewal from Theocritus—"the amorous birds now pair in every brake" —prepares for a generalized *élan* to reanimate the earth:

> Through wood and stream and field and hill and Ocean
> A quickening life from the Earth's heart has burst
> As it has ever done, with change and motion,
> From the great morning of the world when first
> God dawned on Chaos; in its stream immersed,
> The lamps of Heaven flash with a softer light.

[*Adonais,* 163-68]

The keynote is "motion," and we remember not only the god of love from the *Symposium* but that surprising argument in the *Phaedrus,* that motion is the *arché* or fountain of life without which the universe would collapse (245). For Plato, motion is the *sine qua non* of soul, if soul is to exist beyond the perishable world. But even the stars, which Shelley usually treats as spiritual symbols, seem to be implicated in the tricks of mutability. The pastoral pathos is extended, not overcome.

The Adonis myth, expressing a fundamental conception of nature, is being enlarged to become the vehicle for a philosophical problem:

> Nought we know, dies. Shall that alone which knows
> Be as a sword consumed before the sheath.

[177-78]

This is the question Plato raises at the heart and literal center of the *Phaedo* (85e and ff.). What if the soul is only the divine and invisible harmony and the body is its lyre and strings? For readers of the "Defence of Poetry," this question has a peculiarly Shelleyan ring. If spirit is but the highest flowering of corporeal nature, then the human soul is an "intense atom," as the materialists had said:

> ... all we loved of him should be,
> But for our grief, as if it had not been,
> And grief itself be mortal!

[*Adonais,* 181-83]

Or as the Stoic Epictetus also implied, counselling submission to the "will of nature," we are "the actors or spectators" of some indecipherable drama, and "great and mean / Meet massed in death, who lends what life must borrow" (185-86). By the time he came to the writing of *Adonais,* Shelley understood the limitations of arguments based on the rhythm of nature and the psychological laws of memory. He realized with Plato that not only the cycles of nature but the forms of thought might be mere excrescences of matter, and the "secret strength of things which governs thought" might be death. If his solution is no less arbitrary here than it was in *Mont Blanc,* it is at least more illuminating.

The only surprise to the attentive reader of the lyrics and the *Prometheus Unbound* is the inevitability with which his expectations are satisfied. Out of the gloomy melancholy which pervades the contemplation of external events, the elemental feminine figure arises, shrouded in mists. With an echo of Bion's invocation to Aphrodite, Urania is summoned by the dreams which are Keats's poems and experiences. She comes like the Maenad of the *Ode to the West Wind.* Shelley has converted Bion's Aphrodite, wounded by brambles as she rushes mourning through the grove, into Agathon's god of love, afflicted by men's harshness. In short, Shelley's Urania, another goddess of love, is the mythic and emotional mask personifying the *élan* or nature's "naked loveliness"; we need not assign to her any more mystical significance. Indeed, her divinity is, on the literal or dramatic level, a liability, as these lines, paraphrasing Bion's Aphrodite, show:

> . . . I would give
> All that I am to be as thou now art!
> But I am chained to Time, and cannot thence depart!
>
> [*Adonais,* 232-34]

Allegorically this disadvantage of being chained to time may prepare the way for the realization that Adonais has transcended, not only phenomenal nature, but also the immanent principle of its eternal returnings. Through the speech of Urania and the description of her person, Shelley is skillfully modulating into a more comprehensive register, one which is attuned more closely to his own emotional experience. Urania, coming as love but personifying that ambiguous spirit of renewal which looks like death, deflects the whole argument and shifts its focus inward toward the life of men, away from the contemplation of brute nature which the pastoral had revealed. Real men—Byron, Thomas Moore, Shelley himself, and the artist Severn— now replace the conventional mourners of the pastoral procession. But what is more, amid the angry outpourings against the reviewer, Urania formulates the central statement in this section:

> "The sun comes forth, and many reptiles spawn;
> He sets, and each ephemeral insect then
> Is gathered into death without a dawn,
> And the immortal stars awake again;

So is it in the world of living men:
A godlike mind soars forth, in its delight
Making earth bare and veiling heaven, and when
It sinks, the swarms that dimmed or shared its light
Leave to its kindred lamps the spirit's awful night."

[Stanza XXIX]

However inadequate we may feel its expression to be, the effect of this statement is to reverse the conclusion Shelley found in Moschus: human nature corresponds to the whole range of created things, from the celestial lights to the insects, and the great and stalwart and wise, that is, the poets, are imperishable as the stars.

These gleanings stand out; the attack upon the reviewer establishes a contrast which becomes the theme of the sustained if not exalted poetry of the concluding movement. The reviewer, presumably with the mass of mankind, "whose sails were never to the tempest given," remains in the lower air of "carrion kites," while the spirit of Keats, like the eagle in which a Greek epigrammatist had represented the dead Plato's soul, has "awakened from the dream of life" and has "outsoared the shadow of our night."[51] The world from which Keats has fled is a world of "phantoms" and "invulnerable nothings," of wearying pleasures and contagious guilt, of moral as well as physical decay. On the other hand,

. . . the pure spirit shall flow
Back to the burning fountain whence it came,
A portion of the Eternal, which must glow
Through time and change, unquenchably the same. . . .

[*Adonais*, 338-41]

The last eighteen stanzas of *Adonais* continue to bear out our belief that this poem is Shelley's best synthesis of Platonic thought with an array of materials from Greek poetry. In the last of the three hypotheses the pastoral treatment of death is undergoing its final transformation. The result is a view which Plato shared to some extent with the tragic poets. Death, the "veil" called life, becomes a way to true being. It is a necessity for the realization of *areté*, as Sophocles implied,[52] a gateway, as Plato thought, into the real life. The pastoral conventions do not altogether disappear in this ultimate shift in attitude: some of them are sublimated, etherealized. The "inheritors of unfulfilled renown," Chatterton, Lucan, Sidney, greet the spirit of Adonais as the Vesper of their starry bands; thus they enact a sort of pastoral procession "beyond mortal thought / Far in the Unapparent" (398-99). And we remember not only the Platonic epigraph to this poem, but also the myth of the *Phaedrus* (the idea is in the *Timaeus,* too) which says that inspired and virtuous souls are borne by love back to a place they once occupied in the celestial processions of the gods.

Impressions of the phenomenal world are also recalled from earlier hypotheses, but in a new mood: the sense of new dawning and of triumphant release overrules the former grief. In Rome, where Keats was buried, "flowering weeds, and fragrant copses dress / The bones of Desolation's nakedness" (436-37). Rome is phenomenal nature in miniature, and this is the world of elegiac impermanence. Yet this symbol of time's decay has an important place in the ladder of images by which Shelley's argument mounts above the elegiac hypotheses. All of these images show the imprint of the same pattern. It is the relation of the many to the One, of perishable fact to eternal value. The sign of eternity is light or fire, of course. In the Protestant cemetery (a metonymous island of special significance within Rome) the "light of laughing flowers along the grass" indicates a trace of eternal goodness in the world of appearance. Time's "slow fire," its kinship with the eternal, appears, at another stage, "transformed to marble" in the pyramid of Cestius which stands as an almost timeless pavilion over mortal remains. The "light of heaven's smile" over a larger field of death points the same motif still more steeply toward the eternal light associated with the One, the "fire for which all thirst" (485).

The import of all these images is generalized in the metaphysical statement:

> The One remains, the many change and pass;
> Heaven's light forever shines, Earth's shadows fly;
> Life, like a dome of many-coloured glass,

Stains the white radiance of Eternity,
Until Death tramples it to fragments. . . .

[460-64]

This famous assertion inverts the elegiac formulations, though it remains in harmony with the elegiac contexts. Life under this view is a
distortion of truth, an impediment to the attainment of real worth.
But the poet's affinity with nature is more secure than ever. "He is
made one with nature" (370), and his reunion with this primal creative energy is orchestrated like the apotheosis of Oedipus at Colonus,
when, amid sounds of thunder, he was received among the tutelary
powers in a grove where nightingales sang. And nature also is exalted
above the elegiac notion. Complex at least in its manifestations, it is
the power "which wields the world with never-wearied love, / Sustains it from beneath, and kindles it above" (377-78). We may compare it with Virgil's half-Platonic, half-Stoic world mind—especially
if we think of its lower side as the lusty *élan* of stanza XIX:

Principio caelum ac terras camposque liquentis
lucentemque globum lunae Titaniaque astra
spiritus intus alit, totamque infusa per artus
mens agitat molem et magno se corpore miscet.

[*Aeneid,* VI, 724-27]

It is Coleridge's "one spirit within us and abroad," from the *Aeolian Harp*, and it operates like the arts which Prometheus describes.
The instrument of this transcendent love, or perhaps its very essence,
is a cosmic imagination:

He is a portion of the loveliness
Which once he made more lovely: he doth bear
His part, while the one Spirit's plastic stress
Sweeps through the dull dense world, compelling there,
All new successions to the forms they wear;
Torturing th' unwilling dross that checks its flight
To its own likeness, as each mass may bear;
And bursting in its beauty and its might
From trees and beasts and men into the Heaven's light.

[Stanza XLIII]

If eternal nature is the imagination of the world,[53] then the "dome of many-coloured glass," which resembles at once the poetic veils and the Platonic sky or upper world, is a work of art. We come back to the Pindaric lyre which we have already discussed at the end of the last chapter.

Normally in Shelley's poetry such images symbolize order. They correspond to an inner peace to which the poet's spirit comes by a sudden change from chaos or despair. Such images of structure (these may include a unified vision of the celestial vault as well as human architecture) are the outward correlative of the cave. The cave is the heart or inner locus of the imagination. The domes and vaults and towers are its triumphant manifestations in the outer world.[54] These images are achieved in the "moment," when the poet feels himself to be under the beneficent influence of some eternal or transcendent power. Often, though not always, the imaginative simulation of death provides a means of passing under this inspiration. Perhaps recalling the inspiring effluence which he felt among the Euganean Hills, Shelley continues to adumbrate that principle variously as light, beauty, benediction, and sustaining love. To arrive at this state, there must be a transformation of consciousness, as we have shown. In *Adonais,* the dome, the product of the supreme creative power and the image of the transformed consciousness, is realized only to be annihilated in the effort to escape the evils of existence. Real, not imaginary death is the "moment" and the means of passage to the beatitude of union with the One. At its conclusion *Adonais* is cleft by the difficulty which besets any monistic theory.[55] Creation is good only from the vantage point of the creator. The escape from the evil of existence is a flight into non-being, unless one can become a god. But the works, even of the divine artist, are racked by intrinsic wrong. This is the conclusion to which Shelley's lyrical dialectic conducted him at the end of *Adonais.* It has carried the elegiac sense that life is vanity even into the "intense inane," which his imagination has peopled with noble spirits and a friendly power answering to the heart's desire. One consequence of our argument is that the very technique of *Adonais,* as well as its content, transfers to the poetic imagination the activity of the Platonic dialectic. In the *Republic* we are told:

. . . when I speak of the other division of the intelligible, you will understand me to speak of that other sort of knowledge which reason herself attains by the power of dialectic, using the hypotheses not as first principles, but only as hypotheses—that is to say, as steps and points of departure into a world which is above hypotheses, in order that she may soar beyond them to the first principle of the whole. [VI, 511]

Shelley's last complete long poem, however, does not really give a satisfactory answer to the obvious question: how is man to be redeemed by art and converted to love by the power of imagination? In *Hellas* Shelley insists as always that there is a kind of fatality by which ideals are brought to renew themselves in history. Tyranny and the moral effects of slavery are to be overthrown. The Turkish tyrant Mahmud, unlike Jupiter, is even brought to accept the necessity of his downfall,[56] and the liberation of the Greeks is hoped for as a renewal of ancient ideals. But in *Hellas* the ideals from the Greeks' "golden years" never really touch the historical Greece of the nineteenth century.[57] Instead, ancient Greece stands out as a luminous symbol. It is the ideal source of innocence, courage, liberty, and felicitous poetic fictions—the suprahistorical center of values which have civilized the West. Though founded "on the crystàlline sea / Of thought and its eternity" (698-99), classical Greece and its Saturnian dreams are dispelled by the glare of truth, which Shelley associates with Christianity. In the choral lyric which ends the play, the golden age conceived in the imagination, though it is preferred to the Christian truth, seems more remote than ever from the reality which it was once supposed to reform.

THE *CANTI* OF GIACOMO LEOPARDI

Fruitions of Romantic Hellenism

VI

The Heroic *Canzoni*

As we cast our thought back over these pages and thence outward to the numerous romantic attempts to relocate the lyric voice in an alien and unpoetic world, we realize that Chénier and Shelley were not alone in their search for a marriage of poetry and nature which would vindicate the sovereignty of the imagination and the heart's desire. For the poet with learning, for whom his art was his religion, classical Greece—however it might be perceived—was both a symbol and a canonical inspiration.

For Leopardi the historic Greece, its heroism, its culture, its literature, occupy the zenith of human well-being and the summit of human perfection, fulfilling the ideal of happiness in harmony with nature. The historic Greece is possessed of all the main characteristics which identify an ideal world. It is like the Homeric realm of the epic heroes, whose inhabitants are able to hold free and inspiring intercourse with the still higher and paradigmatic world of the gods and the glorious dead. It represents the youth, if not the childhood of the world, as a kind of "civiltà media," as Leopardi said, since it combines the cultural and political advantages of civilization with that closeness to primitive nature, which the romantics had been seeking since Rousseau. But Greece is great and beautiful, from Leopardi's point of view, because it is governed by illusions, which, though they are the gifts of nature, are nevertheless untrue or incompatible with reality in which men now live. For Leopardi, classical Greece is the object of a consciously nostalgic longing, which is the more intense because he knows it cannot be fulfilled. And yet his lyrical task is not to disguise but to exploit this contrast and this irremediable desire. His poetic purpose is not to conquer consciousness but to intensify it and to elicit by the undiminished light of intelligence a lyrical emotion which is both desperate and consoling. Shelley's pessimism is only an undertone, which now and then breaks in upon his Platonized dream of union with nature through the *logos*. For Giacomo Leopardi, the lyric poet's words can sometimes give beautiful form to the otherwise mute and terrible anguish of the enlightened spirit.

We notice an important difference between Shelley and Leopardi. The English poet was an amateur in the best sense of that word.[1] The Italian was a scholar, prematurely grave, who spent in study the principal energy of his youth. His universe, as De Sanctis said, was classical antiquity (this could hardly be said of the young Shelley):

> Separated from the modern world and from all society, he found in his father's library a sort of Pompeii where he shut himself up to dig at will as best he could until he became a citizen there.[2]

A citizen of Pompeii, however, is not an Athenian. At least during Giacomo's youth, the Leopardi library lacked editions of the four Greek dramatists and three historians, and it seems likely that his citations in notes on the language and the thought of these authors, though sometimes copious, must often have been gathered at second hand.[3] His Pindar and his Greek-Latin edition of nine lyric poets, both dating from the Renaissance, could have acquainted him with idea and style but not with the latest criticism.[4] Yet if his resources were limited, his precocity is nevertheless impressive. To take one

example, not long after his sixteenth birthday he completed emenda-
tions and commentary of Porphyry's *Life of Plotinus.* This work
drew the praise "vir illustris" from the scholar Kreuzer.[5] According
to a recent judgment, his philological insights sometimes rivalled the
best work of the day and showed more skill than those of the famous
paleographer Angelo Mai, but Leopardi's scholarship was not on a
plane with Foscolo's or Carducci's.[6] His knowledge of Greek, though
fluent and perceptive, was not really scientific.[7] His interest in philology persisted throughout most of his life; philological notes and ob-
servations continued appearing in *Lo Zibaldone* even after he turned
over his unpublished manuscripts to De Sinner in 1830, when failing
sight, poor health, and lack of success led him to abandon his hopes
for a distinguished career.

Of more obvious importance in his poetic development are his
verse translations. These include principally the first book of the *Odyssey,* the idylls of Moschus, the Triopean inscriptions, the *Batra-
comiomachia,* the battle of the Titans from Hesiod's *Theogony,* and
the *Aeneid,* Book II, all finished between 1816 and 1817. It is scarcely an exaggeration to say that Leopardi wanted to touch and render
the divine worth of poetic expression not tarnished, but quintessen-
tially clear in its revelation of ideal life.[8] But faithfulness to the text
was the way to preserve the inestimable richness. Any word omitted
from Homer, he said, is a lost gem.[9] The principle of fidelity was
generally successful in the translations from Greek. Its application
was less felicitous in the version of the *Aeneid,* Book II, which is
hard reading and quite inferior to Annibal Caro's sixteenth-century
version with its fine swiftness and appropriately Italianate phrasing.
Leopardi's verses are rough and lifeless even in the account of Laocoon's death or of the slaughter within Priam's palace (II, 483 ff.),
where the "indefinite" and the "pathetic" are both to be found.

Whatever Italian critics may say, the foreign reader coming to
Leopardi's translations from the Greek is likely to find himself engaged and instructed.[10] The translation of Book I of the *Odyssey*
certainly bears out this claim. In spite of the disparagements it has
sometimes received, it displays the technique of a remarkable young
craftsman. Leopardi is not above flaunting his achievement in the

preface, where he defies the reader to compare his verses with the
Greek. And the boast is justified. But accuracy is not the only merit.
The tone is right—dignified yet easy in its assurance. There is a real
charm of far away places and the sea, perhaps more than the original
possesses, in this account of Odysseus on Calypso's isle:

> In un'isola d'arbori nutrice
> Tutta cinta dall'acque, ove del mare
> E l'umbilico, e dove in sua magione
> Ha ricetto una Dea figlia d'Atlante
> Cui tutto è noto, che del mar gli abissi
> Tutti conosce, e che la terra e il cielo
> Sopra colonne altissime sorregge.
> La figliuola di lui ritiene a forza
> Il misero piangente, e ognor con dolci
> Molli detti il carezza, affin che il prenda
> D'Itaca obblio. Ma di sua terra almeno
> Veder bramando Ulisse alzarsi il fumo,
> Morir desia. . . .

The occasional touch of artifice beyond the original is usually un-
strained. Some of the speeches, especially those of Telemachus and
Penelope, show surprising richness of character. At the same time
they give a taste of the simplicity and naturalness which Leopardi
never ceased to praise as high values in art.

Though Leopardi's verse translations did not win him immediate
fame as he hoped they would, his philological jokes caused a stir. His
Inno a Nettuno, a dull pastiche of classical allusions, convinced the
Vatican librarian that a genuine Greek manuscript had been stolen
from the archives and translated.[11] The *Odae adespotae,* composed
in Greek with accompanying Latin version and editor's notes, passed
for genuine Anacreontics. The description of the moon is clearly a
preparation, in Greek, for a whole set of lyrical passages, notably this
from *La sera del dì di festa:*

> E queta sovra i tetti e in mezzo agli orti
> Posa la luna, e di lontan rivela
> Serena ogni montagna. . . .

Occasionally, Leopardi's emotional impression of what he took to be the essence of Greek antiquity was at odds with his critical judgment. For instance, he did not know that the Anacreontea, those little lyrics to wine and beauty, were, as we now suppose, poor and late imitations of the Tean poet. He ranked the Anacreon whom these copies were thought to represent, among the first lyric poets of Greece. To describe the pleasure they gave him, the only likeness he could find was a summer breeze.[12] "To appreciate it," he wrote in 1826, still trying to explain this delight, "it is necessary to read them on purpose with a certain haste and with a little or very slight attention. Any one who reads them with deliberation, or pauses over the parts, or examines, or pays heed, sees no beauty and feels no pleasure " (*Zibaldone*, 4177). To his attentive mind these songs are trivial enough. But his imagination is charmed and refreshed because they are supposed to be ancient Greek. Leopardi does not know why the charm vanishes when he reads with care.

Surely part of the attraction for him in the Greek classics was simply their antiquity. The closer they seemed to the dawn at which civilization was born, the stronger was their hold on his imagination. Coming to Hesiod with his head still full of Homer's ideas, manners, and "godlike quality," Leopardi feels that Hesiod is so much more simple, free, and natural that he must have come first: "precisely in Hesiod's work more than in any other, there smiles and breathes that freshness of nature now withered forever."[13] We must not expect too much consistency between this early preface recommending Hesiod to Italian readers and the copious jottings throughout *Zibaldone*. There, in Leopardi's intellectual diary, Homer is the figure that dominates, both early and late. His antiquity and closeness to nature partly explain his greatness. He is the ideal which nature bequeathed to subsequent, civilized generations. He is the prototype of the first poetic spirits and wandered without fetter through the "campi immaginabili." He had no rules; he studied nature, and others study him.[14] Leopardi brings us back to the neoclassical dictum that Homer and nature are the same, but Leopardi is clearly coming to this realization afresh. Homer's language, his characterizations, his pictures of virtue, heroism, sympathy, pathos, or grief, were the continual subjects of criticism, analysis, speculation. They were touchstones by which the critic assayed literature and the moralist passed judgment on life. Achilles was the type for admiration, Hector for sympathy, the Homeric world a model of emotional freedom and imaginative vitality.

The mystery of Homer's art was a great whale over which Leopardi threw various nets of theory. At one phase Homer seemed simple because of his primitiveness. Even when Leopardi concluded that Homer sought to be "ornate," that simplicity, indeed, is the fruit of art, Homer still had "naturalezza," in spite of himself. The sense of something indescribably precious persists through the changes of opinion. Homer is the archetype of the poet; his power transcends the apparatus of criticism as the deity transcends theology. Leopardi's mythic Homer wandered the face of the earth and suffered, like Chénier's "mendiant" and Foscolo's seer, poetic because of his suffering. Here he is more ethereal:

> In Homer all is vague [the Italian word means beautiful and charming, too] ; all is supremely poetic in the largest truth and justness, the greatest force and range of this term; to begin with, this is true of his person and his life, wrapped and shrouded as they are in mystery, beyond the highest antiquity and distance and the ever-increasing difference that divides his age from later ages and especially from ours . . . Homer himself is a vague and therefore poetic idea. This is so much the case that some have doubted and some still doubt whether Homer was ever really anything but an idea. [*Zibaldone*, 3975]

This note, December 12, 1823, is the first reference to the theory that, as Vico put it, "Homer was an idea or a heroic character of Grecian men insofar as they told their history in song."[15] Leopardi rejected this theory in 1823. But he had already noticed the opinion of Longinus that the *Odyssey* was the poem of Homer's old age, and in 1821 he conjectured that the *Odyssey* was a feeble imitation of the *Iliad*. Not until 1828 did he appear to accept the claim that the *Iliad* was written in the youth of Greece itself, the *Odyssey* in its rational and luxurious old age.[16] Confronting the theories of Wolf and his disciples, which Vico had anticipated by half a century, Leopardi conceded that the Homeric epics must have been the fragmentary narrative songs of the rhapsodes, which editors later organized and refined. Thus the Homeric poems were lyrical, at least in their supposed origins. Leopardi found at last in Homer himself a support for his long-standing conviction that the most perfect kind of human discourse, and one of the most primitive, is lyric poetry.[17]

Still, even during the period that concerns this chapter, Leopardi would not have us conclude that the poems of Homer were charming merely because they were ancient. They would not become mere commonplaces if one could take away from them the simplicity of a world beginning. This was Mme de Staël's position.[18] There are certain natural forms, prototypes of human experience, he argued in 1818, and to these the human emotions always respond: "Men's love for these forms is not dead, nor will it cease to exist before the human race ceases."[19] Chénier's theory of allegory was really based on such an assumption. And of course, the everlasting patterns of the imagination were most perfectly realized in the fictions of Greek poetry. Nature and Greek antiquity are correlatives, not absolute equivalents. They belong so often together because the standards of life as well as art held out by ancient Greek poetry derive immediately from eternal nature. The decline of poetry accompanied the human spirit's decay, and a measure of this process could be found in the fact that Greek, a language of nature, had once been universal, whereas the universal language in the nineteenth century was civilized, rational, unpoetic French. Leopardi is especially critical of French translations from Greek. But it is reassuring to read that the province of Italian, as of Greek, is the imagination. Analogies between Italian and Greek intrigued him. To Pietro Giordani, who gave him the idea in 1817, he wrote: ". . . having opened some Greek prose writer, I found with the greatest pleasure that your observation is very true and instructive." Not classical but vulgate Latin, he thought, was the linguistic link.[20]

His devotion to ancient Greece did not exclude some Italian poets from the plane of natural greatness. Dante, "per lo cui verso / Il meonio cantor non è più solo," was Homer's Italian equal. If Homer was, as Petrarch had said, "the first who painted ancient memories," Dante, with that simple ease ("negligenza") which comes from nature could sculpture both feeling and conception before the reader's eyes. Dante's imagination was not merely fertile, as was Ovid's or Ariosto's; he was not like the moderns who replace their somnolent and frozen imagination with egoistic sentiment. Dante's imagination is powerful and vigorous like Homer's (*Zibaldone*, 2523, 3154-55). Dante is the Italian Homer. The Italian lyrist, Chiabrera, for instance, could be compared with Pindar. And Leopardi applies to him some of the standards by which he thought Longinus measured the "sublime." Chiabrera achieves the "sublime" as Homer and Pindar did, "within large but just limits," with fitting Greek simplicity. He collects certain parts or aspects of a thing which taken altogether "swiftly form the sublime."[21] It is not Chiabrera's merit that interests us in this early judgment. Leopardi himself was later to disown any affinity between his *Dieci canzoni* and the traditional Italian lyric.[22] We are concerned with the standard of taste, which, though in modified form, persisted throughout his life, and the direction which that standard dictates.

Pindar was studied more by the youthful philologue than by the mature poet and was to slip from the foreground of ideal antiquity. The theory of the sublime, however, had a lasting impact, not only on Leopardi's judgment, but on his practice. The *Idilli*, especially the *Grandi idilli*, often rise to serene but intense feeling, maintained above the commonplace by the hidden hand of artifice. The necessary conditions of this "poetic" elevation are range and grasp of imagination and harmony of thought. The sublime satisfies a natural instinct to admire what is greater than ourselves—the ocean rather than the potable stream, the stars rather than the fire we cook with. Longinus' intuitive but self-confident standard for the grand style is a prototype and probably a source for Leopardi's poetic of the vague, the indefinite, the half-perceived. The heroic *Canzoni*, the subject of this chapter, seek the sublime with more obvious intent. Their rhetoric, especially the interminable rhetorical questions, is the direct legacy of an oratorical tradition in Italian poetry. But Longinus too had tried to explain how the tropes served sublimity when inspiration commanded them. He was inclined to treat poetry and eloquence together. The onrush of true passion, he thought moreover, required and justified boldness of imagery.

Let *Ad Angelo Mai* be our example. It falls short of the standard because feeling and art are not quite wed. Besides the rest of the rhetoric, it has its bold metaphors, but the automatic eloquence born not from passion but from art neutralizes here, as it weakens elsewhere, the boldness of invention. This is particularly true and particularly disappointing in the stanza addressed to Columbus. Here are the stars and the open sea beyond the pillars of Hercules, and in a moment an "unknown, immense land" is added—all "elements of grandeur." Since "the ancient is an important ingredient in sublime sensations" (*Zibaldone,* 1429), there are fairly deft allusions to legends that the sun drowns each night in the ocean. The imagination reaches out powerfully and swiftly gathers many large ideas. But too much prosaic argument creeps in. The world is measured by the realization that the day is born on the open sea as it sinks from the coasts of Italy. The thesis of the poem infects the style, and we feel that knowledge does indeed nullify imagination and shrink the globe. A lack of choice, a lack, really, of apparent negligence, leaves the sublime scattered in its various members.[23] But clearly sublimity is the intention.

The poem *Ad Angelo Mai* lavishes praise on the "scopritor famoso."[24] But the poem also says that discovery in general destroys imagination and increases the domain of *il nulla,* the palpable, one might say Platonic, non-being.[25] This contradiction represents a tension perhaps unconsciously desired and maintained. It is like other romantic dilemmas: it makes the actual present intolerable. Leopardi's quest for the newness and freshness of nature among the remains of antiquity is one more case in the central paradox of romantic Hellenism. But Leopardi's nostalgia is also different from Shelley's. Shelley, influenced by Plato, conceived origin as a metaphor for archetype. The values of antiquity appeared sometimes as a canopy beneath which the present could take refuge; the many-colored scarf of eternal nature was sometimes the poet's cloak and sometimes his shroud. For Leopardi, the past is a more or less concrete set of facts. His nostalgia[26] in the heroic *Canzoni* recalls persons and historical impressions. His motive is always to depreciate the present life. He shares this inclination with Longinus and to some extent with Chénier. The burden of his message to his contemporaries is a

command to turn back to the ancients and to despise themselves. It
is summed up in the second heroic *canzone, Sopra il monumento di
Dante:*

> Volgiti indietro, e guarda, o patria mia,
> Quella schiera infinita d'immortali,
> E piangi e di te stessa ti disdegna;
> . . . .
> Io mentre viva andrò sclamando intorno,
> Volgiti agli avi tuoi, guasto legnaggio. . . .

* * * * *

I

In the first two *canti* (September and October, 1818), the theme
of Longinus that the ancient is great and glorious, while the modern
is small and mean, mingles with the sense of present moral feebleness
which has persisted in Italian literature even from Dante's time. Like
Shelley, Leopardi asserted that it is absurd to suppose a difference
between the moderns and the ancients in native genius. But genius
cannot thrive because circumstances and fate prepare the desolation
which the modern mind beholds:

> Perchè venimmo a sì perversi tempi?
> Perchè il nascer ne desti o perchè prima
> Non ne desti il morire,
> Acerbo fato? . . .

[*Sopra il monumento di Dante*]

This is variously true throughout the *Canti.* The knowledge of fate
and history rouses in the lyrical consciousness a singular mixture of
pain and pleasure. In the later of the first two *canti, Sopra il monumento di Dante,* the exemplars from Italy's golden past are invoked,
"patrii esempi della prisca etade," but they are mere names. The virtues, the triumphs, the glories of the Latin past give no vitality to the
present. To Shelley, a voluntary exile, the arches and columns of
Pompeii were a temple of Grecian art in harmony with nature, as if

by a living connection Italian ruins could awaken in the noble mind
the memory of life in its ideal season.[27] To Leopardi, the fragments
of architecture are no easy symbolic route which the romantic wanderer may follow out of history. They are the lifeless shells of nobility, reminders above all of destiny, taunting the consciousness in a
world which is emptied of glory.

The opening lines of *All'Italia* give utterance to the theme which
develops throughout the patriotic *canzoni*:

> O patria mia, vedo le mura e gli archi
> E le colonne e i simulacri e l'erme
> Torri degli avi nostri,
> Ma la gloria non vedo. . . .

The underlying attitude is implicitly that of the lyric to Angelo Mai:

> . . . O torri, o celle,
> O donne, o cavalieri,
> O giardini, o palagi! a voi pensando,
> In mille vane amenità si perde
> La mente mia. Di vanità, di belle
> Fole e strani pensieri
> Si componea l'umana vita: in bando
> Li cacciammo: or che resta? . . .

When the subject is Italian, the command to turn back to the exemplars of the past appears to be a helpless gesture. As Leopardi admits
in *Ad Angelo Mai*: "Ahi dal dolor comincia e nasce / L'italo canto."
The principal difference between Italy's past and her present is

> . . . E pur men grava e morde
> Il mal che n'addolora
> Del tedio che n'affoga. . . .

But if, as De Sanctis has said, these first *canzoni* were murmured "a
bassa voce" by the resurgent nationalists of the South, or if, as Settembrini argued, the rhetorical patriotism conveyed the sentiments
for which Italians were to die in the struggle for the unification of
Italy, these additional ironies point to the effects of heightened consciousness in men of action.[28]

It has been said that *All'Italia* echoes the fading pomp of Monti and the eighteenth century. Carducci, on the other hand, thought its language was attuned to the spirit of national awakening.[29] The personification of Italy, the fallen lady, unveiled, dishevelled, wounded, and in chains among the tokens of ancestral pride, was a commonplace. Not only Monti but also the less known Fantone had used a similar device.[30] Borsieri's "cardboard statue" which at a distance seems to wear the peplos is a satirical transformation of this cliché.[31] It is Leopardi's point of view, however, that gives this commonplace a special meaning. He makes the gesture of sacrificing his own blood to rekindle the patriotism of his countrymen. After painting the defections of Italy's sons who died in the service of her conquerors, he turns back not to Rome but to Greece, and his sentiments gain solidity, his verses become simpler, his periods less swollen and protracted, as he remembers the scene at Thermopylae. Each instance of Italian ignominy has a glorious counterpart in a corresponding Greek event. The bitter tenderness in behalf of Italy gives way to a larger and freer pathos which presents the historical picture of the Greek heroes in the mood of the sepulchral epigrams. When Simonides steps into this scene to celebrate their deeds, he does not speak merely in the voice of the Greek poet who wrote the simple arguments of the epitaphs. In addition to narrating his recollection of what took place, Leopardi's Simonides displays his personal sentiments toward heroism:

> . . . Ecco io mi prostro,
> O benedetti, al suolo,
> E bacio questi sassi e queste zolle,
> Che fien lodate e chiare eternamente
> Dall'uno all'altro polo.

Had Leopardi known Chénier's formula, he might have said that his hymn to Italy was ancient verse made from the inescapable perspective of modern sentiment. We cannot abandon our self-knowledge, he would have repeated, or relieve its pernicious hold upon the heart, but we must disguise it. Leopardi's ostensible theme is Simonides' premise, that "to die nobly is the greatest part of virtue."[32] Introducing the ancient poet's speech, Leopardi quotes him directly:

> . . . morendo
> Si sottrasse da morte il santo stuolo . . . .

Or as Simonides himself has said:

> Those who wrapped their beloved country in unextinguished fame
> have donned the black cloud of death. Yet in dying, they are not
> dead, since courage, bestowing honor from above, leads them back
> from the house of Hades. [frg. 126]

The whole declamation is a composite of classical patriotic utterance, including an echo of Pindar's first *Olympian*.[33] In imagining the small band of Spartans going to their death as to a feast, Leopardi may have remembered the moving account in Aeschylus' *Persae* (386 ff.) of the Greek sailors at Salamis, who sang a paean as they bore down at dawn on the outnumbering Persians.[34] The Pindaric line with which the speech closes, signifies a kinship through *areté* between the poet and the hero. Feeling that for the modern poet such a relationship is impossible since heroism is dead, Leopardi has entered imaginatively, through the words of the Greeks, into an ideal though once historically actual world where heroism survives in the memory of immortal fame.

In its content, then, Leopardi's recollection of Thermopylae is faithful to the spirit of Simonides' well-known epitaph:

> Glorious is the fortune of the men that died at Thermopylae; their
> fate is beautiful; their tomb is an altar; their memory takes the
> place of lamentation, and eulogy is pity for them; neither darkness
> nor all-devouring time will obscure their sepulture. This shroud of
> worthy men has gathered to itself the glory that abides in Greece.
> [frg. 21]

But if we attend to the transcription of these lines, we may penetrate Leopardi's disguise:

> Prima divelte, in mar precipitando,
> Spente nell'imo strideran le stelle,
> Che la memoria e il vostro
> Amor trascorra o scemi.

La vostra tomba è un'ara; e qua mostrando
Verran le madri ai parvoli le belle
Orme del vostro sangue. . . .

The mood and scope of this statement, its historical consciousness and the argument that the dead are a source of almost religious inspiration for the living, remind us as much of Foscolo's *Sepolcri* as of the ancient whom Leopardi seems to imitate. *All'Italia* is not, as many critics have thought, a mere juxtaposition of modern decadence and ancient glory. Leopardi does not forget Italy any more than he forgets himself. The Pindaric technique of balancing symbolic analogues or counterparts with opposite values, negative against positive, enables the modern poet to participate however remotely in that age when there was communication between the living and the dead, and the past was an efficacious influence on men's lives. In presenting the two faces of history, the true and the ideal, the real and the beautiful, the seasons of the living and the dead, *All'Italia* confronts us with the lyrical antithesis which is at the heart of Leopardi's *Canti* and his thought.

The *canzoni* of November and December, 1821, present the basic antithesis and define the heroic ideal with sharper clarity. The poem to Paolina Leopardi, on the occasion of her wedding (which later failed to take place), is a sort of ode on the roles of women in modern and ancient societies. It is a partially disguised contrast between the inspiration which ancient women could offer and the impossibility of such inspiration in modern times. The premise of the poem is that civilization has created an absolute opposition between heroism and life as it is to be lived under the sway of fate. Then the poem turns to women in general, to describe their power in lines which echo the Anacreontea and Petrarch,[35] and to indict their failure to exercise this capacity: "Ragion di nostra etate / Io chieggo a voi." The hope that noble examples may renew the ancient spirit of Rome would be the typical ending for an ode on such an occasion, when explicit despair would be inappropriate or even unkind. But Leopardi's real conclusion is that heroism, like the "beate larve" and "antico error" which Paolina was about to leave behind, belonged to an ideal time when the light of heaven was more benign: ". . . più bello a' tuoi di spendesse il sole / Ch'oggi non fa." That light was the light of nature, which in historical times shone above all on classical Greece.

In the second patriotic ode of 1821, we notice the same pattern of conflicting intentions. The occasion of *A un vincitore nel pallone* was Leopardi's acquaintance with a celebrated young athlete of the day, Carlo Didimi di Treja. Its ostensible message is that bodily exercise is a concomitant of patriotic heroism. Leopardi noted the Greek belief that physical vigor was necessary for the health of the spirit.[36] Carlo Didimi's athletic prowess might have been a fine example with which to educate Italian youth in the ways to ancient nobility. Thus Leopardi begins, remembering Pindar and Chiabrera's three *canzoni* on soccer, as Karl Vossler points out.[37] The athlete is called by his country to perform noble deeds and renew the examples from antiquity. But once again Leopardi's memory takes the same turn. He recalls the example of Greek athletes. He thinks of the victory at Marathon as if it was a result of the skill which Greeks acquired in the Hellenic games. But this memory, instead of leading to a vision of heroism, intensifies the recognition that the deeds of mortals are a futile game. It is not that the young athlete's achievements are less fine in themselves, but rather that they cannot be related to anything equally noble in their own time. *Areté* has no context. It is negated in the moral void that surrounds it. What Pindar had and what Leopardi lacks is an emotional atmosphere alive with nobility. The light of imagination had been extinguished:

> · . . . A noi di lieti
> Inganni e di felici ombre soccorse
> Natura stessa: e là dove l'insano
> Costume ai forti errori esca non porse,
> Negli ozi oscuri e nudi
> Mutò la gente i gloriosi studi.

In classical Greece, the imagination was still alive; reason had not yet prevailed, though as Leopardi admits in *Ad Angelo Mai* the first inquiries of the human mind contain the fatal seeds of scientific knowledge. Thus in the age of Pericles, heroic sacrifice might receive a monument more lasting than marble within the human heart. Pin-

dar's poems were such monuments in words. His myths were paradigmatic examples from a legendary *illo tempore,* or from what might
be called archetypal time.[38] But for Leopardi, antiquity itself is *illud
tempus.* Its deeds and examples have the value of myth. But these
cannot penetrate current history because knowledge precludes belief
in those desires and strivings which antiquity displays. Therefore the
promise which opens *A un vincitore* must inevitably be unfulfilled.
The athlete's prowess would have been glorious in a time when the
voice and countenance of glory spoke as sovereign realities to the
living imagination. Then virtue could be saved from the swift river of
time on the stream of song. But in an unpoetic age the occasions of
poetry are causes of nostalgia.

There is in these *canzoni* a discord between memory and imagination which Leopardi resolves through what we should term the irony
of inverted imitation. *A un vincitore* is not Pindaric, as Leopardi reminds us. Nevertheless, it has the shape of an ancient ode. Making
one event the center of reflection, it moves through contrasting
planes of thought and feeling reaching out to find a context for its
subject and its dominant emotion. But this poem's climax, its myth,
is a vision of ruin whose grandiloquence, as De Sanctis said, has not
been equalled in Italian poetry. Echoing lines in which Horace exalted the Roman Capitol by contrast with the crumbling tomb of
Priam, Leopardi reverses Horace's intention,[39] and anticipates a future in which Rome will become a wilderness once again:

> Tempo forse verrà ch'alle ruine
> Delle italiche moli
> Insultino gli armenti, e che l'aratro
> Sentano i sette colli; e pochi Soli
> Forse fien volti, e le città latine
> Abiterà la cauta volpe, e l'atro
> Bosco mormorerà fra le alte mura . . . .

And just when we would expect a Pindaric flight showing how individual virtue might regain its power—"ma per te stesso al polo ergi
le mente"—Leopardi asks: "Nostra vita a che val? solo a spregiarla."[40]
As if to parody Simonides' argument that heroic death is like a gar-

ment of *areté,* Leopardi concludes that life is happiest in the midst of perils which may bring it to an end.

* * * * *

II

Leopardi conceives the whole course of history as a decline from an indefinite time of fabulous creativity to the tedium of scientific realism. Shelley too had outlined such a progression in the "Defence of Poetry," where he noted that spontaneously creative language, the work of the imagination, gives way inevitably to algebraic generality. Within the period of the heroic *canzoni,* imagination equals nature, and, although Leopardi would later contradict this equation, nature still equals life (*Zibaldone,* 3813). History, as Leopardi conceived it, is the history of the human mind.[41] It is mythical, a philologue's history, and is preserved, therefore, not so much in the exact record of men's deeds as in the embodiment of their thoughts and of their reactions to their circumstances and to themselves.

In *Alla primavera o delle favole antiche,* as Leopardi perceives the signs of life returning with the spring, he seems to hear the "maternal voice" ("materna voce") of nature. He translates his yearning for the old life of the spirit into the language of ancient memories, which through study had become the familiars of his own youth. The three central stanzas are a tissue of ancient myths. Touching them lightly, he leads us through a highly generalized composite picture of the milieu in which nature spoke the language of the imagination: "What a beautiful time that was in which every thing was alive according to the human imagination, and humanly alive, that is, inhabited or formed by beings like ourselves!" (*Zibaldone,* 63-64). Not only the reading of Ovid, to whom many of these fables can be traced, but the meticulous, even pedantic study of the ancient stories entered into this imaginative re-creation of nature's vitality.[42]

Leopardi's reflections, moreover, on the semi-philosophical assumption that primitive life is to the ages of humanity what childhood is to the years of a single man,[43] shows close resemblances to the statements of Vico. "The first peoples," as Vico said, "who were the children of the human race, founded first the world of the arts; then the philosophers, who came a long time afterwards and so may be regarded as the old men of the nations, founded the world of the sciences, thereby making humanity complete."[44]

In this remark of Vico's we recognize the polarizing terms of Leopardi's thematic opposition. We perceive foreshadowings of Leopardi's pessimism in Vico's assertions that "in the world's childhood men were by nature sublime poets," that it was "deficiency of human reasoning power that gave rise to poetry so sublime that the philosophies which came afterwards, the arts of poetry and of criticism, have produced none equal or better, and have even prevented its production."[45] For Vico, it is axiomatic that "because of the indefinite nature of the human mind, wherever it is lost in ignorance, man makes himself the measure of all things," and that "whenever men can form no idea of distant and unknown things, they judge them by what is familiar and at hand."[46] In man's "grossest and most bodily instincts" lies the "veiled image" of his reflective life of mind, which develops "under the pressure of his needs and interest and passions."[47]

These ideas of human development, taken together with Vico's three ages, of gods, heroes, and men, might serve as the headings in an outline of Leopardi's philosophy of history. But for Leopardi, both men and the world have survived to endure a fourth age, in which the machinery of reason is so far "encrusted" on primitive vitality that the sleeping world is like a watch with a broken spring, while man is "a dream of a shadow." The attention of an automaton, he adds, should be quite sufficient for such an existence.[48]

The encounter of imagination with nature created ethics and theology. Reason reduces guilt and innocence to a merely personal or subjective matter and renders nature indifferent to good and bad alike. One of the evils in man's "dark intellect" is that it separates him from the life of instinct. The pursuit of virtue is part of the "giovanile error," the imaginative falsehood, by which both Leopardi and the whole race were happily deceived in their youth. This conviction is implied in the framework of *Alla primavera* and gives that poem its intellectual force. In that period of human history when the dialogue between man's growing consciousness and his natural circumstances formed the imaginative fables which classical literature has preserved, nature seemed to recognize the difference between the innocent and the guilty. The exile found sympathy from the fabulous inhabitants of the trees; the nightingale's song seemed to preserve the memory of ancient wrongs:

> . . . E te d'umani eventi
> Disse la fama esperto,
> Musico augel che tra chiomato bosco
> Or vieni il rinascente anno cantando,
> E lamentar nell'alto
> Ozio de' campi, all'aer muto e fosco,
> Antichi danni e scellerato scorno,
> E d'ira e di pietà pallido il giorno.

> [*Alla primavera*]

These ancient stories were caused by nature itself,[49] and the religion with which they were associated, that religion whose errors Leopardi had exploded in his youth, contained an inherent system of values. Vico's pronouncement, that the mythical theology of the Greeks was "the science of the language of the gods,"[50] suits Leopardi's conception exactly. The Ovidian tale, on which the passage just quoted was partly based, is but one illustration of the ancient belief that nature's living beings express a strict divine law of punishments and rewards (*Metamorphoses,* VI, 424 ff.). The metamorphoses interpret nature in accord with man's predispositions. While the imagination still responded to these symbols of the mythical past, Leopardi argues in *Alla primavera,* men took the measure of their innocence from the feelings which accompanied their encounters with nature.

Leopardi's philosophical name for the laws behind these responses is "credenze," beliefs, which are implanted by nature and arise out of innate dispositions. They are not Platonic ideas. They are rather like Epicurean "prolepses,"[51] the psychological preconditions of perception, action and thought. If a man is to have fixed motives for decisive action, these beliefs are necessary, and unlike the civil law, which one can forget, this law, which nature writes on the heart, has the force of instinct. The religious and philosophical beliefs of the natural man derive from the same instinctive source as the animal's appetites. And if these beliefs and the myths that embody them are illusions, Leopardi's attitude was:

> I consider illusions as things which have a certain reality, inasmuch as they are essential ingredients in the system of human nature, and are given by nature to many men in such a way that it is not right to disparage them as the dreams of an individual, but rather they are proper to man and are intended by nature, and without them our life would be the most miserable and barbarous thing, . . . wherefore they are necessary and enter substantially into the order and composition of things.[52]

Illusions were the realities by which the ancients lived. The fables or myths of the ancients were the incarnation of those primitive mental dispositions with which nature both gifted and deceived the earliest men for their own good. "There must in the nature of human things," Vico says, "be a mental language common to all nations, which uniformly grasps the substance of things feasible in human social life, and expresses it with as many diverse modifications as these same things may have diverse aspects."[53]

The history of language is the history of human thought, and of its moral as well as its emotional laws. The course of that history in every people is a continual progress from nature to reason, which, as Leopardi affirmed, are joined as contraries. But in the Greeks, more than in any other people, the cultural movement between these contraries can be traced. It is the movement from the "naturalezza" of Homer or the early lyric poets to the rationalism, melancholy, and artifice of Alexandrian times. But at the height of Greek culture, in what Leopardi called the Greek "civiltà media," the contraries of reason and nature are momentarily harmonized. In Plato, whose works are the meeting point of nature and reason and examples of the most elegant Greek prose (*Zibaldone*, 2150), we can in fact discern, as Leopardi must have done, the process of transition.

* * * * *

III

The prose elegance of the "civiltà media" may be sublime and even beautiful; a philosopher, indeed, needs imagination to be great. But the development of philosophy, the increased knowledge, the added experience of men and of things all lead away from poetry and ultimately away from nature. They lead, in fact, to the "sentimental" (Leopardi's use of this term is about the same as Schiller's). The reflex reasonings of the heart are a condition of modern thought and consequently of modern poetry, and it is this self-consciousness that we hear throughout the five last heroic *canzoni*.

As long as Leopardi remained reluctant to blame nature either for reason or for the ills which it discovers or creates, he had the usual monistic difficulty with the problem of evil. That difficulty (How does evil arise from a good source?)[54] is not solved in the heroic *canzoni*. The special merit of these five poems is that they treat the change from illusion to enlightenment not merely as a fact to be lamented, though it is always that, but rather as a fact to be experienced. All of these poems display the "aging of our spirit" (*Zibaldone,* 17). The sort of change he means seems to have happened whenever things grew bad for man. It is Vico's change from poetic to philosophic mentality. It is Peacock's or Shelley's or Rousseau's. It is basically the change which Wordsworth described eloquently as the loss of the "splendor in the grass" and the acquisition, as a consolation for the advancement into the shades of the prison house, of the "philosophic mind." However we describe it, whether on the plane of the individual life or on the stage of history, it is a moment of awakening—or at least this is how the poets who believe in such a change tend to treat it. For what they all have in mind is an alteration in basic consciousness, a radical change in point of view.

Leopardi had undergone such a change himself, in 1819, when poor health, strained eyes, and mental fatigue cut him off from study and left him without work or diversion. He filled long hours of tedium by speculating on a world scheme that could deface an ardent spirit with a hunchback's constitution and reward talent and work with disappointment.[55] Thus, in his own terms, he passed from poet to philosopher (*Zibaldone,* 144). He became separated from the ancients, he says, and became more like the moderns. He descended into despair and concluded that death was the only cure for life (a mood which coincides with Bruto's and Saffo's). And then he went still lower, to "noncuranza" or absolute indifference.[56] At least as poet, however, Leopardi was capable of being like Bruto and Saffo, who come to us still partially clad in the freshness of ancient illusion. The despair of Bruto and Saffo was an ancient unhappiness:

> That was a sorrow without the remedy which our grief has. Misfortunes did not come upon the ancients as though they belonged to our nature by necessity, as though they were a mere nothing in this wretched life. They came rather as impediments and obstacles to that happiness which to the ancients did not seem a dream, as it does to us. . . . The ancients seemed hated by the gods when they were in trouble. Therefore, their sorrow was desperate as it is wont to be in nature and as it is now in barbarians and in country folk, without the comfort of sensibility, without the sweet resignation to misfortunes, which are known by us, but not by them, to be inevitable. [*Zibaldone*, 76-77]

If we must think of his development as a steady progression (which is especially rare in a mind that cannot conclude),[57] then the five last heroic poems return in memory to an earlier phase than the *noncuranza* of 1821.

The emotion, perhaps the whole argument, of *Alla primavera*, had been anticipated by an experience reported to Pietro Giordani in March, 1820:

> A few evenings ago before I went to bed, my bedroom window was open, and I saw the clear sky and the beautiful moonlight, felt the mild air, and heard some dogs barking far off; and there were awakened in me some ancient images. I seemed to feel a stirring in my heart, so that I began to cry out like a man who has lost his senses, appealing for mercy from nature whose voice I seemed to be hearing after so long a time.[58]

The close of *Alla primavera* expresses this appeal to nature in a delicately structured plea:

> Tu le cure infelici e i fati indegni
> Tu de' mortali ascolta,
> Vaga natura, e la favilla antica

Rendi allo spirto mio; se tu pur vivi,
E se de' nostri affanni
Cosa veruna in ciel, se nell'aprica
Terra s'alberga o nell'equoreo seno,
Pietosa no, ma spettatrice almeno.

This is an almost, but not quite, ironical prayer. It reflects the design of the poem that creates or imitates a complex (we might well call it sentimental) consciousness. In *Alla primavera* reason does not suspend its operations, but imagination or memory overcome the effects of reason, almost as Shelley's elegiac flowers hide the "bulk of death." Ancient images, or remembered fables, seem to endow the world again with physiognomy,[59] with divine countenance. They create a domain of externalized human feeling, enlarged and responsive to the mind of man. The fables are concrete examples of *credenze*. These are hypotheses of the ancient imagination which made life worth choosing, at least as a rule. On the other hand, Leopardi could note that the consequence of reasonableness in the extreme is suicide; madness, or the extreme of imagination, is necessary for life (*Zibaldone*, 183). *Alla primavera*, though, does not tumble into the realm of the fables by negating them. Fantasies about nature ("inquiete larve"), piety, and virtue both public and private are all woven together in the illusory veil of the ancient world. The closing sentence of *Alla primavera* sums up these ingredients and shows the change:

Ahi ahi, poscia che vote
Son le stanze d'Olimpo, e cieco il tuono
Per l'atre nubi e le montagne errando,
Gl'iniqui petti e gl'innocenti a paro
In freddo orror dissolve; e poi ch'estrano
Il suol nativo, e di sua prole ignaro
Le meste anime educa. . . .

The sacredness of the native soil is one sign of animation once projected by the human spirit and now remembered poignantly. The myths of Daphne and of Phyllis, suggesting as they do that a consciousness in the forest once consoled even the outcast, are part of the realization of the lost *credenze*.[60] Bruto's "ululati spechi" untroubled by our misfortune are, as it were, turned inside out in *Alla primavera,* where Echo, "non vano error de' venti," is the bearer of human anxieties and quarrels. Man, of course, is the measure of all things, and in his decline, even the nightingale is "men caro assai." This is a consistent yet surprising touch and one that shows how carefully Leopardi has controlled his use of the ancient myths, even in saying again and again his regret over the loss of the "happy pieties." The image of the "happy pieties" remains, balancing the effects of knowledge. While truth's stern challenge shows how value has drained from the world, we still perceive life for a moment through the old spectacles of myth. *Alla primavera* is Leopardi's *Ode to Psyche.*

It is from the opposite direction that Leopardi's Saffo arrives at the mental state of *Alla primavera.* Saffo appears to be leaving her union with the "larve" or fantasms, and entering an imprecise and still poetic—a sentimental—estrangement from nature. She, too, makes a rhetorical plea which deserves comparison with the closing lines of *Alla primavera.* She says:

> Bello il tuo manto, o divo cielo, e bella
> Sei tu, rorida terra. Ahi di cotesta
> Infinita beltà parte nessuna
> Alla misera Saffo i numi e l'empia
> Sorte non fenno. A' tuoi superbi regni
> Vile, o natura, e grave ospite addetta,
> E dispregiata amante, alle vezzose
> Tuo forme il core e le pupille invano
> Supplichevole intendo. . . .

Here are clear notes of artifice, of oratory.[61] It is more apparent than in Leopardi's similar plea in his own voice. This is not the delicately controlled yet genuine cry of the wintered heart awakening. The rotundity of Saffo's questions is like an ancient mask that amplifies the voice. At most there is only a hint of tender places in the really injured soul, and that hint comes when the projected emotion, not unlike Bruto's wrath, reverberates back on the larger-than-life, but ultimately helpless, woman. Leopardi tells us in his annotations to the *Dieci canzoni,* that *L'ultimo canto di Saffo* "purports to represent the unhappiness of a delicate and tender spirit . . . placed in a body

that is ill-favored, though it is young."[62] It is well known that Leopardi could have seen himself in such a portrait. It is a variation on
the theme, familiar enough to the romantics, that the great spirit is
too fine to fit into the world of consciousness. Leopardi knew no
famous writer who had treated this difficult subject, except Mme de
Staël. But his Saffo bears the marks of the romantic artist-hero. She
is like the hero of *Alastor* (especially in her love of nature, her estrangement from it, and even her futile longing for the ideal beloved); and she is like the Shelleyan Prometheus. Indeed, the prototype of such figures is the Platonic Socrates, whose other-worldly
soul was a prisoner in unhandsome flesh.

Saffo belongs to a state which Leopardi called "mezza natura,"
half nature or medium nature. Apparently regardless of their historical period, people in this condition have strong feelings deep within
them; but finding no natural outlet, these passions become destructive or at least tormenting (*Zibaldone*, 268). Indeed, "mezza natura,"
like "civiltà media," is the condition of all the figures in these last
heroic *canzoni*, including in a sense Leopardi himself. But to show
the genesis of Saffo's feelings in particular, we should quote from a
note in *Zibaldone* (718-19) dated March 5, 1821:

> The man of imagination, feeling, and enthusiasm who is deprived
> of bodily beauty stands toward nature in about the same relation
> as an ardent and sincere lover has to his beloved when his love is
> not returned. He throws himself at the feet of nature; he deeply
> feels all her force, her magic, her charms, her beauty; he loves her
> with every transport. But as if he was not answered, he feels that
> he has no share in this beauty which he loves and wonders at. He
> sees that he is outside the sphere of beauty, like the lover excluded
> from the heart, the caresses, and the company of the beloved....
> He feels as if beauty and nature are not made for him but for
> others.

All this fits Saffo; she is a sentimental philosopher. Saffo half-con-
sciously makes her own feelings the basis of a world view. Her reasonings consist largely of a comparison between herself and the world
around her. She experiments with imaginary scenes in an effort to
find an analogue for the turbulence in her mind:

. .˙. già non arride
Spettacol molle ai disperati affetti.
Noi l'insueto allor gaudio ravviva
Quando per l'etra liquido si volve
E per li campi trepidanti il flutto
Polveroso de' Noti, e quando il carro,
Grave carro di Giove a noi sul capo,
Tonando, il tenebroso aere divide.
Noi per le balze e le profonde valli
Natar giova tra' nembi, e noi la vasta
Fuga de' greggi sbigottiti, o d'alto
Fiume alla dubbia sponda
Il suono e la vittrice ira dell'onda.

We know that Saffo is stepping back into the milieu of the *favole antiche,* or rather, into the psychological milieu of Leopardi's youth.[63] Then, as a consequence of learning that beauty in the world is not for her, she lapses into deliberate pathos:

. . . dove all'ombra
Degl'inchinati salici dispiega
Candido rivo il puro seno, al mio
Lubrico piè le flessuose linfe
Disdegnando sottragge,
E preme in fuga l'odorate spiagge.

The fleeing stream, of course, is an outrageous instance of the pathetic fallacy. But what is interesting about this passage is that the pathetic fallacy is also a moral fallacy—a trace of the very kind of illusion whose loss marked in Leopardi's mind the end of heroism.[64] Saffo obviously feels that her alienation is accompanied by some vague guilt. Her next question furnishes the proof:

Qual fallo mai, qual sì nefando eccesso
Macchiommi anzi il natale, onde sì torvo
Il ciel mi fosse e di fortuna il volto?
In che peccai bambina, allor che ignara
Di misfatto è la vita. . . .

In June, 1822 (*L'ultimo canto di Saffo* had been composed in May), Leopardi observed the force and sublimity of the Greek response to beauty. Beauty was taken for "part and name of virtue," and the term *kala* was assigned to "all things good, honest, virtuous, useful" (*Zibaldone*, 2486). On March 17, 1822, he had quoted Xenophon: "Everything is good and beautiful according to how well it serves its purpose, and everything is bad and ugly according to how poorly it serves its purpose."[65] To the Greeks of the "new" city states, as Werner Jaeger tells us, *kalokagathia* meant the ideal of "civic virtue" that was best exemplified in the person of Achilles (though it may be rather hard for us to see how that solitary hero could be a model of good citizenship). This concept "comprehended both a fine stature . . . and true *areté*."[66] Thus outer beauty was associated with inner worth. The convention had also been invoked by the Greek Sappho:

> He that is fair is fair to outward show;
> He that is good will soon be fair also.[67]

Leopardi, of course, agreed with Theophrastis that beauty is a "silent deceit," for "all that beauty promises and seems to show—virtue, frankness of manner, sensibility, greatness of spirit—all of it is false" (*Zibaldone,* 306). Yet in a mood like his Saffo's Leopardi reflected that a man must have much experience to realize that "a handsome face may cover a wicked soul" (*Zibaldone,* 1594). In brief, then, Leopardi took seriously the *kalokagathia.* How seriously appears in his noting that the confusion of nature and reason, the beautiful and the true, is the fountain of errors (*Zibaldone*, 341). It is certainly a key to Saffo.[68] She feels that the *kalos kagathos* is the law of the universe. As we have already said, she senses a terrible mystery behind the beauty of nature; it becomes concrete in the "cieco dispensator dei casi." Saffo points also toward the mysterious law—"Arcano è tutto, / Fuor che il nostro dolor." Her language about casting off the "unworthy veil" of this life and her hints of the awareness that true worth is within are Platonic, whether or not Leopardi in 1822 knew the judgment myth of the *Gorgias.* Saffo speaks the language of an ancient from the heart of a sentimental philosopher. Her mask is the countenance of just-awakening disillusionment.

Having grasped the frames of Saffo's consciousness, we can also understand the two voices which readers have heard in her utterance.

These voices, one beseeching, the other bitterly wise,[69] make up the polyphony of sentimental thought. Sentimentality, philosophy, irreligion, and moral relativism are all signs of the advancing consciousness. And this penetration of mysteries is the destructive work of the Promethean intellect. In a larger sense the name Promethean fits the significant changes in all these poems. Bruto directly calls the human race "figli di Prometeo" and blames our "tenebroso ingegno" for reverencing laws contrary to nature. The analogous phrase in *Alla primavera* is the "black torch of truth." In *Inno ai patriarchi* it is the "unquiet intellect"; and surely in that poem "l'invitto nostro furor," which "educates" the noble savage to civilized misery, is a Promethean effect, if not another name for the cause. And if in *Inno ai patriarchi* Leopardi somewhat scornfully denies the Greek myth of the golden age, he nevertheless asserts its reality in principle and even uses its language: "aurea corse nostra caduca eta'."

Alla sua donna laces together diverse contexts. The *donna* is associated hypothetically with dreams, with the golden age, with the future life, with youth, with Platonic ideas, and with a better world, neighbor to a happier star than ours.[70] She is symbolically associated with virtue and glory, like the fantasms that haunted Bruto. The *donna* floats like an apparition through this most delicate of the heroic *canti.* Her image is confounded with the laughter of nature or recalled by it. And the plea to her at the end of this hymn shows her to be a remote but perhaps tender goddess, like the nature in *Alla primavera.* The plea is in the same style of restrained beseeching, a tone of imagined naïveté. Instead of the obvious classical language that appears in *Saffo* and especially in other pieces such as *Alla primavera,* one finds that the tone of this poem is less rhetorical, less "eloquent." It is of secondary importance that "or leve intra la gente / Anima voli" puts the *donna* explicitly among Hesiod's golden generation who roam over the countryside, wrapped in mist.[71] This feigned naïveté, of course, runs the risk of collapsing into clumsy periphrasis. Leopardi comes close to that pitfall as he beings his evocation of Hesiod's golden age: "Forse tu l'innocente / Secol beasti che dall'oro ha nome." But for some reason difficult to ascertain, the whole texture of the poem is so perfect that one does not feel the danger that it might fail.

In *Alla sua donna,* as in other *canti,* the contrast of youth and age appears side by side with the larger historical myth of the golden age. This, after all, is one version of the story that progress through time is a falling out of blessedness. In the next chapter, we shall turn this telescope around and look at the smaller end, for the *Idilli* are personal poems, and they treat the elegiac theme, another version of this same story, in the particular experience of that poet himself. *Donna,* being both heroic and idyllic, helps to turn our thoughts in that direction.

VII

Idyll and Elegy:
A Further Transformation

The criticism which accepts an alienation from the classics as a cultural inevitability has blamed the heroic *Canti* for being too classical. Although these poems contain much that would be called *pensers nouveaux,* much psychological insight and a philosophical view which the ancients did not have, they reveal modern man through poetic mannerisms and personae which no longer speak to us directly. Even in the dramatic lyrics, too much premeditation and too much oratory betray the philologue speaking for the poet. Is not Leopardi only half-improving on the neoclassicism of Vincenzo Monti? Leopardi chastised Monti for saying what the ancients had said, by means of a hundred fragments gleaned from their writings. These objections have greater cogency for the Italian reader who regards poetic diction as anathema. They have some truth, however, even for readers of English (though we remember that the allegory of allusion was a technique important to Milton as well as to André Chénier). In truth, the highroad of neoclassicism never carried Leopardi very far from the romantic landscape or from the romantic melancholy. The gesture of self-sacrifice in *All'Italia* was but the patriotic expression of that romantic mood in which, seated by a well, the youthful poet had called on death "di cessar dentro quell' acque / La speme e il dolor mio" (*Le ricordanze*). Leopardi's imagination might have revived the transfiguration of the Greek dead at Thermopylae, while the poet sat on Monte Tabor, in meditation. The real setting for the monologues of Saffo and Bruto was the solitary hill and the large vistas which were familiar to Leopardi from his childhood in Recanati. The heroic *Canti* are Leopardi in disguise.

The *Idilli* to which we turn our attention now are Leopardi revealed, or so it seems. The *Idilli* are "esperimenti, situazioni, affezioni, avventure storiche del mio animo."[1] In the *Idilli,* the analogy between personal life and the history of the race is turned around, so that the modern individual becomes the central secret to be unfolded. Youth rather than antiquity appears now to be the ideal. The landscape near Recanati, the village itself, and the stars which he contemplated in his youth, provide the symbolic vehicles through which the poet discloses the postures and adventures of his own spirit. The *Idilli*, which developed alongside the heroic *canzoni* and extended beyond them to mature in the *grandi idilli* of 1828-29, appear to be the work of Leopardi the romantic. They contain no Greek fables or ancient personages, no remnants of Greek or Roman architecture. No traces of ancient poetry are immediately audible. Their periods follow the rhythms of meditation.[2] We seem to hear the poet in his own words re-creating his profound melancholy and transforming the pain of conscious life into pleasure through the contemplation of nature.

Surely melancholy glimpsing itself in the contemplation of certain natural sensations is romantic, as Leopardi understood this term. Nature is not Cynthea or Philomel or Sicilian herds. Instead, nature is the phenomena actually perceived, as the Italian romantic, Lodovico di Breme, told the poets that it ought to be. It is the moon shining over a wooded grove, or this scene from *La sera del dì di festa:*

Dolce e chiara è la notte e senza vento,
E queta sovra i tetti e in mezzo agli orti
Posa la luna, e di lontan rivela
Serena ogni montagna. . . .

It is the sparrow sending its song over the springtime landscape from a solitary tower, or the peasant's song, heard but not seen, as it fades into the distance, "morire a poco a poco." And both di Breme and Leopardi include in this class of naturally poetic things the bell, heard in one's native place, which, like Dante's "squilla di lontano / Che paia il giorno pianger che si more" (*Purgatorio,* VIII, 5-6), wakes melancholy memories, brings comfort, and foreshadows the final transformation of anxiety into repose:

Viene il vento recando il suon dell'ora
Dalla torre del borgo. Era conforto
Questo suon, mi rimembra, alle mie notti,
Quando fanciullo, nella buia stanza,
Per assidui terrori io vigilava,
Sospirando il mattin. . . .

[Le ricordanze]

Or la squilla dà segno
Della festa che viene;
Ed a quel suon diresti
Che il cor si riconforta.

[Il sabato del villaggio]

As the notes in *Zibaldone* attest, these examples from the *Canti* are all fragments of Leopardi's personal experience which he turned into poetry.[3] Like the daily call of the herb vender, the screech of a cart starting off again on its way or the tinkle of cowbells far off as life takes up its normal course after a storm, these examples are all nature.

The measure of naturalness in this sense was the effect such objects produce in the sentimental heart. It was also termed pathetic. An emotional response was to be the ultimate criterion for judging nature. In his early attack on romanticism as he knew it, this conception of poetic nature was the one point on which Leopardi agreed with di Breme. Indeed, Leopardi's *Idilli* lend a peculiar force to di Breme's insistence that the poet is nature: instead of rehearsing conventions which humanity has outgrown, he ought to be nature's "interpreter," her partner in fresh creation, and her "rival in morals, sensibility, and imagination."[4] Despite the confusion which the term "nature" has always introduced into aesthetic, not to say philosophical, discussions, di Breme is emphasizing the very point which Leopardi was to accept and to develop. On a late page of *Zibaldone*, Leopardi was to write:

> It is a false notion that treats and defines poetry as an imitative art, classing it with painting, etc. The poet imagines, and the imagination sees the world as it is not, constructs a world that is not, fashions, invents, . . . creator, inventor, not imitator—this is the essential character of the poet.[5]

And Leopardi's prime example of the pathetic, "la vista di una campagna, di una torre diroccata" (*Zibaldone*, 15), is not only a seminal image in which the dominant emotion of the *Idilli* sketched itself; this image is, indeed, the similitude with which, in *Il pensiero dominante*, the poet represents his thought of beauty, standing in the midst of his mind "as a tower in a solitary field." The setting of the "poétique des ruines" becomes the symbol for the ideal of subjective beauty, and this ideal, as we shall see, assumes the shapes of romantic melancholy.

But let us continue to examine the images and the language from which the *Idilli* were fashioned. The romantics whom Leopardi read in Italian periodicals between 1816 and 1818 were arguing that liberation from the classics should stimulate the creation of a literature which would be cognizant of the Enlightenment and the modern expansion of knowledge. The subjects available to nineteenth-century poets, Visconti said in one of these articles, were by comparison with the subjects which Virgil and Lucan knew, as the Atlantic Ocean is to Lake Como.[6] As di Breme put it, the characteristic of modern poetry is the infinite:

. . . and if our religious, ethical, and scientific doctrines, our customs, and our new sentiments have so greatly enlarged the domain of invention, let us measure the whole extent of that horizon: let us plunge into that immensity, and with courage let us explore the realms of that infinity which have been granted to us.[7]

The optimism in this statement recalls not only Chénier's wish to make poetry the companion of advancing knowledge but his enthusiastic flights of imagination as well. According to Leopardi's theory of civilization, however, the progress of learning gradually contracts the horizons of feeling and imagination. Knowledge shows the limits of things and robs them of their suggestiveness. Infinity is not to be discovered in the things of phenomenal nature, but rather in the emotion with which primitive man or the child responds to nature. From a few incomplete hints, imagination sketches endless possibilities. As Leopardi said,

. . . a rustic landscape, for example, depicted by the ancient poet in a few strokes and, as I may say, without its horizon, stirred up in the imagination that divine surge of confused yet radiant ideas which are indefinably romantic—the excessively dear and pleasant soaring, that wonder, which was wont to make us ecstatic during our childhood. The moderns, on the other hand, limiting everything and showing all the boundaries, are almost entirely lacking in this infinite emotion; instead they waken only that feeling of finiteness and circumscription which comes from knowledge of the whole object. [*Zibaldone,* 100]

In short, the ancients had greater success in achieving that poetic effect which the moderns claim as the special province of romantic poetry. Leopardi's examples from Homer and Virgil are prophetic of the scenes which we have already noticed in the *Idilli.* Is not the vision of a clear, silent moonlit night sentimental?—he asks the romantics. Then, with careful fidelity to the original, he translates the following simile from the *Iliad*:

Sì come quando graziosi in cielo
Rifulgon gli astri intorno della luna,
E l'aere è senza vento, e si discopre

Ogni cima de' monti ed ogni selva
Ed ogni torre; allor che su nell'alto
Tutto quanto l'immenso etra si schiude,
E vedesi ogni stella, e ne gioisce
Il pastor dentro all'alma.[8]

We could not say that Leopardi has altered a single detail, unless one wished to scruple over a slight change in the order with which the items lighted by the moon are mentioned, or to insist that Homer's towers are really watchtowers and therefore contain some trace of that human presence which the Greeks usually work into their descriptions of nature.[9] He feels those sentimental stirrings which he elsewhere calls melancholy and identifies as the characteristic tone of modern poetry (*Zibaldone*, 3976). This Homeric passage contains many examples of the poetic indefiniteness, of painting things with minimal detail and without their horizon, as Leopardi said, in order that the imagination might venture among half-formed fictions beyond the limits of sense (*Zibaldone*, 100). Any object seen in a diffused light, a balcony of the Palazzo Leopardi as well as Homer's towers and mountaintops and groves, would stir the imagination with hints of the unknown. Too much direct perception cuts short the imaginative adventure. But objects "half-seen" rouse ideas of immensity, infinity, antiquity, eternity, ideas whose mere names filled Leopardi with "poetic" pleasure. "This pleasure is enhanced by the variety, by the uncertainty, by the inability to see the whole, and therefore by the power of the imagination to enlarge upon that which is not seen" (*Zibaldone*, 1744-48). Homer's sky, seen in relation to the earth, a multitude of stars giving the impression of particularity, but suggesting an invisible immensity beyond, must have had this effect, which Leopardi describes in *Le ricordanze,* referring to the "vaghe stelle dell'Orsa":

Quante immagini un tempo, e quante fole
Creommi nel pensier l'aspetto vostro
E delle luci a voi compagne! . . .

It is probable that Leopardi's conception of nature derived from such poetic passages in the works of the ancients. Though he realized that the philosophical and sentimental poet knew more of nature's secret than the ancients, part of the poetic game was the pretense of ignorance for the sake of the imagination. Poetry depends on "lieti inganni," "felici ombre," "forti errori," with which nature tricks and yet comforts the primitive poet and the child.[10]

Sounds, too, may reverberate in the imagination with similar aesthetic results, when the poet introduces them into his argument spontaneously, as if he did not know their power to please by suggesting the infinite. The whir of the wind, "when it shivers confusedly in a forest or among the various objects of a countryside," is analogous to Homer's moonlight: "Any sound whatever (even the homeliest) is pleasing, if it is widely and vastly diffused, . . . especially when one does not see the object whence it comes " (*Zibaldone*, 1928). But this principle applies not only to the sounds of nature but to the human voice or the noises of labor. When they are perceived as if almost lost or losing themselves in the vastness of space, or, being heard at night, are undetermined by precise sensation or circumstantial detail, these impressions become resonant with vague significance:

> D'in su i veroni del paterno ostello
> Porgea gli orecchi al suon della tua voce,
> Ed alla man veloce
> Che percorrea la faticosa tela.
> Mirava il ciel sereno,
> Le vie dorate e gli orti,
> E quinci il mar da lungi, e quindi il monte.
> Lingua mortal non dice
> Quel ch'io sentiva in seno.

> [*A Silvia*]

In these lines from *A Silvia* and a similar passage of *Le ricordanze*, the effects of sound and light when they are half-perceived harmonize and enhance each other, being controlled by a single artistic conception.

Yet in these lines, which seem to be the casual accompaniment of youthful recollections, we catch a glimpse of the meditative process by which Leopardi's reflections on his literary models merge with the experience of his daily life, enabling him to fit that experience into his sentimental perspective. Virgil, like Homer, was one of his teachers in this technique, as he acknowledges in *Zibaldone* (1930),[11] where he cites the same passage which he had used to show the romantics how the ancient poets were sentimental:

> adspirant aurae in noctem, nec candida cursus
> luna negat, splendet tremulo sub lumine pontus.
> proxima Circaeae raduntur litora terrae,
> dives inaccessos ubi Solis filia lucos
> adsiduo resonat cantu,tectisque superbis
> urit odoratam nocturna in lumina cedrum,
> arguto tenues percurrens pectine telas.

[*Aeneid,* VII, 8-14]

In this description we find the literary basis of scenes which recur throughout the *Canti,* climaxed by the opening lines of *Il tramonto della luna:*

> Quale in notte solinga,
> Sovra campagne inargentate ed acque,
> Là 've zefiro aleggia,
> E mille vaghi aspetti
> E ingannevoli obbietti
> Fingon l'ombre lontane
> Infra l'onde tranquille
> E rami e siepi e collinette e ville. . . .

It is in Virgil's verses that the lines to Silvia find their origin. One can hardly tell whether an impression of life in Recanati or the vivid response to Virgil's words more strongly influenced the description of the moonlit garden, the song of the coachman's daughter in the Leopardi household, the sounds of her shuttle and her loom, the nocturnal light. Into such patterns of imagery Leopardi translated both feeling and observation, because as he said, "an image in one poem is often pleasing thanks to the abundant memories of the same or similar images seen in other poems" (*Zibaldone,* 1804-8). The technique of allusion, though concealed, still further enlarges the response to the most familiar things. The lesson which Leopardi learned from Homer and Virgil enabled him to transform commonplace impressions into symbolic vehicles of his dominant concerns. Thus, in *Il sabato del villaggio,* the whistle of a day-laborer returning to his rest, the sound of a carpenter's hammer and saw coming across the darkened and silent village, ring with the pathos of the poet's argument. The picture of the *zapatore,* borrowed as it is from Petrarch, has been simplified, generalized, made slightly vaguer, to get the effects of the half-perceived.[12] At once classical and sentimental, this technique of the half-perceived controls perception in order to create beautiful falsehoods, as Leopardi told the romantics. Thus it serves in the chief work of poetry, which is to give pleasure, to delight with wonder, and to refresh or console the heart by freeing the imagination from the fetters of truth. It is through such activities that poetry imitates or carries out nature's kindly plan to deceive men and keep them from the truth.

Pleasure, the only source of human happiness, is incompatible with clear rationality and perception of the real. These are the domain of consciousness. *Il vero,* the real, the object of memory and sense which are the basic components of consciousness, is matter. But matter has the property of having known and certain limits. A conformity with the limited is the requirement of memory and sense and also of their instrument, language (*Zibaldone,* 1764-65). Consciousness is of things that can be perceived, grasped, defined. Pleasure, on the other hand, is the actual or anticipated satisfaction of desire. But desire is infinite. Desire, therefore, cannot be satisfied in the real world, since satisfaction would require an infinite object. Even if such an object could be had, the perception necessary to enjoy it would fail: the pleasure would escape us; we would not know we were having it, since our cognitive faculty cannot embrace the infinite, but can have only a dim sense of indefiniteness:

> . . . the good, the object of joy, is merely imaginary: and because joy would be such as to overcome the capacity of our spirit, it would require, as in children and primitive men, a strength and freshness of imagination and illusion, which are no longer compatible with the life of today. [*Zibaldone,* 717]

It follows, then, that desire, in the material world, is pain: "the greatest and most lively desire is the greatest and most lively pain, and constant desire, which is never satisfied, is constant pain " (*Zibaldone*, 3445). Here is the fundamental romantic premise, the premise of *Alastor* and *Prometheus Unbound,* drawn as a solemn conclusion from a hundred mazy reasonings, which sound like the debate of hedonism versus *areté* and mind in the Platonic dialogues. (One cannot summarize these arguments without thinking especially of the *Philebus*.) Leopardi is no Shelleyan Platonist. He does not shy away from his conclusion or dress desire in the clothes of mind. Pleasure is the only good; pleasure is impossible in adult life; desire yoked to consciousness is painful in proportion to its intensity and duration. Again and again he repeats these findings. The birth of desire, he says in *Il primo amore* (1817), brings such anguish that tedium is "all contentment" by comparison:

> Ahi come mal mi governasti, amore!
> Perché seco dovea sì dolce affetto
> Recar tanto desio, tanto dolore?

Love, a primary desire, is as always a crucial instance. It is one of the desires which youth promises, but even while it is as yet only anticipated, it causes fears, because complete union with the beloved would be impossible (*Zibaldone,* 3443-46). "Love, alas! within my breast / Hath got an ever-building nest," where the greater passions nourish the lesser, as Leopardi no doubt read in one of the Anacreontea which he might have had in mind while writing *Il passero solitario*.[13] And as with love, so with all delights; in the world as we know it, pleasure is "the child of woe." This is the law of nature, which gradually unfolded itself to Leopardi:

> . . . Uscir di pena
> E diletto fra noi.

> [*La quiete dopo la tempesta*]

We have a special case of this law in the relationship of love and death. The desire for death is the twin of love:

Quando novellamente
Nasce nel cor profondo
Un amoroso affetto,
Languido e stanco insiem con esso in petto
Un desiderio di morir si sente . . . .

[*Amore e morte*]

Hindered from positive satisfaction, desire seeks release from "un-pleasure,"even in extinction. To a race tormented by such incompatible opposites, death was a blessing and a healer of all pain:

. . . beata
Se te d'ogni dolor morte risana.

[*La quiete dopo la tempesta*]

As Leopardi said in *Ad Angelo Mai,* "tutto è vano altro che il duolo." In this philosophy which judges the world in relation to man's emotional economy, pain is the only positive reality.

Questo io conosco e sento,
Che degli eterni giri,
Che dell'esser mio frale,
Qualche bene o contento
Avrà fors'altri; a me la vita è male.

[*Canto notturno di un pastore errante dell'Asia*]

There is a deep consistency between the inner life of the individual and the course of human history, because the theory of the emotions is basic to the understanding of both. It was desire, with its accompanying hopes and fears, that generated the heroic illusions, not only the fables but also the virtues by which the ancients lived. Similarly, it was youthful desire still intact that urged Leopardi to strive after honor, glory, literary success, and love. These were the values that guided him while he was still able to believe that desire could be satisfied in the real world.

But if the extension of desire brings a proportionate increase of pain, leading to a wish for the annihilation of consciousness, the expansion of consciousness has an analogous effect upon desire. "E discoprendo, / Solo il nulla s'accresce." These words from *Ad Angelo Mai* can be applied to the advance of individual experience as well as to the development of science in history.

> Vano è saper quel che natura asconde
> Agl'inesperti della vita, e molto
> All'immatura sapienza il cieco
> Dolor prevale. . . .
>
> *[Il sogno]*

Knowledge, in the double sense of science and experience, constrains us with the limits of truth. By stifling or freezing the imagination, it robs us of the illusions on which desire depends. Just as the exploration of the sea puts an end to those imaginings of an "immensum . . . aequor," which to Virgil were one sign of the golden age,[14] so experience brings the recognition that all the "distant hopes where mortal nature takes support" are empty (*Il tramonto della luna*). Whether it is the "conoscenza" of Dante's Ulysses (*Inferno* XXVI, 90 ff.) or di Breme's expanded learning about nature and the human heart, knowledge causes that *taedium vitae* which Leopardi's philosopher-shepherd describes:

> Ed io pur seggo sovra l'erbe, all'ombra,
> E un fastidio m'ingombra
> La mente, ed uno spron quasi mi punge
> Sì che, sedendo, più che mai son lunge
> Da trovar pace o loco.
> E pur nulla non bramo,
> E non ho fino a qui cagion di pianto.
>
> *[Canto notturno di un pastore]*

This is *la noia,* which swallows youth, hope, positive desire, even pain, and which, in draining the world of value, is a moral and emotional old age:

> Or poserai per sempre,
> Stanco mio cor. . . .
> . . . .

> . . . Non val cosa nessuna
> I moti tuoi, nè di sospiri è degna
> La terra. . . .

[A sè stesso]

This state is at once the bizarre sign of human dignity and a torment of a modern inferno:

> *Noia* is in some ways the most sublime of human sentiments. . . .
> to be unable to find fullness in any earthly thing or, so to speak,
> in the whole earth; to consider the incalculable reaches of space,
> the number and wondrous mass of the worlds, and to find that all
> is little or slight by comparison with the capacity of a man's own
> spirit; to imagine the number of worlds and the universe infinite
> and to feel that our spirit and desire would be greater still than a
> universe formed to such a conception; and always to charge things
> with insufficiency and nothingness, and suffer lack and emptiness
> —all this, and therefore *noia*, seems to me the greatest sign of
> grandeur and nobility that appears in human nature. [*Pensieri
> LXVIII*]

The intuition that the human spirit cannot be measured is present in Greek literature. As Heraclitus said: "You could not in your going find the ends of the soul though you traveled the whole way; so deep is its law [*logos*]."[15] In these words of Heraclitus one can hear the unsolved mystery of the human spirit; there is the un-self-consciousness that Leopardi and Schiller called naturalness. But Leopardi's *noia* conceives an infinity arrived at by self-consciousness. Here the spirit preoccupied with itself has overpowered everything that is outside itself. Even desire, if not altogether absent, is somehow anticipated, somehow foreknown and therefore frustrated. And to a mind in this state, the outer world loses its worth because no value is acknowledged in the inner world. All, or most, of this philosophy is present in the *Idilli*. But the conclusions of the *Idilli* are inferred from precisely fashioned aesthetic settings. Indeed, Leopardi's doctrines become aesthetically plausible, because the poet has control over the sphere of experience by which they are implied. They become profoundly moving even to a reader who does not accept them as philosophical statements. In the midst of consciousness, the *Idilli* recapture the harmony of imagination and desire. They imitate the irony of nature, revealing her secrets through her own illusions and pretenses. Our attempt in the remaining pages of this study will be to point to some sources or at least parallels in early Greek thought through which the *Idilli* may be related to the work of the other poets treated in these chapters.

* * * * *

II

It is well known that the idylls of Moschus, which Leopardi translated, and the idylls of Theocritus, in which he saw a revival of the classical Greek creativity after a decline during the time of the Sophists, furnished the frames for several of the first *Idilli*.[16] The feigned dialogue, not infrequently used by the bucolic writers to portray the overflow of strong passion deluding itself, is the device which Leopardi found to be especially appropriate in the *Idilli*.[17] It is evident in nearly all of them. Sometimes there is only a trace of dialogue, as in *La quiete dopo la tempesta,* where the poet addresses nature and then the human race. Sometimes the device is more fully exploited. Thus Silvia seems to live, though she is only remembered. By this means, addressing Nerina and, as it were, reporting to her his dialogue with himself, Leopardi can make her memory a companion of his life. The pretense of dialogue gives human life to inanimate things, as Leopardi believed that the ancient imagination had done. The things of nature become "physiognomic," as they had been in antiquity.[18] "Mia diletta luna" receives a sort of mythic life, as the poet explains—as if to a being like himself—how pleasure comes from the recollection of past sorrows.[19] The simulated dialogue differs in its effect from the apostrophes in the *Hymn to Intellectual Beauty,* the *Ode to the West Wind,* or for that matter in *Alla primavera* and *Alla sua donna.* These hymns force the image upon the mind by recalling names and powers associated more or less conventionally with the being which is invoked. In the *Idilli,* on the other hand, there is a dramatic naïveté. The hypotheses about the moon in *Canto notturno di un pastore*, for example, appear to be spontaneous extensions of the shepherd's thoughts about his own life and the world around him. The moon seems almost to answer, certainly to qualify his conjectures. The form of direct address, while providing an emotional bridge, objectifies a clearly definable portion of feeling and thought.

The imagination can soar; the "pastore errante" can guess what it would be like to fly among the clouds or wander like thunder from peak to peak. But Leopardi does not distort either symbol or feeling by forcing them together. He does not have to say to the solitary sparrow, "bird thou never wert." Nor does he make reverie a precondition for poetic vision. Consciousness holds on to truth, even to pain, while the symbols with which it has intercourse belong to an ideal plane. The moon and the "passero solitario" are models, which idealize the pattern of the speaker's experience in a clear symbolic form:

> Sorgi la sera, e vai,
> Contemplando i deserti; indi ti posi.
>
> > [*Canto notturno di un pastore*]

> Non compagni, non voli,
> Non ti cal d'allegria, schivi gli spassi;
> Canti, e così trapassi
> Dell'anno e di tua vita il più bel fiore.
>
> > [*Il passero solitario*]

The argument of these poems proceeds by measuring man's life against the ideal models which nature provides. For Leopardi, the contemplation of such natural symbols reinforces the reality of old age, of *noia,* and of death itself, the "abisso orrido, immenso" which is the human analogue for the moon's descent. The symbolism is associative rather than metaphorical. Like Aeschylus' Cassandra, Leopardi cannot forget that his individuality, which separates him from the rest of nature, is both a curse and a dignity:

> Tu, solingo augellin, venuto a sera
> Del viver che daranno a te le stelle,
> Certo del tuo costume

Non ti dorrai ; che di natura è frutto
Ogni vostra vaghezza.
A me, se di vecchiezza
La detestata soglia
Evitar non impetro,
. . . .
Ahi pentirommi, e spesso,
Ma sconsolato, volgerommi indietro.

[*Il passero solitario*]

Poetry must return to the vague beauty of the forms which the primitive mind struck off as it encountered nature with the full strength of its *ragione immaginativa*. The poetic intention is to renew the intuition of boundless possibility. In this effort, Leopardi, like Chénier, shares the situation of the Alexandrian poets. They too had felt alienated from the large poetic energies of their predecessors, which they sought to recapture with study and highly developed and self-conscious technique. They too had cultivated conscious illusion (which in Callimachus at least was qualified by a wry irony), in order to preserve poetry in spite of the metaphysical malaise which accompanied the advance of knowledge.[20] They too had taken refuge in the artificial assumption that man and nature are emotionally akin. But Leopardi strips away the conventions with which the bucolic writers had fostered the pretense that they were suspending disbelief. The literary mores of Arcadia, the symbolic rustic and his unreal milieu, were ornaments, beautiful once, perhaps, because they were appropriate to an age, but worn-out now and enfeebled by the passage of time so as to be faded emblems only, lacking the familiarity and contemporaneousness which the poetic image must have. From the Greek idyll Leopardi retains only the hints of design with which he organizes the elements of his composition. The direct borrowings of language or situation are compressed and distilled until only a vestige of the original remains.

Leopardi is refashioning and simplifying the idyll in order to regain a conception of man and nature which was a central concern both to the Alexandrian writers of the pastoral and to the earliest poets of whom Greek literature has preserved any record. The theme, the "musical and poetic motif" of the *Idilli* as De Sanctis said, "is the fresh and immediate impression which solitary and melancholy souls receive from the contemplation of nature."[21] In a lyric translated by Leopardi and included among the *Canti* as a clue to the ancient authenticity of his views, Simonides (or Semonides of Amorgus) commended this theme as Homer's finest saying:

> Umana cosa picciol tempo dura,
> E certissimo detto
> Disse il veglio di Chio,
> Conforme ebber natura
> Le foglie e l'uman seme.

[*Canti XLI*]

For the early Greeks, this pathos was the response to a reflective consideration of man's condition. Homer had seen the valor and nobility of his heroes against this background of flux. From Homer the early lyric poets learned that pathos arises from the contrast of what is loved or admired for its beauty, its excellence, its vigorous vitality with the consciousness of imminent loss through change or suffering or death. In the Alexandrian idyll, a miniature world of artifice remotely mirrors and at the same time mitigates the facts of human decay. Pathos was the essence of the poetic, as Leopardi told the romantics, and in addition to the images which suggest infinity, he had pointed to the lines of Moschus which view man's death in the context of nature's recurring seasons. But this, as we have already seen, is only a variant of the Homeric formula.

Simonides developed the Homeric theme along lines which Mimnermus had laid down in passages from which we have also quoted before.[22] If the race of men is as the generations of the leaves, youth is the flower of our time. The delight in life which belongs to youth is no more enduring than the brief sunshine that revives the flowers in the spring. Youth is "dell'arida vita unico fiore," the time "che l'acerbo indegno / Mistero delle cose a noi si mostra / Pien di dolcezza," as Leopardi says in *Le ricordanze*. Or in the words of Mimnermus: "For a little time, like flowers, we take delight in youth in the presence of the gods, and we know neither evil nor good." Simonides stresses the emotional side of the analogy, using natural growth as a metaphor. Hope flourishes in the youthful breast, he says, and the young and lighthearted thinks his joys are immortal (frg. 97). Youthful hopes for Leopardi are the "ameni inganni della mia prima età" (*Le ricordanze*), symbolized in the mirages of indistinct sensation. They are the impulses toward love or fame or virtue, which in the nature of things cannot be possessed.

Simonides wishes to call the attention of his audience to the facts of their condition, lest they fail to catch the few brief goods that are allotted them: "Ma stolto è chi non vede / La giovanezza come ha ratte l'ale," as Leopardi somewhat freely translates. But this is precisely the message of *Il sabato del villaggio*: "Godi, fanciullo mio; stato soave, / Stagion lieta è cotesta." But in *Il sabato*, Leopardi leaves to inference what he and the elegiac poets explain elsewhere. Two destinies stand ever by, as Mimnermus said; of these, death is to be preferred to old age, which brings shame in the presence of lovers, disease, a weakening of the eyes, so that there is no pleasure even in the sunlight; cares beset the mind, and the journey to the grave sees one's greatest desire unfulfilled. In the *Idilli* Leopardi's chief preoccupations are the sorrows that come with advancing life:

> . . . muti questi occhi all'altrui core,
> E lor fia vòto il mondo, e il dì futuro
> Del dì presente più noioso e tetro,

he says in *Il passero solitario*. Or again, in *Le ricordanze*:

> . . . o mie speranze antiche,
> . . . .
> . . . quando la terra
> Mi fia straniera valle, e dal mio sguardo
> Fuggirà l'avvenir; di voi per certo
> Risovverrammi; e quell'imago ancora
> Sospirar mi farà, farammi acerbo
> L'esser vissuto indarno, e la dolcezza
> Del dì fatal tempererà d'affanno.

This, then, is the elegiac view, as we may call it, though as Leopardi knew, elegy is only a name for that lyric meter which alternates heroic and iambic verses. This view arises from the Homeric comparison of man and the generations of the leaves, and wishes to emphasize the consequences of that comparison in order to make men conscious of their life, or, as it were, to give life significance by means of pathos.[23] But the best example of how Leopardi synthesizes this ancient lyrical view with the spirit and technique of the Alexandrian idyll is *Il sabato del villaggio.* In this exquisite little poem we see how Leopardi's art seems to become detached, how it mingles the motifs and frames which we have discussed, and naturalizes them in the setting of Italian life in Recanati. The asperities of irony, the bitterness of personal grief, even the crude hedonism of the elegiac view are here softened and almost forgotten. There is a gentleness and a sense of mystery half-unfolded. The opposition of youth and age develops gradually through the juxtaposition of typical figures in familiar scenes. Moschus' Europa may be the young girl coming in from the countryside at the end of the day, carrying her bundle of grasses and holding in her hand a bunch of flowers with which on the day of rest she will adorn her bosom and her hair. She is pictured with a few touches, with *negligenza,* as Leopardi would say. There is no comment, no elaboration. If Leopardi was really thinking of Europa gathering flowers in the springtime meadow or of the lines "Breve diletto! omai non più dai fiori / Trarra piacer, nè la verginea fascia / Intatta serberà"[24] to represent the passage from youth into experience, he does not say so much. He turns from the *donzelletta* to the old woman sitting on the steps to spin and chat with neighbors and recall her own youth—how she decked herself with flowers and danced among her companions. The setting sun and deepening shadows measure the span of life across which her memory reaches and suggest the difference between herself and the girl.

This is not Mimnermus or Moschus. Yet Leopardi's mood has something from both of them besides a deeper, unspoken melancholy of Recanati. The other pictures, too, some of them drawn from sketches in Leopardi's notes on personal observation, belong first to Recanati and the present. They are the sound of the bell from the village tower, the children playing in the little square, the laborer returning home at nightfall, even the noises of the carpenter's shop.

But we are not told the ultimate meaning. Art is not to conceal art, but to hide the very truth which it proposes. From the account of *Il sabato*, Leopardi has constructed a symbolic model which contains the typical patterns of pathos—hopes that are to be disappointed and the loss of youth which is remembered. From this model, as from those half-perceptions which lead the imagination to conceive infinity, the statement of the ultimate pathos, the elegiac law of human life, is to be inferred.

But in "Cantico del gallo silvestre," one of the *Operette morali*, Leopardi had seen the life of an individual man and the universe as a whole imaged in a single day. He had stated the elegiac law or what he called a "poetic" conclusion concerning the nature of existence in general form: "Pare che l'essere delle cose abbia per suo proprio ed unico obbietto il morire." "Every part of the universe tirelessly hastens toward death," he says.

> . . . siccome i mortali, se bene in sul primo tempo di ciascun giorno racquistano alcuna parte di giovanezza, pure invecchiano tutto dì, e finalmente si estinguono; così l'universo, benché nel principio degli anni ringiovanisca, nondimeno continuamente invecchia. Tempo verrà, che esso univerceo, e la natura medesima, sarà spenta. E nel modo che di grandissimi regni ed imperi umani, e loro maravigliosi moti, che furono famosissimi in altre età, non resta oggi segno né fama alcuna: parimente del mondo intero, e delle infinite vicende e calamità delle cose create, non rimarrà pure un vestigio; ma un silenzio nudo, e una quiete altissima, empieranno lo spazio immenso. ["Cantico del gallo silvestre"]

Everything that exists emerges from some material element, earth, water, air, fire, or from the infinite unspecified element; the individual takes shape for a moment; then it drops back into the general reservoir of being, which to the particular thing is the same as nonexistence. In this hypothesis of the pre-Socratic philosophers, the elegiac view receives its philosophical statement. "Coming-to-be and passing-away, which have furnished the lyric poets of the time with a theme for sighing and plaintive melancholy, are here objectively vindicated," as Werner Jaeger said.[25] In this larger view, the elegiac clinging to life gives way to a sense that life is evil. Existence is war or strife, as Heraclitus said. Existence is an imbalance, an injustice or having too much, as Anaximander said, and death is a restitution or compensation for this excess, or in Nietzsche's interpretation, an a-tonement for "apostasy" from the primordial one.[26] *L'infinito* shows how Leopardi synthesized this philosophical version of the elegiac theme with an aesthetic design borrowed from the Alexandrian idyll.

In this early idyll of 1819, the argument is perfectly general, almost abstract. Though his senses are occupied with concrete, definite perception, Leopardi does not allow himself even so much detail as he found in Greek poetry. There is only the sketch of a landscape, the hillside, the shrub, the whir of the wind through the branches. There is only enough reality to anchor the senses, while his mind expatiates in the unrelieved immensity of the sky. He does not look beyond the bush, which cuts off the view of the extreme horizon. He hears no sound but the wind. He only knows that the immensity is there. Through a series of contrasts, the mind is expanded in an extreme but pleasurable tension between sensation and thought. The declared relationship between the poet and the scene is reduced to "sempre caro mi fu." Thought is attenuated and stretched across the immeasurable gulf between perception and the negation of all. The poet, on his hill in Recanati, may be re-creating in his imagination the world vision of the pre-Socratic philosopher and elegiac poet, Xenophanes.[27] Xenophanes had said "the earth had cast deep roots into the bosom of the infinite, and thus sustained itself like a plant or a mountain, of which men occupied the summit."[28] The scene stands for the whole world, conceived in elegiac awareness of human impermanence which the ancient philosopher had generalized as an ontological opposition between individual existing things and the infinite, unspecified element whence all things come and whither they return.

L'infinito is a dialogue carried on within the imagination between these extremes. This is what we might call its aesthetic design or composition, by which the vast philosophical hypothesis of Xenophanes is shaped. This is how the illusion even of infinite non-being becomes almost palpable. This device shows its descent from the bucolic poetry. The "landsman" in the fifth idyll of Moschus, which

Leopardi translated, had found pleasure in comparing his actual situation with its opposite.[29] When the sea is calm, he likes to leave the earth, but when the sea is rough and the winds blow, he runs to the land and likes to fall asleep amid sounds that are not frightening in themselves, though they remind him of the perils he has escaped. One intention in this idyll is to display the pathos in the hardships of the fisherman's life set off against the safety and comfort of the pastoral life. But Leopardi saw in this trivial composition the means for expressing the universal pathos, the human condition and relentless ruin. The wind singing in the pine becomes the voice of history and floods the mind with the memory of life's seasons, both the present and the *annos eternos* and *dies antiquos* of the Psalms.[30] But the mind has already embraced the eternal silence and infinite annihilation which awaits all things. It has made itself the image of Xenophanes' infinite. Through memory, the mind becomes the symbolic vessel or container of existence. But if pleasure comes from a throng of vague memories, it comes also with forgetting and from the total calm of passion (*Zibaldone*, 1777-79). Then Leopardi watches the extinction of his own consciousness,[31] following the course which it has conceived for all things, not into a terrible nothingness, but into a more comforting imaginary analogue. Leopardi's "naufragar . . . dolce in questo mare" is comparable to Rousseau's annihilation of ordinary consciousness amid the flux and reflux of reduced sensation. But *L'infinito* transposes the romantic withdrawal from consciousness into a classical key.

In this first of the *Idilli* to reflect Leopardi's original synthesis of bucolic technique with the theme of the early Greek lyrists, the elegiac law becomes the "symbolic form" for that melancholy which, according to Leopardi, sets the tone of the best modern poetry. We might therefore be inclined to describe Leopardi with Jaeger's words about the early Greek lyric poets. "Personality, for the Greeks," Jaeger said,

> gains its liberty and its consciousness of selfhood not by abandoning itself to subjective thought and feeling, but by making itself an objective thing; and, as it realizes that it is a separate world opposed to the external law, it discovers its own inner laws.[32]

At the same time, however, it must be clear that melancholy is here masking itself in the objectivity of Greek pathos, and that this transformation of the personality into a symbolic vessel containing the whole world, is the act of a consummate egoism. There are two emotional ways to look on truth, Leopardi thought. One of these is *noia*, the unpoetic state, which amounts to indifference or feigned indifference, at least. The other way, which we have already traced in the elegies of Chénier and Shelley's middle lyrics, is the last route to pleasurable illusions still open to the sceptical mind. For Leopardi, *noia*, the death of the spirit, takes the place of that destruction of consciousness or simulation of death through reverie, which was the pre-lyrical state of mind for Shelley and Chénier. *Noia* is the subjective devaluation of all things outside the ego. It brings about the estrangement of the ego from the objective world. After this separation has taken place, the imagination is freed from the limitations of normal consciousness. Then the imagination can re-create the subject's relations with the objective world on congenial terms. But melancholy is the catalytic agent which volatilizes sensation and thought. It adapts perception to symbolize the heart's desire. Melancholy is therefore the subjective complement to the world-pathos of the elegiac Greeks. Pathos is the perception of something valued together with the awareness of its decay or end. Melancholy introduces the self into this sense of perishing. As Leopardi wrote less than a year after the composition of *L'infinito* and while he still believed that nature formed man to enjoy the life of imagination:

> Melancholy, the modern sensibility, etc., are so delicious precisely for this reason, that they immerse the soul in an abyss of unlimited thoughts, whose depth and boundary it cannot see. . . . in that time the soul expatiates in a beautiful infinity. The type of this beauty and these ideas does not exist in reality, but only in the imagination, and illusion alone can represent them to us: reason has no power to do it. But our nature was very fertile in them and intended that they should have been the elements of our life. [*Zibaldone*, 170]

Indeed, this emotion is "angelica beltade." This "angelic semblance," last of the benign illusions, is Leopardi's "intellectual beauty":

Dolcissimo, possente
Dominator di mia profonda mente;
Terribile, ma caro
Dono del ciel; consorte
Ai lúgubri miei giorni,
Pensier che inn'anzi a me si' spesso torni.

[*Il pensiero dominante*]

This is the emotion that rules the human heart:

. . . Solo un affetto
Vive tra noi: quest'uno,
Prepotente signore,
Dieder l'eterne leggi all'uman core.

[*Il pensiero dominante*]

And if in this connection we remember Shelley's sovereign passion, we must also notice Leopardi's argument that the natural root of all man's strivings and indeed of all his unhappiness is the self-love, "amor proprio," with which nature gifts and torments all her creatures. Aesthetically considered, however, this passion is deified and invoked under the names which Shelley had given to it.

Da che ti vidi pria,
Di qual mia seria cura ultimo obbietto
Non fosti tu? quanto del giorno è scorso,
Ch'io di te non pensassi? ai sogni miei
La tua sovrana imago
Quante volte mancò? Bella qual sogno,
Angelica sembianza,
Nella terrena stanza,
Nell'alte vie dell'universo intero,
Che chiedo io mai, che spero
Altro che gli occhi tuoi veder più vago?
Altro più dolce aver che il tuo pensiero?

[*Il pensiero dominante*]

We might think that Leopardi had been reading Shelley's *Hymn to Intellectual Beauty,* though of course Shelley was unknown to him.

But if, for a time in the spring of 1831, Leopardi was willing, like the Torquato Tasso of the *Operette morali,* to withdraw into the paradise of his own dreams, his intention in the *Idilli* and perhaps throughout his major lyrics is not to retreat into a Shelleyan island of the blessed but to suffuse perception and experience with the aesthetic emotion. But experience in itself is not poetic. He realized with increasing force the truth of the elegiac warning that "precious youth is fleeting as a dream" (Mimnermus, frg. 5). When youth is ended, the melancholy poet has recourse to memory. Memory becomes the poetic faculty, as Leopardi wrote in December, 1828:

> Any object whatever, a place, for example, a site, a countryside, no matter how beautiful it may be, is not poetic merely because it is seen, unless it also awakens some recollection. The same landscape and even a site, indeed any object whatever, though it be utterly unpoetic in itself, will be quite poetic when it is remembered. Recollection is a primary and indispensable ingredient in the aesthetic feeling, precisely because the present, whatever it may be, cannot be poetic, and the aesthetic, in one way or another, is found always to consist in the distant, in the indefinite, in the ideal.[33]

Melancholy, then, is the aesthetic emotion. It is, moreover, the modern, psychological equivalent for that response to nature which the early elegists formulated as a universal law. Melancholy is the cosmic pathos transferred to the ego, where suffering detached from its real causes becomes an ideal pleasure.

Poetry requires a transformation of consciousness, or to put in other terms this point which has been at the center of our discussion from the beginning, poetry reshapes the impressions from the domain of adult experience, so that things and the names of things become symbolic of thought and the emotional life. Scientific reason compelled the mind to stoop and conform itself to the contours of things and to submit to the exigencies of seeing things as they are. The poetic mind either conceives or refashions things after its own likeness and in accord with what Wordsworth called the "grand elementary principle of pleasure." Leopardi had told the romantics ten years earlier that he would himself be a "divine poet," if he could recapture the impressions which certain familiar scenes and pictures had made on his imagination in childhood and youth.

The familiar images from childhood are poetic because childhood is the time of imagination. But aesthetic pleasure also comes from the remembrance of these past images which come to us again by association from fresh impressions or from the words of the poets. Poetry, for Leopardi, is recollection, not of emotion, but of the forms in which our emotional life first discovered itself through contact with the world outside: "When we are children, if a view, a sound, a description, a dream pleases or delights us, that pleasure is always vague and indefinite" (*Zibaldone,* 514). The child forms his general ideas from the first individual examples he sees. The ideas which we carry through life are modifications of these first images, so that the character of a man and his way of looking at the world are fixed by the slightest details in his childhood. Even an adult's present sensation "does not derive from things but from the childhood image"; perception itself is "a recollection, a reverberation or reflection of an old image" (*Zibaldone,* 515). Memory, then, is a two-way street, along which we return to the origins of our thought and come back again, carrying the warmth of past pleasure into the present. Thus memory controls both the meaning and the quality or value of immediate perception. "The recollections of images and things, which in childhood were grievous or fearful to us, are pleasant because of their vividness," Leopardi notes, "and for the same reason, the memory of grief is pleasant to us in life, even when the cause of the grief is not passed, even when the memory causes or increases it" (*Zibaldone,* 1987).

In *La sera del dì di festa,* the bucolic dialogue artificially produces the tension between desire and pain which the lyric seeks to resolve and convert to pleasure. The cry of personal despair over the grief that has infected the poet's youth is at first only a subjective recognition that it is better to see the light for a short time and then pass quickly away. But this personal sorrow becomes a melancholy which embraces the whole world and a universal lament through the intervention of poetic memory. The distant song of a workman returning home after the diversions of his holiday catches at the poet's heart. The song recalls the elegiac truth that all of history, the triumphs of ancestral Rome, and every human accident vanish like the holiday in the simplest life. The memory has altered the emotional power of the personal experience by placing it in a general context and by relating it to a law. Indeed, the memory is doing that work which Leopardi was to leave partially to inference in *Il sabato del villaggio*. It is as if "all is contained in each," as Shelley said in *Hellas*. Then the peace and silence of the present scene, even the present life itself, carrying the mind back to the soft calm of the moonlit night, become a symbol of the "infinito silenzio" into which remembered history has subsided. By means of a recollection which includes the processes of inference as well as association of ideas, the picture of the present awakes the echo of that which is not. And the song which began this chain of metamorphic reflections is also symbolic:

> Nella mia prima età, quando s'aspetta
> Bramosamente il dì festivo, or poscia
> Ch'egli era spento, io doloroso, in veglia,
> Premea le piume; ed alla tarda notte
> Un canto che s'udia per li sentieri
> Lontanando morire a poco a poco,
> Già similmente mi stringeva il core.

> [*La sera del dì di festa*]

The song of the *artigian* recalls a prototype or paradigm, formed unreflectively in the poet's youth, but containing, nevertheless, the elegiac principle, of which the present experience is but an image.

But the *logos* is the image, the likeness, or as we might say, the model of an event, and it is also the statement formulating the law. But here in the *Idilli,* the model is tied by memory to a prototype from the heart's first responses to the ways of the world. And this mental type, for Leopardi, is an intuition in which, from the slightest hints, the heart discerns the course of life. But the mental type was a necessary portion of the *logos* in the Greek sense. For Plato, mental type was the *orthos logos,* the correct, inner symbolic formulation by which the soul grasps and preserves its vision of the absolute truth (*Phaedo,* 73a). And the Platonic recollection, which brings this formulation to the mind, is a general explanation of the symbolic process of learning. It may be summed up in the statement that when we perceive one thing, we think of something else, whether by arbitrary association, by analogy, as when the mind fills out a ratio or comparison, or by inference, as when the mind steps to a conclusion from an organized survey of fact or argument. Anamnesis is the general name for the process by which thought relates perception to paradigm, things to the laws of things, words to thoughts, and arguments to their conclusions. For Plato, after all, the world itself was but a symbol, a copy of the truth, and he who knew how to read that symbol and to construct an appropriate model, in diagram or word, would recognize in his own mind the pattern of truth. For Leopardi, the ideal is that which is not perceived but only imagined, that which is not present but only remembered. But it would seem that memory in the broad Platonic sense is the symbolizing process by which the *Idilli* convert pain to pleasure. Instead of being the likeness of eternal forms, the *logos* has become the Lockean image, engraved upon the *tabula rasa* in the earliest years of life (*Zibaldone*, 1676).

This, at any rate, is how we may think of Leopardi's nostalgia in the *Idilli*, coming to them from our study of Shelley and from our reading of the *Zibaldone*. We must emphasize, of course, that Leopardi's recollection developed as much in reaction against Plato's philosophical theory as in sympathy with it. For Leopardi, the opposition between ideal and real has a quite different content from that which we have seen in Shelley. For Leopardi, the poetic use of memory is a means of achieving personal melancholy in the midst of consciousness. What we have called the *logos* also has a different value for Leopardi. As expression derived from ancient thought, it is a kind of film through which life can be experienced. Insofar as Leopardi adopted the ancient elegiac language and thought, he was cloaking himself in a partially alien expression which was comforting in spite of its sorrowful message.

Conclusion

In the foregoing studies we have concentrated for the most part on concrete relationships between certain poems and the literature and thought of classical Greece. Chénier, Shelley, and Leopardi were unknown to one another, and such beliefs, attitudes, and techniques as they display in common were shared without the help of mutual influence. Yet certain important subjects and themes have recurred in our discussions. We have dealt repeatedly with idyllic, elegiac, and heroic poetry, if this last term can be stretched to include Shelley's *Prometheus Unbound* as well as Leopardi's heroic *canzoni*. And we have touched upon our poets' conceptions of reason and imagination in their relation to nature. Above all, we have been concerned to realize that classical Greece was a source of value as well as models and ideas to these poets—that to all three it was an ideal, however variously they saw and interpreted it. Now it is desirable, in a few words, to recall their attitudes and to make some comparisons.

In an age that was often nostalgic, all three of these poets looked back to Greece, highly civilized as it was, with admiration and considerable longing for what they conceived to be its primitive naturalness. This quality meant freedom and nobility of spirit based not on reason primarily but on imagination. It meant a higher life which had been lost and was to be recovered perhaps only in poetry. Even for Shelley, who sometimes thought he could almost perceive the Greek ideal renewing itself in the modern world, the ideal, in fact, remained outside of time, in the past or in some future golden age, never really to be present. And Chénier and Leopardi, assuming diverse Greek voices, entered the Greek world in imagination in order to criticize or to exhort the world around them.

Indeed our poets all saw a fundamental opposition separating the actual present and normal realm of conscious life from the ideal, imaginative life of value. We do not greatly oversimplify if we say that the poetry, mostly lyric poetry, which we have examined, sought either to close or to cross the gap which divides these extremes. Chénier's bucolics, broken off from specimens of antiquity, seem to stand on the ancient side of the historical gulf. They are little pictures from the past, charged with literary memories. But as such, by a vaguely universalizing allegory, they are also tied to the common emotional life of all men. His elegies, though less Greek, often express the modern spirit with the help of ancient language. His famous formula in *L'Invention,* "sur des pensers nouveaux faisons des vers antiques," is one expression of the basic antithesis with which these chapters have been concerned. If this formula did not guide him to success in his attempt to prepare a didactic scientific poem and a great modern epic to rival those of the ancients, the broader synthesis which this formula suggests might describe his accomplishments in his lyric poetry.

An analogous pair of opposites provides an approach to Shelley, though Shelley, the most sentimental of our poets, is also the least nostalgic in his attitude toward Greece. For Shelley the fundamental opposition is that between the world as it is and the world as it ought to be. In some of his lyrics and in *Prometheus Unbound,* a poetic enthusiasm and the characteristically human emotion, love, are fused or identified with the Greek notion of *areté*, that is, with excellence or power, though in Shelley's hands this ideal loses something of its original heroic significance. Shelley's masters include Aeschylus especially, as well as Pindar and Sophocles and the bucolic poets. But it was Plato who lent dignity to his melancholy and his sentiments, confirmed his views of love, consciousness, and the meaning of death, and in general provided the principal Hellenic ingredients in his thought.

It might be argued that in this group of poets Shelley most often borrowed directly from the writers of that period from the birth of Pericles to the death of Aristotle, which he considered the central period in classical Greece. But it must also be said that Shelley is the poet whose works least clearly embody the outstanding values which we find in the writings of this period. Leopardi had the clearest vision of Greek life and the most effective sense of the creative vitality in Greek poetry. This judgment, of course, needs qualification. We must accept the conclusion at which Sebastiano Timpanaro arrived from his study of Leopardi's philological works. Leopardi learned much of Greece through the writers of the Hellenistic period and later.[1] He sometimes reacted against his ancient models, inverted their intention, or used his sense of their imaginative kinship with nature to point out the misfortunes brought on the modern world by reason. And though he could not be called a primitivist in any strict sense, his love of the antique extended farther beyond classical Greece than did the corresponding feeling in either of our other poets.

Yet from his contact with classical Greece he drew a poetic strength which Shelley and Chénier usually lacked. In his heroic lyrics he often produced what Emilio Bigi has aptly called an "aristocratic music."[2] In the *Idilli* he went beyond the Greek models, unobtrusively synthesizing several Greek elements. He applied to his own poetry his theory of the infinite suggestiveness which ancient poets achieved through the control of perception. He expanded the conception of the idyll to include a philosophical view of man's life and destiny. And his elegiac melancholy, which expressed itself partly through the formulas of ancient Greek writers, led not to an escape from the pain of consciousness, but to a transformation of consciousness through the power of half-Platonic, half-Lockean recollection. In the *Idilli* the Greeks are virtually hidden. Yet these more than any other of the poems which we have examined realize the spirit if not the literal intention of Chénier's commandment for the modern disciple of classical antiquity. And in Leopardi's poetry generally, in his control of perception and his rigor of thought and expression, we may find the signs of that intellectual poise and that creative force which we are accustomed to associate with classical Greece.

All this is not to say that Leopardi's view of classical Greece was more accurate than Shelley's or Chénier's. We mean only to suggest that Leopardi's absorption of Greek culture was more poetically successful. And while we grant that the lens of nostalgia through which our poets looked on Greece may have distorted or sometimes blurred their vision, the intellectual background of their poetry has been our chief concern.

Notes

NOTES FOR INTRODUCTION

1. Frank E. Manuel, *The Eighteenth Century Confronts the Gods* (Cambridge, Mass., 1959), pp. 259-62.

2. Paul Dimoff, *La Vie et l'oeuvre d'André Chénier jusqu'à la Révolution française, 1762-1790* (Paris, 1936), I, 77. F. Baldensperger, "Un Témoignage allemand sur la mère d'André Chénier," *Revue de littérature comparée*, XXI, no. 83 (July-September, 1947), 89-92.

3. Gustave Lanson, *Histoire de la littérature française* (Paris, 1912), p. 846.

4. *The Cambridge History of English Literature*, ed. Sir A. W. Ward and A. R. Waller (New York and Cambridge, 1916), XII, 359. Gaudence Megaro, *Vittorio Alfieri: Forerunner of Italian Nationalism* (New York, 1930), p. 86.

5. Sebastiano Timpanaro, *La filologia di Giacomo Leopardi* (Florence, 1955), pp. 14-16, 31.

6. Johann Joachim Winckelmann, *The History of Ancient Art*, trans. G. Henry Lodge (Boston, 1880), p. 315.

7. *Ibid.*, pp. 355-56.

8. Ibid., pp. 320-21.

9. Ibid., p. 320.

10. R. B. Farrell, "Classicism," in *Periods in German Literature,* ed. J. Ritchie (Great Britain, 1967), I, 114, 116.

11. Winckelmann, p. 307.

12. Ibid., pp. 294-97.

13. *Shelley's Prose, or the Trumpet of a Prophecy,* ed. David Lee Clark (Albuquerque, 1954), p. 221.

14. Mircea Eliade, *Cosmos and History: The Myth of the Eternal Return,* trans. Willard R. Trask (New York, 1959), pp. 20-21.

15. "Defence of Poetry," in *Shelley's Prose,* ed. D. L. Clark, p. 283. See note 60, Chapter VI.

16. *Tutte le opere di Giacomo Leopardi,* ed. Francesco Flora, 5 vols. (Milan, 1961).

17. "A Discourse on the Manners of the Ancient Greeks Relative to the Subject of Love," in *Shelley's Prose,* ed. D. L. Clark, p. 218.

18. Nello Carini, *Giacomo Leopardi critico e traduttore di Omero* (Assisi, 1964), p. 43.

19. Friedrich von Schiller, "On Simple and Sentimental Poetry," in *Criticism: The Major Texts,* ed. Walter Jackson Bate (New York, 1952), p. 410.

20. M. H. Abrams, *The Mirror and the Lamp: Romantic Theory and the Cricital Tradition* (New York, 1958), pp. 273-74.

21. Ibid., p. 261.

22. Friedrich August Wolf, *Prolegomena ad Homerum: sive de operum homericorum prisca et genuina forma variisque mutationibus et probabili rationi et emendandi,* ed. Immanuel Bekker (Berlin, 1876), p. 35. Manuel, p. 303.

23. *The Complete Works of Samuel Taylor Coleridge,* ed. W. G. T. Shedd (New York, 1853), VI, 312-13. Cf. M. H. Abrams, p. 257.

24. *The New Science of Giambattista Vico,* trans. from 3rd ed., 1744, by Thomas Goddard Bergin and Max Harold Fisch (Ithaca, 1948), p. 290.

25. Mark Schorer, "The Necessity of Myth," *Daedalus: Journal of the American Academy of Arts and Sciences,* LXXXVIII, no. 2 (Spring 1959), 360: "A myth is a large, controlling image that gives philosophical meaning to the facts of ordinary life; that is, which has organizing value for experience."

26. David Hume, *The Philosophical Works,* ed. Thomas Hill Green and Thomas Hodge Grose (Aalen, 1964), III, 183. Peter Gay, *The Enlightenment: An Interpretation. The Rise of Modern Paganism* (New York, 1966), p. 36.

27. *The New Science of Giambattista Vico,* pp. 64, 108.

NOTES FOR CHAPTER I

1. Emile Zola, letter to Baille, June 15, 1860, *Les Oeuvres complètes: Correspondance, 1858-1871* (Paris, 1928), p. 95.

2. Other authors have argued that in reality the poem was finished some days before Chénier's execution. Cf. André Chénier, *Oeuvres complètes*, ed. Gérard Walter (Paris, 1958), p. 890. Henceforth quotations of Chénier's works will be cited from this edition, referred to as *Oeuvres*.

3. Charles-Augustin Sainte-Beuve, *Oeuvres*, ed. Maxime Leroy (Paris, vol. I in 1956, vol. II in 1951), I, 798.

4. Ibid., I, 801.

5. Ibid., I, 799.

6. René Canat, *L'Hellénisme des romantiques* (Paris, 1951), p. 208.

7. Ibid., p. 209.

8. Quoted by Gérard Walter in Chénier's *Oeuvres*, p. 846.

9. Basil Willey, *The Eighteenth Century Background: Studies in the Idea of Nature in the Thought of the Period* (London, 1941), p. 27.

10. *L'Invention, Oeuvres*, p. 127.

11. For the classical sources of Chénier's poetry I have generally followed the notes of Gérard Walter in *Oeuvres*.

12. *Nine Classic French Plays*, ed. Joseph Secondo and Henri Peyre (Boston, 1936), p. 575.

13. *Oeuvres*, p. 692.

14. Friedrich von Schiller, "On Simple and Sentimental Poetry," in *Criticism: The Major Texts*, ed. Walter Jackson Bate (New York, 1952), p. 411. Cf. *Oeuvres*, pp. 645-46: "Les anciens étaient nus . . . leur âme était nue. . . . Pour nous, c'est tout le contraire. . . . Dès l'enfance, nous emmaillotons notre esprit; nous retenons notre imagination par des lisières; des manchettes et des jarretières gênent les articulations et les mouvements de nos idées (et notre âme est emprisonnée dans des culottes)."

15. Walter Jackson Bate, ed., *Criticism*, p. 360, introduction to Coleridge.

16. *Oeuvres*, p. 684.

17. Ibid., p. 680.

18. Ibid., p. 685.

19. Ibid., p. 685.

20. Ibid., p. 708.

21. Cf. Maurice Badolle, *L'Abbé Jean-Jacques Barthélemy et l'hellénisme en France dans la seconde moitié du XVIII'e siècle* (Paris, 1927), p. 215. This line does not disrupt the underlying alexandrine rhythm, as Chénier's verses sometimes do.

22. Renato Poggioli, "The Oaten Flute," *Harvard Library Bulletin*, XI (Spring 1957), 149.

23. Walter W. Greg, *Pastoral Poetry and Pastoral Drama: A Literary Inquiry, with Special Reference to the Pre-Restoration Stage in England* (New York, 1959), p. 10.

24. *Oeuvres*, p. 867. Cf. Virgil, *Eclogue VI*, 13-14.

25. Zeph Stewart, "Song of Silenus," *Harvard Studies in Classical Philology*, LXIV (1959), 189.

26. Gustave Lanson, *Histoire de la littérature française* (Paris, 1912), p. 852.

27. Gotthold Ephraim Lessing, *Laocoon: An Essay upon the Limits of Painting and Poetry*, trans. Ellen Frothingham (New York, 1961), p. 85.

28. Ibid., p. 90.

29. Ibid., p. 92.

30. Ibid., p. 90. E. M. Butler, in *The Tyranny of Greece over Germany* (Cambridge, England, 1935), p. 59, says of Lessing: "He had seen almost no pictures and virtually no sculpture. . . . It is even doubtful whether his eyes had ever flickered over a plaster-cast reproduction of the Laocoon group when he was writing the book which was to turn it into a household word."

31. Lessing, p. 91.

32. Ibid., p. 92.

33. Ibid., p. 114.

34. Walter Jackson Bate, ed., *Criticism*, p. 243.

35. Johann Joachim Winckelmann, *The History of Ancient Art*, trans. G. Henry Lodge (Boston, 1880), I, 361-62; V, iii, 13-15.

36. Irving Babbitt, *The New Laokoon: An Essay on the Confusion of the Arts* (Boston, 1924), p. 3.

37. Ibid., p. 9 and pp. 14-15.

38. Quoted by Badolle, p. 208.

39. Ellen Frothingham in the translation of the *Laocoon* already cited quotes the following passage (p. 229) from the *avertissement* to *Tableaux tirés de l'Iliade*: "On est toujours convenu, que plus un poëme fournissait d'images et d'actions, plus il avait de supériorité en poésie. Cette réflexion m'avait conduit à penser que le calcul des différens tableaux, qu'offrent les poëmes, pouvait servir à comparer le mérite respectif des poëmes et des poëtes. Le nombre et le genre des tableaux que présentent ces grands ouvrages, auraient été une espèce de pierre de touche, ou, plutot, une balance certaine du mérite de ces poëmes et du génie de leurs auteurs."

40. Badolle, pp. 401-03.

41. Winckelmann, V, iii, 4; I, 356.

42. Louis-Marie-Émile Bertrand, *La Fin du classicisme et le retour à l'antique dans la seconde moitié du XVIII'e siècle et les premières années du XIX'e en France* (Paris, 1897), p. 258, calls Chénier "le plus pur modèle de style Louis XVI que nous avons en littérature." For the plastic character of this style, cf. Lanson, p. 844 and *passim*.

43. Denis Diderot, *Oeuvres esthétiques*, ed. Paul Vernière (Paris, 1959), p. 641.

44. Walter Pater, *The Renaissance: Studies in Art and Poetry* (London, 1919), p. 201.

45. Leonidas of Tarentum, 98, in *Analecta veterum poetarum Graecorum*, ed. Richard Franz Phillip Brunck (Argentorati, 1772-76), I, 246.

46. W. K. C. Guthrie, *The Greeks and Their Gods* (Boston, 1951), p. 260.

47. Translated from Leonidas of Tarentum, loc. cit.

48. "Sepulchral Epigrams" VII, 291, in *The Greek Anthology*, trans. W. R. Paton, Loeb Classical Library (Cambridge, Mass., 1960), II, 158.

49. For a clear example of this composite technique, see *La Lampe, Oeuvres*, pp. 120-22. Cf. Bertrand, pp. 238-40.

50. Cf. Chénier, *La République des lettres*.

51. Sainte-Beuve notes that this passage and the lines immediately following were pieced together from fragments of Mimnermus (Sainte-Beuve, *Oeuvres*, I, 806, note). Cf. Mimnermus, frgs. 1 and 2, in *Elegy and Iambus*, trans. J. M. Edmonds, Loeb Classical Library (Cambridge, Mass., 1969), I.

52. *Oeuvres philosophiques de Condillac*, in *Auteurs modernes, XXXIII*, ed. George Le Roy (Paris, 1947), I, 329-31. Cf. Paul Hazard, *La Pensée européenne au XVIIIème siècle, de Montesquieu à Lesing* (Paris, 1946), II, 26.

53. Compare *Les Amours, Lycoris*, 1, with Propertius, III, 5, 19-26, and see Chénier's note, *Oeuvres*, p. 870. This elegiac theme is contained in several of the *Amours* to Lycoris and to Camille.

54. Henri Potez, *L'Élégie en France avant le romantisme (de Parny à Lamartine) 1778-1820* (Paris, 1898), p. 272.

55. In reading such a passage, one thinks of Shelley rather than the ancients. But compare Ovid, *Amores*, I, 10, 1-8. Perhaps Chénier had some of the classical journeys in mind, such as that at the end of the *Georgics*. Henri Potez says: "Sa Muse a quelquefois un moment de songerie, mais à la manière de La Fontaine" (pp. 272-73).

56. Jean-Jacques Rousseau, "Cinquième Promenade," in *Les Confessions: Les Rêveries du promeneur solitaire*, ed. Pierre Grosclaude (Paris, 1954), p. 419.

57. Yet they resemble the "formosae . . . heroinae" of Propertius (I, 19, 13) whose somber imaginings of love in the world beyond the grave Chénier amplified and adapted in one of his *Amours* (*Lycoris*, 4): "Venez me consoler, aimables héroïnes: / O Léthé! fais-moi voir leurs retraites divines; / Viens me verser la paix et l'oubli de mes maux." Compare *Ébauches d'élégies, VIII:* "Doux et cruels tyrans, brillantes héroïnes, / Femmes, de ma mémoire habitantes divines, / Fantômes enchanteurs, cessez de m'égarer."

58. Poggioli, p. 154.

59. *Oeuvres*, p. 858.

60. See Stewart, "Song of Silenus."

NOTES FOR CHAPTER II

1. André Chénier, *Oeuvres complètes,* ed. Gérard Walter (Paris, 1958), p. 404.

2. C. Kramer, "Les Poèmes épiques d'André Chénier, III, *Hermès,*" *Neophilologus,* VI, no. 1 (1920), 14. Kramer says that astronomy "intéressait André Chénier . . . autant que les poètes érudits d'Alexandrie, Callimaque, Aratus et Eratosthène, à qui il avait emprunté le titre de son poème."

3. *Oeuvres,* p. 414.

4. Ibid., p. 391.

5. Ibid., p. 127.

6. Zeph Stewart, "Song of Silenus," *Harvard Studies in Classical Philology,* LXIV (1959), 198.

7. *L'Invention, Oeuvres,* p. 125.

8. Ibid., p. 126.

9. Ibid., p. 127.

10. Louis-Marie-Émile Bertrand, *La Fin du classicisme et le retour à l'antique dans la seconde moitié du XVIIIe siècle et les premières années du XIXe en France* (Paris, 1897), p. 238.

11. *Oeuvres,* p. 125.

12. Quoted by Basil Willey, *The Eighteenth Century Background: Studies on the Idea of Nature in the Thought of the Period* (London, 1941), p. 156.

13. *Oeuvres,* p. 435.

14. Ibid., p. 441. C. Kramer, "Les Poèmes épiques d'André Chénier. IV. *L'Amérique,*" *Neophilologus,* VI, no. 3 (1921), 155: "Il metra dans la bouche de quelques personnages du poème des allusions un peu détaillées de quelques révolutions intéressantes, mais pas assez importantes pour leur donner un article à part. Là encore il se réclame de l'exemple d'Homère dont les personnages entremêlent dans leurs discours des récits de choses qui leur sont arrivées dans leur jeune âge."

15. *Oeuvres,* p. 431.

16. Cedric Whitman, *Homer and the Heroic Tradition* (Cambridge, Mass., 1958), pp. 126-27.

17. Ibid., p. 17.

18. Lónginus, *On the Sublime,* in *Criticism: The Major Texts,* ed. Walter Jackson Bate (New York, 1952), p. 66.

19. Cf. Bertrand, p. 258 ff.

20. Edward Young, "Conjectures on Original Composition," in *Criticism,* ed. Bate, p. 242. Jean Fabre, *André Chénier: L'Homme et l'oeuvre* (Paris, 1955), pp. 131-32, argues that Chénier's wish to avoid slavish imitation of the ancients was based partly on the injunction to imitate Homer the man rather than the *Iliad,* a precept which Chénier learned from Pope and Edward Young. Fabre also cites

Voltaire: ". . . il faut peindre avec des couleurs vraies comme les anciens, mais il ne faut pas peindre les mêmes choses."

21. *L'Invention, Oeuvres,* p. 124.

22. Ibid., p. 127.

23. Ibid., p. 128.

24. *Oeuvres,* p. 438.

25. Ibid.

26. The following passage is from the early epistle to the Marquis de Brazais (*Oeuvres,* p. 133):

> Déjà dans les hameaux, silencieux rêveur,
> Une source inquiète, un ombrage, une fleur,
> Des filets d'Arachné l'ingénieuse trame,
> De doux ravissements venaient saisir mon âme.
> Des voyageurs lointains auditeur empressé,
> Sur nos tableaux savants où le monde est tracé,
> Je courais avec eux du couchant à l'aurore.
> Fertile en songes vains que je chéris encore,
> J'allais partout, partout bientôt accoutumé,
> Aimant tous les humains, de tout le monde aimé.

27. Fabre, p. 131.

28. *L'Invention, Oeuvres,* p. 128.

29. Ibid., p. 131.

30. Longinus, p. 68.

31. *L'Invention, Oeuvres,* p. 127.

32. Ibid.

33. Ibid.

34. *Oeuvres,* pp. 427-28. Compare, for example: "Through this opaque of nature and of soul, / This double night, transmit one pitying ray, / To lighten, and to cheer. O lead my mind" "Night the First," 43-45, *Young's Night Thoughts,* ed. Rev. George Gilfillan (Edinburgh, 1853). *Night Thoughts,* as well as Thomson's *The Seasons,* were translated into French in 1769. Cf. René Jasinski, *Histoire de la littérature française* (Paris, 1947), II, 23.

35. "Defence of Poetry," in *Shelley's Prose,* ed. David Lee Clark (Albuquerque, 1954), p. 279.

36. Cf. Fabre, pp. 122-23.

37. For a discussion of Chénier's political views, see Fabre, pp. 80-88.

38. Ibid., p. 80.

39. Though the alternating long and short verses of the *Iambes* may have been intended as a formal link with the iambic and elegiac meters of the Greeks, we may compare the following passage from Gilbert's *Ode imitée de plusieurs psaumes* (1780), quoted by Henri Potez, *L'Elégie en France avant le romantisme (de Parny à Lamar-*

tine)1778-1820 (Paris, 1898), p. 71:

> Au banquet de la vie, infortuné qu'on vive,
> J'apparus un jour, et je meurs.
> Salut, champs que j'aimais, et vous, douce verdure,
> Et vous, riant exil des bois,
> Ciel, pavillon de l'homme, admirable nature,
> Salut pour la dernière fois!

The substance of these verses might be compared with *La Jeune Captive*.

40. Werner Jaeger, *Paideia: The Ideals of Greek Culture*, trans. Gilbert Highet (New York, 1960), I, 118.

41. Ibid., I, 88.

NOTES FOR CHAPTER III

1. "Proposals for an Association of Philanthropists," *Shelley's Prose, or the Trumpet of a Prophecy,* ed. David Lee Clark (Albuquerque, 1954), pp. 61, 66, 60; "An Address to the Irish People," p. 45. Hereafter this work will be referred to as *Prose*. All quotations from Shelley's prose will be taken from this work, unless otherwise specified.

Quotations from Shelley's poetry will be taken from *The Complete Poetical Works of Percy Bysshe Shelley,* ed. Thomas Hutchinson (Oxford, 1923). Hereafter this work will be referred to as *Poetical Works*.

2. James A. Notopoulos, in *The Platonism of Shelley: A Study of Platonism and the Poetic Mind* (Durham, N. C., 1949), p. 177, says that the *Timaeus* is the ultimate source for the idea of a world soul.

3. Letter to Elizabeth Hitchener, October 12, 1811, *The Letters of Percy Bysshe Shelley*, ed. Roger Ingpen (London, 1912), I, p. 145. Hereafter this work will be referred to as *Letters*. All quotations from Shelley's letters will be taken from this work, unless otherwise specified.

4. *Poetical Works*, p. 201.

5. Cf. *Prose*, pp. 103-8, Clark's notes.

6. William Godwin, in his *Enquiry Concerning Political Justice and Its Influence on Morals and Happiness,* ed. F. E. L. Priestley (Toronto, 1946), I, 363, sees necessity, which he equates with determinacy and predictability, operating in the moral as well as the physical world. Whereas freedom would be man's "bane and his curse" (I, 382-83), necessity should produce intellectual tranquility and release from anxiety (I, 395-96).

7. Joseph Barrell, *Shelley and the Thought of His Time* (New

Haven, 1947), p. 71. This discussion of *Queen Mab* is largely indebted to Barrell.

8. For Platonic elements in Locke, see Paul Shorey, *Platonism Ancient and Modern* (Berkeley, 1938), p. 206. In language that has a Platonic tone, though the premises of the argument are materialistic, Godwin, I, 382, says: "Man being, as we have found him to be, a creature, whose actions flow from the simplest principle, and who is governed by the apprehensions of his understanding, nothing further is requisite but the improvement of his reasoning faculty, to make him virtuous and happy."

9. Notopoulos, p. 35.

10. Ibid., p. 137.

11. Barrell, p. 72.

12. *Queen Mab*, VIII, 53-54, 88-100, 234-38. Cf. Barrell, p. 75.

13. Letter to Hogg, March 16, 1814, *Letters*, I, 417.

14. Ibid., p. 419.

15. *The Dialogues of Plato*, trans. B. Jowett (New York, 1937), I, 236. Unless otherwise specified, translations from Plato are Jowett's.

16. Harold Lloyd Hoffman, *An Odyssey of the Soul: Shelley's Alastor* (New York, 1933), pp. 63 ff.

17. "A Discourse on the Manners of the Ancient Greeks Relative to the Subject of Love," *Prose*, p. 220.

18. "Essay on Love," *Prose*, p. 170.

19. Anthony Ashley Cooper, Earl of Shaftsbury, "A Letter Concerning Enthusiasm," *Characteristics of Men, Manners, Opinions, Times, etc.* (London, 1900), p. 35: "The lymphatici of the Latins were the *nympholepti* of the Greeks. They were persons said to have seen some species of divinity, as either some rural deity, or nymph, which threw them into such transports as overcame their reason."

20. *Prose*, p. 170.

21. Carlos Baker, *Shelley's Major Poetry: The Fabric of a Vision* (Princeton, 1948), p. 54.

22. This is a point which Neville Rogers frequently makes in *Shelley at Work: A Critical Inquiry* (Oxford, 1956).

23. "On the Manners of the Ancient Greeks," *Prose*, p. 221.

24. Ibid., p. 222.

25. Hoffman, p. 44.

26. Irving Babbitt, *The New Laokoon: An Essay on the Confusion of the Arts* (Boston, 1910), pp. 90-91. Notopoulos, p. 27.

27. *Symposium*, 206, Shelley's translation in Notopoulos, p. 445.

28. Ibid., 206c, in Notopoulos, p. 445.

29. Ibid., 218, in Notopoulos, p. 455.

30. Quoted by George Thomson, *Aeschylus and Athens* (London, 1941), pp. 319-20. Cf. *An Essay on the Beautiful from the Greek of Plotinus*, trans. Thomas Taylor (London, 1917), p. 10.

31. Cedric Whitman, *Sophocles* (Cambridge, Mass., 1951), chap. VII.

32. Preface to *Prometheus Unbound, Poetical Works,* p. 201.

33. The edition of Aeschylus used throughout these chapters is *Aeschylus,* ed. Gilbert Murray (Oxford, 1957).

34. For a detailed account of a similar pattern in the corresponding movements of the *Prometheus Bound,* see Thomson, pp. 323-46.

35. N. Rogers, p. 150.

36. Cited by Carl Kerenyi, *Prometheus: Archetypal Image of Human Existence,* trans. Ralph Manheim, Bollingen Series, LXV (New York, 1963), pp. 22, 42.

37. *Prometheus Unbound,* II, iv, 63-65; I, 772; I, 780. *Symposium,* 195d. Notopoulos, p. 244.

38. Plato in the *Sophist* (247) defines being as nothing else but power. The notion that the world of common experience is one of separations is in complete agreement with Plato's statements about the unintelligibility of the "many" of perception and opinion.

39. *Prometheus Unbound,* I, 200-10. Compare Thomas Taylor's note on Lethe (*Republic,* 621) in his translation, *The Works of Plato* (London, 1804), I, pp. 477-78: "By Lethe we must understand the whole of a visible nature, or, in other words, the realms of generation, which contain, according to Empedocles, oblivion and the shadow of Ate; and, according to the Chaldaean Oracles, the light-hating world, and the winding streams, under which many are drawn." The "souls descending into the plain of Lethe" are "alone conversant with things analogous to the delusions of dreams."

40. Baker, p. 96.

41. See note 26 above.

NOTES FOR CHAPTER IV

1. Neville Rogers, *Shelley at Work: A Critical Inquiry* (Oxford, 1956), p. 21.

2. Ibid., p. 52. Cf. Shelley's translation of *Symposium,* 196b, in James A. Notopoulos, *The Platonism of Shelley: A Study of Platonism and the Poetic Mind* (Durham, N. C., 1949), p. 435.

3. "A Discourse on the Manners of the Ancient Greeks Relative to the Subject of Love," *Shelley's Prose, or the Trumpet of a Prophecy,* ed. David Lee Clark (Albuquerque, 1954), p. 217. Hereafter this work will be referred to as *Prose.* All quotations from Shelley's prose will be taken from this work, unless otherwise specified.

4. "Defence of Poetry," *Prose,* p. 279.

5. Ibid., pp. 283-84; "On the Manners of the Ancient Greeks," *Prose,* p. 219. See also Preface to *Prometheus Unbound, The Complete Poetical Works of Percy Bysshe Shelley,* ed. Thomas Hutchin-

son (Oxford, 1923), p. 202. All quotations from Shelley's poetry will be taken from this work, unless otherwise specified.

6. "On the Manners of the Ancient Greeks," *Prose,* p. 217.

7. Preface to *The Revolt of Islam, Poetical Works,* p.34.

8. Olwen Ward Campbell, *Shelley and the Unromantics* (London, 1924), p. 78. Cf. Notopoulos, p. 55.

9. Douglas Bush, *Mythology and the Romantic Tradition in English Poetry* (New York, 1957), p. 132.

10. Letter to Elizabeth Hitchener, October 12, 1811, *The Letters of Percy Bysshe Shelley,* ed. Roger Ingpen (London, 1912), p. 145. Hereafter this work will be referred to as *Letters.* All quotations from Shelley's letters will be taken from this work, unless otherwise specified.

11. N. Rogers, p. 24, cites Coleridge, *Biographia Literaria,* ed. J. Shawcross (Oxford, 1907), II, 258. Letter to Godwin, December 11, 1817, *Letters,* p. 574.

12. Cf. Notopoulos, pp. 206-07.

13. *The Timaeus and Critias, the Thomas Taylor Translation,* foreword by R. C. Taliaferro (New York, 1944), pp. 157-58.

14. Ibid., p. 65.

15. N. Rogers, p. 15, *Oedipus Tyrannus,* 67. The translation of Sophocles' line is Rogers' correction of Shelley's version.

16. *Prose,* p. 174.

17. Letter to Thomas Love Peacock, July 12, 1816, *Letters,* p. 497.

18. Bush, p. 148.

19. Plato's statesman stands for the "form" of being, as the sophist represents the "form" of non-being.

20. *Prometheus Unbound,* II, i, 53, 31, 70. Cf. also *The Revolt of Islam,* II, 875, where Cythna is called Laon's "second self."

21. N. Rogers, pp. 162-63.

22. "Defence of Poetry," *Prose,* p. 282.

23. Edgar Wind, *Pagan Mysteries in the Renaissance* (New Haven, 1958), p. 114. Pindar, *Pythian X,* 28 ff.; cf. N. Rogers, p. 100. *Odyssey,* VIII, 557-63.

24. *The Revolt of Islam,* IX, 3699; *Epipsychidion,* 455-56

25. David Perkins, *The Quest for Permanence: The Symbolism of Wordsworth, Shelley and Keats* (Cambridge, Mass., 1959), p. 156.

26. Gilbert Norwood, *Pindar* (Berkeley, 1945), p. 23: "Here [in a fragment of *Paean VI*] are lines which, beyond all others of Pindar, seem to prophesy of Shelley."

27. *Olympian VI,* 53-57. For further evidence that Agathon was speaking like the poets, compare his speech with Sophocles, *Antigone,* 781 ff., where love is said to prevail through all the living beings, to be inescapable even by the immortals, and to be enthroned beside the great laws. Cf. also Euripides, *Hippolytus,* 525 ff. There is every

reason to suppose that Shelley was familiar with these passages. There is strong likelihood that the speech of the Earth (*Prometheus Unbound*, III, iii, 114 ff.) which expands the picture of the "bowers" of Asia's lyric was composed with the help of the Pindaric passages we have already quoted (frgs. 129-30 and *Olympian VI*, 53-57).

28. *Symposium*, 197; *Prometheus Unbound*, II, v, 72-110. Cf. N. Rogers, pp. 135-36.

29. Shelley's translation, Notopoulos, p. 436.

30. *Symposium*, 209; "Defence of Poetry," *Prose*, p. 279.

31. "Essay on Christianity," *Prose*, p. 202.

32. M. H. Abrams, *The Mirror and the Lamp: Romantic Theory and the Critical Tradition* (New York, 1958), p. 51.

33. *Cratylus*, 400c; *Phaedrus*, 250c; *Gorgias*, 493c; B. Jowett trans., *The Dialogues of Plato* (New York, 1937), I, 190, 254, 552.

34. Norwood, pp. 102 ff.

35. *Phaedo*, 110 b.

36. N. Rogers, pp. 18-19, cites Euripides, *Hercules Furens*, 342; see also p. 227.

37. *Pythian VIII*, 96-97; Cedric Whitman's translation in *Sophocles: A Study of Heroic Humanism* (Cambridge, Mass., 1951), p. 72. For Shelley's quotation of this passage, see N. Rogers, p. 260.

NOTES FOR CHAPTER V

1. J. A. K. Thomson, *The Art of the Logos* (London, 1935), has suggested the title of this chapter. I have decided to use the term *logos* as a convenient verbal container for much of Shelley's poetic theory and some of his practice. Each sense of the term referred to in this chapter has an established Greek meaning and an analogous application in the discussion of Shelley. The danger which lurks in the use of such a term is that readers may suppose Shelley was consciously guided by it. Of course, I do not wish to make this claim. Nor do I want the term *logos* to assume here the altogether mystical meanings which it derived from the Hermetic writings and the Gospel of St. John. The following quotation from *The New Science of Giambattista Vico*, translated from the third edition, 1774, by T. G. Bergin and M. H. Fisch (Ithaca, 1948), p. 114, helps to explain the basic meaning of the term and gives indirect support for my use of it: "The word logic comes from *logos*, whose first and proper meaning was *fabula*, 'fable,' carried over into Italian as *favella*, 'speech.' In Greek the fable was also called *mythos*, 'myth,' whence comes the Latin *mutus*, 'mute.' For speech was born in mute times as mental [or sign] language, which Strabo in a golden passage says existed before vocal or articulate [language]; whence *logos* means both 'word' and 'idea'." The resemblances between Vico's theory and Shelley's deserve to be explored. In another passage Vico says: "There must in

the nature of human things be a mental language common to all nations, which uniformly grasps the substance of things feasible in human social life, and expresses it with as many diverse modifications as these same things may have diverse aspects" (p. 60).

2. *Sophist,* 266c; *Republic,* X, 602, 605.

3. Thomson, Chapters I and II.

4. For example, *Phaedo,* 70c, 76d-e, 99d-100a. Simonides, frg. 65, *Lyra Graeca,* ed. J. M. Edmonds, Loeb Classical Library (Cambridge, Mass., 1958), II, 321.

5. For a full discussion of the *logos* and its meanings see W. K. C. Guthrie, *A History of Greek Philosophy* (Cambridge, 1962), pp. 38, 205, and especially pp. 419 ff.

6. "Defence of Poetry," *Shelley's Prose, or the Trumpet of a Prophecy,* ed. David Lee Clark (Albuquerque, 1954), pp. 279, 281. Hereafter this work will be referred to as *Prose.* All quotations from Shelley's prose will be taken from this work, unless otherwise specified. Vico, p. 142.

7. "The Four Ages of Poetry," *The Works of Thomas Love Peacock,* ed. H. F. B. Brett-Smith and C. E. Jones (London, 1934), VIII, 4, 11. To indicate the kind of attitude against which Shelley was reacting, we might quote the following passage from "The Four Ages of Poetry": ". . . thus they are not only historians but theologians, moralists, and legislators: delivering their oracles *ex cathedra,* and being indeed often themselves (as Orpheus and Amphion) regarded as portions and emanations of divinity: building cities with a song, and leading brutes with a symphony; which are only metaphors for the faculty of leading multitudes by the nose" (VIII, 6). For a discussion of Peacock's essay in comparison with Shelley's "Defence" see M. H. Abrams, *The Mirror and the Lamp* (New York, 1958), pp. 126-27.

8. *Lyra Graeca,* II. 258.

9. Sir Philip Sidney, "The Defence of Poesy" in *Poetry of the English Renaissance,* ed. J. W. Hebel and Hoyt H. Hudson (New York, 1929), p. 885.

10. Preface to *Prometheus Unbound, The Complete Poetical Works of Percy Bysshe Shelley,* ed. Thomas Hutchinson (Oxford, 1923), p. 202. Hereafter this work will be referred to as *Poetical Works.* All quotations from Shelley's poetry will be taken from this work, unless otherwise specified. *Prose,* p. 281.

11. "Defence of Poetry," *Prose,* p. 278.

12. Ibid., p. 281.

13. James A. Notopoulos, *The Platonism of Shelley: A Study of Platonism and the Poetic Mind* (Durham, N. C., 1949), pp. 472-73.

14. A. E. Taylor, *Plato* (New York, n.d.), pp. 90, 94.

15. Carl Grabo, *Prometheus Unbound: An Interpretation* (Chapel Hill, 1935), p. 46.

16. "Defence of Poetry," *Prose,* p. 281.

17. Ibid., p. 283.

18. Ibid.

19. Abrams, p. 42.

20. *Ennead V*, viii, 1, in Plotinus, *The Six Enneads*, trans. Stephen MacKenna and B. S. Page (Chicago, 1952), p. 239.

21. Notopoulos, p. 25: ". . . there is no evidence that he read any of the Neoplatonists."

22. For example, compare *Prometheus Unbound*, III, iii, 168-74, with the note on *Republic*, 328, in *The Works of Plato*, trans. Thomas Taylor (London, 1804), I, 520.

23. *The Works of Plato*, I, 447-48. For Taylor's support for Shelley's reversal of the Platonic irony in the treatment of the poets, see his note on the first sentence in the tenth book of the *Republic* (I, 438-47).

24. N. I. White, *Portrait of Shelley* (New York, 1945), p. 402.

25. Douglas Bush, *Mythology and the Romantic Tradition in English Poetry* (New York, 1957), p. 140.

26. Neville Rogers, *Shelley at Work: A Critical Inquiry* (Oxford, 1956), pp. 102, 128.

27. Thomas Taylor, trans., *The Works of Plato*, I, 520.

28. "Defence of Poetry," *Prose*, p. 279; *Prometheus Unbound*, II, iv, 1. Olwen Ward Campbell, *Shelley and the Unromantics* (London, 1924), p. 216.

29. *Prometheus Unbound*, ed. G. Lowes Dickinson (London, 1910), introduction.

30. *Poetical Works*, p. 478.

31. Milton, *Paradise Lost*, II, 964. Cf. Notopoulos, pp. 245-46. Dickinson, *loc. cit.*, cites Lactantius on Statius, *Theb.*, II, 516; Boccacio, *Genealogia Deorum*, I, chap. I, vi, vii; and Spenser, *Faery Queene*, IV, 2, 47, and I, 5, 22.

32. *Republic*, VI, 508; *Prometheus Unbound*, II, iv, 3-4.

33. Cf. also Thomas Taylor's introduction to the *Parmenides*, *The Works of Plato*, III, 25.

34. Bush, p. 146.

35. "Defence of Poetry," *Prose*, p. 282.

36. R. S. Brumbaugh, *Plato on the One* (New Haven, 1961), p. 149.

37. For the discussion of the one in the moment see *Parmenides*, 156d ff.

38. For the philosopher as imitator and painter of ideal patterns see *Republic*, 500e, 540c. Cf. Werner Jaeger, *Paideia: The Ideals of Greek Culture*, trans. Gilbert Highet (New York, 1960), II, 258, 277.

39. *Poetical Works*, p. 473.

40. H. J. Rose, *Handbook of Greek Mythology* (New York, 1959), p. 124.

41. For a late nineteenth-century account of Orpheus as a sun god, see Mallarmé, *Les Dieux antiques*.

42. *The Greek Bucolic Poets*, trans. J. M. Edmonds, Loeb Classical Library (Cambridge, Mass., 1950), Bion I, 96. All citations of the Greek bucolic writers will refer to this edition.

43. Matthew Arnold, *Essays in Criticism: Second Series* (New York, 1930), p. 118.

44. Carlos Baker, *Shelley's Major Poetry: The Fabric of a Vision* (Princeton, 1948), pp. 244-45.

45. Moschus III, 109-12.

46. "Defence of Poetry," *Prose*, p. 278. We might illustrate this passage by referring to Vico's similar argument in *The New Science*, pp. 138-39, 150.

47. Earl R. Wasserman, "*Adonais*: Progressive Revelation as a Poetic Mode," *ELH*, XXI (1954). The following discussion is heavily indebted to Wasserman's analysis of *Adonais*, which I shall try to locate in the context of Shelley's Hellenism.

48. Bion I, 54-55; 96.

49. Bion I, 29.

50. Moschus III, 105.

51. *Anth. Pal.*, VII, 62. For Shelley's translation in 1821 after the death of Keats, see *Poetical Works*, p. 712. Also cf. N. Rogers, p. 258.

52. This inference is drawn from discussions in Cedric Whitman's *Sophocles* (Cambridge, Mass., 1958); see especially pp. 76 ff.

53. Giuseppe Toffanin, *La fine del logos*, vol. 3 in *Storia dell'-umanesimo* (Bologna, 1959), p. 185.

54. See David Perkins, *The Quest for Permanence: The Symbolism of Wordsworth, Shelley and Keats* (Cambridge, Mass., 1959), pp. 179-89; N. Rogers, pp. 154-55; 118-19.

55. Paul Elmer More, *Hellenistic Philosophies* (Princeton, 1923), pp. 153-54, 157-58, 233 ff.

56. Bush, p. 164.

57. "The Historical and Personal Background of Shelley's Hellas," *South Atlantic Quarterly*, XX (1921), 54-55. For a discussion of *Hellas* in comparison with the *Persae* and other sources of the poem, see Bush, pp. 163-65.

NOTES FOR CHAPTER VI

1. *The Life of Percy Bysshe Shelley: As Comprised in "The Life of Shelley" by Thomas Jefferson Hogg, "The Recollections of Shelley & Byron" by Edward John Trelawny, "Memoirs of Shelley" by Thomas Love Peacock* (London, 1933), II, 196. Cf. Olwen Ward Campbell, *Shelley and the Unromantics* (London, 1924), p. 177.

2. Francesco De Sanctis, "La prima canzone di Giacomo Leopardi," *Saggi critici*, ed. Luigi Russo (Bari, 1957), II, 344.

3. Sebastiano Timpanaro, *La filologia di Giacomo Leopardi* (Flo-

ence, 1955), pp. 30-31. Karl Vossler, *Leopardi*, translated into Italian by Thomas Gnoli (Naples, 1925), p. 66.

4. Giovanni Setti, *La Grecia letteraria nei "Pensieri" di Giacomo Leopardi* (Livorno, 1906), pp. 70-71.

5. Francesco Moroncini, *Studio sul Leopardi filologo* (Naples, 1891), p. 65.

6. Timpanaro, pp. 50-51, 66, 201.

7. Nello Carini, *Giacomo Leopardi critico e traduttore di Omero* (Assisi, 1964), pp. 24, 61.

8. Cf. Emilio Bigi, "Il Leopardi traduttore dei classici," *Giornale storico della letteratura italiana*, CXVI (1964), 208, 210.

9. *Poesie e prose*, II, 593, in *Tutte le opere di Giacomo Leopardi, Le poesie e le prose*, 2 vols., *Zibaldone di pensieri*, 2 vols., *Le lettere*, 1 vol., ed. Francesco Flora (Milan, 1961). All quotations from Leopardi's writings will be taken from this edition, unless otherwise specified. Hereafter, the two volumes of *Le poesie e le prose* will be referred to as *Opere*. The page numbers for references to *Zibaldone* are Leopardi's.

10. Later, when we treat the *Idilli*, we shall have to take up Leopardi's versions of Moschus. For now suffice it to say that they are generally clear, graceful, uncluttered, and freer from rhetorical artifice than the *Eneide*, II.

11. Moroncini, p. 193.

12. *Zibaldone*, 30-31.

13. *Opere*, I, 557.

14. Setti, pp. 14, 18-19. *Zibaldone*, 40, 693.

15. *The New Science of Giambattista Vico*, trans. from 3rd ed., 1744, by Thomas Goddard Bergin and Max Harold Fisch (Ithaca, 1948), p. 289. Timpanaro, p. 216.

16. Ibid., p. 290.

17. *Zibaldone*, 70, 1448-50, 4, 4326-27, 2544-45, 803, 4395-97, 4355-57, 4372, 245. For discussion of these points see Nello Carini, pp. 28, 34-35, 39, 43, 45, 57, 61.

18. Anna Luisa Staël-Holstein, "Sulla maniera e l'utilità delle traduzioni," *Discussioni e polemiche sul romanticismo (1816-26)*, ed. Egidio Bellorini (Bari, 1943), I, 5-6.

19. *Opere*, II, 479.

20. 30 May, 1817, *Le lettere*, ed. Francesco Flora (Milan, 1961). Timpanaro, pp. 90-92, 172. Timpanaro (p. 187) says that Leopardi was less well prepared in old Italian than in Latin and Greek.

21. The passage paraphrased from *Zibaldone*, 24 includes a somewhat compressed citation of Longinus' *Treatise on the Sublime*, Chapter X. Leopardi seems to refer to the following passage from Chapter XL: "Among the chief agents in the formation of the grand style is the proper combination of the constituent members—as is true of the human body and its members. Of itself no single member, when dissociated from any other, has anything worthy of note about

it, but when they are all mutually interconnected, they make up a perfect whole. Similarly, when the elements of grandeur are separated from one another, they carry the sublimity along with them, dispersing it in every direction; but when they are combined into a single organism, and, moreover, enclosed within the bonds of harmony, they form a rounded whole, and their voice is loud and clear, and in the periods thus formed the grandeur receives contributions, as it were, from a variety of factors" *Classical Literary Criticism*, trans. T. S. Dorsch (Baltimore, 1965), p. 152.

22. *Opere*, I, 151: ". . . in somma non si rassomigliano a nessuna poesia lirica italiana."

23. Longinus, pp. 146-47, 151-52. Vossler, p. 159. Cesare Galimberti, *Linguaggio del vero in Leopardi* (Firenze, 1959), pp. 12-14, 19, 30-31, 45, 51 ff. *Zibaldone*, 1429, 1 August, 1821, quoted by Galimberti, pp. 30-31.

24. Though Leopardi disparaged the *De Republica* when he saw it, much of his own philological work followed Mai's. Timpanaro, pp. 42, 102.

25. Cf. Galimberti, pp. 51-52.

26. See Vossler, p. 69.

27. Letter to Thomas Love Peacock, January 26, 1819, *The Letters of Percy Bysshe Shelley*, ed. Roger Ingpen (London, 1912), pp. 664-65.

28. Francesco De Sanctis, II, 342. Settembrini quoted in Ferdinando Giannessi, *La critica leopardiana* (Milan, 1957-58), p. 32.

29. *Opere di Giosue Carducci* (Bologna, 1939), XX, 133.

30. J. H. Whitfield, *Giacomo Leopardi* (Oxford, 1954), pp. 200-3.

31. Grazia Avitabile, *The Controversy on Romanticism in Italy* (New York, 1959), p. 38.

32. Simonides, frg. 127, *Lyra Graeca*, ed. J. M. Edmonds, Loeb Classical Library (Cambridge, Mass., 1958), II, 358.

33. Carducci, XX, 134.

34. Leopardi cryptically mentions the *Persae* in "Ricordi d'infanzia e di adolescenza," *Opere*, I, 677.

35. Anacreontea 24, *Elegy and Iambus*, ed. J. M. Edmonds, Loeb Classical Library (Cambridge, Mass., 1961); Bonaventura Zumbini, *Studi sul Leopardi* (Florence, 1902), I, 256.

36. *Zibaldone*, 115; in 2204 Leopardi cites Xenophon on the value of bodily exercise.

37. Vossler, p. 252.

38. Mircea Eliade, *Cosmos and History* (New York, 1959), pp. 20-21. Alfred Croiset, *La Poésie de Pindare et les lois du lyrisme grec* (Paris, 1886), pp. 411-12.

39. Horace, III, 3, 40-44. Cf. Piero Bigongiari, *L'elaborazione della lirica leopardiana* (Firenze, 1937), p. 32.

40. Francesco De Sanctis, "Le nuove canzoni di Leopardi," *Saggi critici*, ed. Luigi Russo (Bari, 1957), III, 227.

41. *Zibaldone*, 2591. Igino Tanga, *La teoria della lingua nel Leopardi* (Rome, 1959), p. 14.

42. Ovid, *Metamorphoses*, I, 750–II, 336; III, 144 ff.; VI, 424 ff.; *Heroides*, II. Aeschylus, *Agamemnon*, 1140 ff. H. J. Rose, *Handbook of Greek Mythology* (New York, 1959), pp. 261, 283. *Opere*, I, 174; II, 280 ff.

43. *Opere*, II, 478.

44. Vico, p. 150.

45. Ibid., pp. 64, 108.

46. Ibid., p. 54.

47. Francesco De Sanctis, *History of Italian Literature*, trans. Joan Redfern (New York, 1959), II, 802.

48. *Opere*, I, 837.

49. *Opere*, II, 535-36.

50. Vico, pp. 106-7.

51. Norman Wentworth De Witt, *Epicurus and His Philosophy* (Minneapolis, 1954), pp. 146 ff.

52. *Zibaldone*, 51. For the notion of *credenze* discussed here, cf. *Zibaldone*, 118-19, 414-15, 439.

53. Vico, p. 60.

54. Paul Elmer More, *Hellenistic Philosophies* (Princeton, 1923), pp. 233 ff., 153-54, 157-58.

55. Francesco De Sanctis, "Le nuove canzoni di Leopardi," *Saggi critici*, III.

56. *Le lettere*, p. 320.

57. Paul Hazard, *Giacomo Leopardi* (Paris, 1913), p. 100.

58. Letter no. 143, *Le lettere*, p. 246. See Giuseppe Chiarini, *Vita di Giacomo Leopardi* (Florence, 1905), p. 193. Giovanni Gentile, *Poesia e filosofia di Giacomo Leopardi* (Florence, 1939), p. 23.

59. Ernst Cassirer, *An Essay on Man: An Introduction to a Philosophy of Human Culture* (New Haven, 1944), pp. 76-77.

60. The same argument, held at a different angle in *Inno ai patriarchi*, shows Cain, who, "fleeing both solitary shades and the secret wrath of the winds in the deep forests, first raised the civil roof, the shelter and the realm of devouring cares."

61. Vossler, p. 264.

62. *Opere*, I, 151.

63. Vossler, p. 259. Cf. "Errori popolari," *Opere*, II, 385, 398-99.

64. The feeling of unhappiness or sensibility usually proceeds from the loss of the "grandi e vive illusioni"; *Zibaldone*, 232, September 6, 1820.

65. *Recollections of Socrates and Socrates' Defense before the Jury*, trans. Anna S. Benjamin (Indianapolis, 1965), p. 87. *Zibaldone*, 2395.

66. Werner Jaeger, *Paideia: The Ideals of Greek Culture*, trans. Gilbert Highet (New York, 1960), I, 112, 444, 416, 11-12, 276.

67. Frg. 58, *Lyra Graeca*, I, 225.

68. Iris Origo, *Leopardi: A Study in Solitude* (London, 1953), pp. 194-95

69. Carlo Muscetta, "L'ultimo canto di Saffo," *La rassegna della letteratura italiana*, LXVIII (1959), 207.

70. De Sanctis, "'Alla sua donna.' Poesia di Giacomo Leopardi," *Opere*, ed. Niccolò Gallo, vol. 56, *La letteratura italiana: Storia e testi* (Milano, 1961), pp. 904-5.

71. Vossler, p. 264.

NOTES FOR CHAPTER VII

1. Giuseppe Chiarini, *Vita di Giacomo Leopardi* (Florence, 1905), p. 150.

2. Karl Vossler, *Leopardi*, translated into Italian by Thomas Gnoli (Naples, 1925), p. 221.

3. See Giuseppe De Robertis, *Saggio sul Leopardi* (Florence, 1960), pp. 167 ff.

4. Lodovico di Breme, "Intorno all' ingiustizia di alcuni giudizi letterari italiani," *Discussioni e polemiche sul romanticismo (1816-26)*, ed. Egidio Bellorini (Bari, 1943), I, 45.

5. *Zibaldone*, 4358. *Zibaldone*, 4372: "Il poeta non imita la natura: ben è vero che la natura parla dentro di lui e per la sua bocca. *I' mi son un che quando Natura parla* ec., vera definizione del poeta. Cosi il poeta non è imitatore se no di se stesso." Cf. Vossler, pp. 152-53.

6. Grazia Avitabile, *The Controversy on Romanticism in Italy* (New York, 1959), p. 111.

7. Di Breme, I, 44: "... e se le nostre dottrine mistiche, morali, scientifiche, se i nostri usi, i recenti affetti nostri hanno ampiato di tanto il campo dell' invenzione, misuriamo noi tutta l'ampiezza di quell'orizonte, lanciamoci in quella immensità, e tentiamo animosi le regioni dell'infinito che ci sono concedute." Cf. also I, 261.

8. *Iliad*, VIII, 555-59, *Le poesie e le prose*, II, 515, in *Tutte le opere di Giacomo Leopardi*, *Le poesie e le prose*, 2 vols., *Zibaldone di pensieri*, 2 vols., *Le lettere*, 1 vol., ed. Francesco Flora (Milan, 1961). All quotations from Leopardi's writings will be taken from this edition, unless otherwise specified. Hereafter, the two volumes of *Le poesie e le prose* will be referred to as *Opere*. The page numbers for references to *Zibaldone* are Leopardi's.

9. Cf. Moses Hadas, *Hellenistic Culture: Fusion and Diffusion* (New York, 1959), p. 212.

10. *A un vincitore nel pallone*, *Opere*, I, 26.

11. Cf. *Opere*, II, 515.

12. It is well known that *Il sabato del villagio* and *Il canto notturno del pastore errante dell'Asia* borrow considerably from *In vita*, L.

13. Anacreontea 25, *Elegy and Iambus,* trans. J. M. Edmonds, Loeb Classical Library (Cambridge, Mass., 1961), II, 553.

14. *Georgics,* II, 536 ff. Cf. *Zibaldone,* 2256.

15. Frg. 45, *Ancilla to the Pre-Socratic Philosophers,* a complete translation of the fragments in Diels, *Fragmente der Vorsokratiker,* by Kathleen Freeman (Cambridge, Mass., 1952).

16. For details cf. *I canti di Giacomo Leopardi,* commentati da Alfredo Straccali, terza edizione corretta e accresciuta da Oreste Antognoni (Florence, 1934).

17. Cf. Andrew Gow, *The Greek Bucolic Poets* (Cambridge, 1953), p. 9.

18. Ernst Cassirer, *An Essay on Man: An Introduction to a Philosophy of Human Culture* (New Haven, 1944), pp. 76-77.

19. De Robertis (p. 166) finds *Alla luna* "una patina d'antico." He observes (p. 164) that in the early *Idilli* sorrow is elevated into an unreal atmosphere.

20. Cf. Hadas, p. 23. Sebastiano Timpanaro in his *La filologia di Giacomo Leopardi* (Florence, 1955), p. 156, points out that Leopardi favored the Hellenistic philosophies and their "arte di vincere la paura e il dolore e di raggiungere l'imperturbabilità. Questo fu l'aspetto della grecità che il Leopardi sentì e comprese appieno; e nella prefazione al volgarizzamento di Epitteto colse con perfetta lucidità il carattere di 'morale dei deboli' della filosofia stoica e in genere di tutta la filosofia ellenistica."

21. De Sanctis, *Giacomo Leopardi,* in *La letteratura italiana nel secolo XIX* (Bari, 1953), II, 84-85.

22. Cf. Mimnermus, frgs. 1, 2, and 5, *Elegy and Iambus,* I. Giovanni Setti, *La Grecia letteraria nei "Pensieri" di Giacomo Leopardi* (Livorno, 1906), p. 90, concludes that Leopardi did not know Mimnermus, frgs. 1 and 5, since none of the classical texts in the Leopardi library contained them. But inasmuch as Leopardi spent a number of years away from Recanati before he wrote the *Idilli* of 1828-29, it seems unnecessary to suppose that his father's books were the only ones the poet read.

23. *Zibaldone,* 4236. Georg Luck, *The Latin Love Elegy* (London, 1959), pp. 18 ff.

24. *Poesie di Mosco, Idillio secondo, Europa, Opere,* I, 590.

25. Werner Jaeger, *The Theology of Early Greek Philosophers* (Oxford, 1948), p. 36.

26. Ibid., pp. 34-35.

27. J. H. Whitfield, *Giacomo Leopardi* (Oxford, 1954), p. 223, quotes Pascal (*Pensées,* 428) in connection with *L'infinito:* "Le silence éternel de ces espaces infinis m'effraie." Whitfield comments: "But terror is not really the motive-power of *L'Infinito. . . .*" Also cf. *Zibaldone,* 2242-43.

28. "Saggio sopra gli errori popolari degli antichi," *Opere,* II, 349.

29. De Sanctis, III, 84-85.

30. Riccardo Bacchelli, "L'infinito di Leopardi e l'esercizio della buona morte di Carl-Ambrogio Cattaneo," *Leopardi: Commenti letterari* (Milan, 1960), p. 381.

31. De Sanctis, III, 87.

32. Werner Jaeger, *Paideia: The Ideals of Greek Culture,* trans. Gilbert Highet (New York, 1960), I, 117.

33. *Zibaldone,* 4426. Cf. *I canti di Giacomo Leopardi,* commentati da Alfredo Straccali, p. 180.

NOTES FOR CONCLUSION

1. Sebastiano Timpanaro, *La filologia di Giacomo Leopardi* (Florence, 1955), p. 31 and *passim.*

2. Emilio Bigi, *Dal Petrarca al Leopardi: Studi di stilistica storica* (Naples, 1954), p. 106.

Bibliography

CHÉNIER

Chénier, André. *Oeuvres complètes,* ed. Gérard Walter. Paris, 1958.
————————, *Oeuvres complètes de André Chénier,* ed. Paul Dimoff. 3 vols. Paris, 1908-19.

Badolle, Maurice. *L'Abbé Jean-Jacques Barthélemy et l'hellénisme en France dans la seconde moitié du XVIIIe siècle.* Paris, 1927.
Baldensperger, F. "Un Témoignage allemand sur la mère d'André Chénier," *Revue de littérature comparée,* XXI, No. 83 (July-September, 1947), 89-92.
Becq de Fouquières, L. *Documents nouveaux sur André Chénier et examen critique de la nouvelle édition de ses oeuvres.* Paris, 1875.
————————, *Lettres critiques sur la vie, les oeuvres, les manuscrits d'André Chénier.* Paris, 1881.
Bertrand, Louis-Marie-Émile. *La Fin du classicisme et le retour à l'antique dans la seconde moitié du XVIIIe siècle et les premières années du XIXe en France.* Paris, 1897.
Brunetière, Ferdinand. *Etudes critiques sur l'histoire de la littérature française.* 6 vols. Paris, 1896-99.

Canat, René. *L'Hellénisme des romantiques*. Paris, 1951.

——————. *La Renaissance de la Grèce antique (1820-1850)*. Paris, 1911.

Chateaubriand, Francois-René de. *Génie du christianisme*. Paris, 1869.

Chénier, Mme Elisabeth Santi Lomaca. *Lettres grecques de Mme Chénier*, ed. Robert de Bonnières. Paris, 1879.

Dimoff, Paul. *La Vie et l'oeuvre d'André Chénier jusqu'à la Révolution française, 1762-1790*. 2 vols. Paris, 1936.

——————. "Winckelmann et André Chénier," *Revue de littérature comparée*, XXI (1947), 321-33.

Egger, Émile. *L'Hellénisme en France*. Paris, 1869.

Fabre, Jean. *André Chénier: L'Homme et l'oeuvre*. Paris, 1955.

Faguet, Emile. *André Chénier*. Paris, 1902.

Kramer, C. "Les Poèmes épiques d'André Chénier," *Neophilologus*, VI (1920-21), 13-28, 149-61.

Lanson, Gustave. *Histoire de la littérature française*. Paris, 1912.

Legros, René P. "André Chénier en Angleterre," *Modern Language Review*, XIX (1924), 424-34.

Potez, Henri. *L'Elégie en France avant le romantisme (de Parny à Lamartine) 1778-1820*. Paris, 1898.

Sainte-Beuve, Charles-Augustin. *Etudes des lundis et des portraits: XVIIIe siècle. Auteurs dramatiques et poètes*, ed. Maurice Allem. Paris, 1930.

——————. *Oeuvres*, ed. Maxime Leroy. 2 vols. Paris, vol. I in 1956, vol. II in 1951.

Zola, Émile. *Les Oeuvres complètes: Correspondance, 1858-1871*. Paris, 1928.

SHELLEY

Shelley, Percy Bysshe. *The Works of Percy Bysshe Shelley in Verse and Prose*, ed. Harry Buxton Forman. 8 vols. London, 1880.

——————. *The Complete Poetical Works of Percy Bysshe Shelley*, ed. Thomas Hutchinson. Oxford, 1923.

——————. *The Complete Works of Percy Bysshe Shelley*, ed. Roger Ingpen and Walter E. Peck. 10 vols. The Julian Editions. London, 1926-29.

——————. *Shelley's Prose, or the Trumpet of a Prophecy*, ed. David Lee Clark. Albuquerque, 1954.

——————. *The Letters of Percy Bysshe Shelley*, ed. Roger Ingpen. 2 vols. London, 1912.

——————. *Prometheus Unbound*, ed. G. Lowes Dickinson. London, 1910.

Baker, Carlos. *Shelley's Major Poetry: The Fabric of a Vision.* Princeton, 1948.

Barrell, Joseph. *Shelley and the Thought of His Time.* New Haven, 1947.

Bloom, Harold. *Shelley's Myth-Making.* New Haven, 1959.

Bowra. C. M. *The Romantic Imagination.* Cambridge, Mass., 1949.

Brooke, Stopford Augustus. *Studies in Poetry.* London, 1910.

Campbell, Olwen Ward. *Shelley and the Unromantics.* London, 1924.

Chayes, Irene H. "Plato's Statesman Myth in Shelley and Blake," *Comparative Literature,* XIII (1961), 358-69.

Fogle, Richard Harter. "Imaginal Design of Shelley's *Ode to the West Wind,*" *ELH,* XV (1948), 219-26.

Grabo, Carl. *A Newton among Poets: Shelley's Use of Science in Prometheus Unbound.* Chapel Hill, 1939.

——————. *Prometheus Unbound: An Interpretation.* Chapel Hill, 1935.

Hack, Arthur. "The Psychological Pattern of Shelley's *Prometheus Unbound,*" *Dissertation Abstracts,* XXVIII (1967), 1078a.

Hildebrand, William H. *A Study of Alastor.* Kent, 1954.

Hoffman, Harold Leroy. *An Odyssey of the Soul: Shelley's Alastor.* New York, 1933.

Hughes, D. J. "Potentiality in *Prometheus Unbound,*" *Studies in Romanticism,* II (1963), 107-26.

Hunter, Parks C. Jr. "Undercurrents of Anacreontics in Shelley's *To a Skylark* and *The Cloud,*" *Studies in Philology,* LXV (1968), 677-92.

Hurt, James R. "*Prometheus Unbound* and Aeschylean Dramaturgy," *Keats-Shelley Journal,* XV (1966), 42-48.

Ingpen, Roger. *Shelley in England, New Facts and Letters from the Shelley-Whitton Papers.* 2 vols. Boston, 1917.

Knight, G. Wilson. *The Starlit Dome: Studies in the Poetry of Vision.* New York, 1960.

The Life of Percy Bysshe Shelley: As Comprised in "The Life of Shelley" by Thomas Jefferson Hogg, "The Recollections of Shelley & Byron" by Edward John Trelawny, "Memoirs of Shelley" by Thomas Love Peacock, introduction by Humbert Wolfe. 2 vols. London, 1933.

McGill, Mildred S. "The Role of Earth in Shelley's *Prometheus Unbound,*" *Studies in Romanticism,* VII (1968), 117-28.

Mahony, Patrick J. "An Analysis of Shelley's Craftsmanship in *Adonais,*" *Studies in English Literature, 1800 to 1900,* IV (1964), 555-68.

Notopoulos, James A. "New Texts of Shelley's Plato," *Keats-Shelley Journal,* XV (1966), 99-115.

——————. *The Platonism of Shelley: A Study of Platonism and the Poetic Mind.* Durham, N. C., 1949.

Peck, Walter E. *Shelley, His Life and Work*, 2 vols. Boston, 1927.
Perkins, David. *The Quest for Permanence: The Symbolism of Wordsworth, Shelley and Keats*. Cambridge, Mass., 1959.
Reiman, Donald H. "Structure, Symbol, and Theme in 'Lines Written among the Euganean Hills'," *PMLA*, LXXVII (1962), 404-13.
Rogers, Neville. *Shelley at Work: A Critical Inquiry*. Oxford, 1956.
Silverman, Edwin B. "Poetic Synthesis in *Adonais*," *Dissertation Abstracts*, XXVII (1967), 2162a.
Stovall, Floyd. *Desire and Restraint in Shelley*. Durham, N. C., 1931.
Vitoux, Pierre. "Jupiter's Fatal Child in *Prometheus Unbound*," *Criticism*, X (1968), 115-25.
Wasserman, Earl R. "*Adonais*: Progressive Revelation as a Poetic Mode," *ELH*, XXI (1954), 274-326.
White, Newman Ivey. "The Historical and Personal Background of Shelley's Hellas," *South Atlantic Quarterly*, XX (January, 1921), 52-60.
—————. *Portrait of Shelley*. New York, 1945.
————— *The Unextinguished Hearth: Shelley and His Contemporary Critics*. Durham, N. C., 1938.
Wilson, Milton. *Shelley's Later Poetry*. New York, 1959.
Woodman, Ross G. "Shelley's Changing Attitude to Plato," *Journal of the History of Ideas*, XXI (1960), 497-510.

LEOPARDI

Leopardi, Giacomo. *Giacomo Leopardi opere,* ed. Sergio Solmi, vol. 52, *La letteratura italiana: Storia e testi*. Milan, 1956.
————— *Tutte le opere di Giacomo Leopardi,* ed. Francesco Flora. *Le poesie e le prose,* 2 vols. (7th ed., 1962), *Zibaldone di pensieri,* 2 vols. (6th ed., 1961), *Le lettere,* 1 vol. (1st ed., 1949). Milan, 1961.
————— *I canti di Giacomo Leopardi,* commentati da Alfredo Straccali, terza edizione corretta e accresciuta da Oreste Antognoni. Florence, 1934.
————— *I canti,* ed. Luigi Russo. Florence, 1945.
————— *Il libro delle prose di Giacomo Leopardi,* ed. Oreste Antognoni. Livorno, 1926.
————— *Epistolario di Giacomo Leopardi,* ed. G. Piergili of the edition by Prospero Viani. 3 vols. Florence, 1924.

Arangio-Ruiz, Vladimiro. "La siepe dell'Infinito," *Letteratura moderna*, I (1950), 99-102.
Avitabile, Grazia. *The Controversy on Romanticism in Italy*. New York, 1959.
Bacchelli, Riccardo. *Leopardi: Commenti letterari*. Milan, 1960.

_____ "Sugli aggettivi determinativi dell' 'Infinito'," *Lettera-tura moderna,* I (1950), 235-39.

Bigi, Emilio. *Dal Petrarca al Leopardi: Studi di stilistica storica.* Naples, 1954.

_____. "Il Leopardi e l'Arcadia," *Leopardi e il settecento. Atti del I convegno internazionale di studi leopardiani.* Firenze, 1964.

_____. "Il Leopardi traduttore dei classici," *Giornale storico della letteratura italiana,* CXVI (1964), 186-234.

Bigongiari, Piero. *L'elaborazione della lirica leopardiana.* Florence, 1937.

Binni, Walter. *La nuova poetica leopardiana.* Firenze, 1962.

_____. "La poesia eroica di Giacomo Leopardi," *Il ponte,* XVI (1960), 1729-51.

Carducci, Giosue. *Giacomo Leopardi.* Bologna, 1911.

_____ *Leopardi e Manzoni,* vol. 20, *Opere di Giosue Carducci.* 28 vols. Bologna, 1939.

Carini, Nello. *Giacomo Leopardi critico e traduttore di Omero.* Assisi, 1964.

Cechetti, Giovanni. "Aspetti dell'elaborazione dei *Canti* leopardiani," *Italica,* XXXV (1958), 167-76.

Chiarini, Giuseppe. *Vita di Giacomo Leopardi.* Florence, 1905.

Consoli, Domenico. *Cultura, conscienza letteraria e poesia in Giacomo Leopardi.* Firenze, 1967.

Crispo d'Asdia, Alfonsina. *Il pensiero estetico di Giacomo Leopardi.* Palermo, 1925.

Croce, Benedetto. *European Literature in the Nineteenth Century,* trans. Douglas A. Ainslie. London, 1925.

De Lorenzo, Giuseppe. "The Cosmic Conceptions of Leopardi," *East and West,* V (1954), 198-204.

De Robertis, Giuseppe. *Saggio sul Leopardi.* Florence, 1960.

De Sanctis, Francesco. *Giacomo Leopardi,* ed. Walter Binni, vol. 3, *La letteratura italiana nel secolo XIX.* 3 vols. Bari, 1953.

_____ *History of Italian Literature,* trans. Joan Redfern, 2 vols. New York, 1959.

_____ *Opere,* ed. Niccolò Gallo, vol. 56, *La letteratura italiana: Storia e testi.* Milano, 1961.

_____ *Saggi critici,* ed. Luigi Russo. 3 vols. Bari, 1957.

Discussioni e polemiche sul romanticismo (1816-26), ed. Egidio Bellorini. 2 vols. Bari, 1943.

Flora, Francesco. "Concordanza grammaticale," *Letteratura moderna,* I (1950), 240-42.

_____. "La 'tanta parte' e gli 'interminati spazi'," *Letteratura moderna,* I (1950), 102-4.

Frattini, Alberto. *Cultura e pensiero in Leopardi: Due contributi.* Rome, 1958.

Galimberti, Cesare. *Linguaggio del vero in Leopardi.* Firenze, 1959.

Gentile, Giovanni. *Poesia e filosofia di Giacomo Leopardi.* Florence, 1939.

Giannessi, Ferdinando. *La critica leopardiana.* Milan, 1957-58.

Gullace, Giovanni. "Pascal and Leopardi: Some Relationships," *Italica,* XXXII (1955), 27-37.

Hazard, Paul. *Giacomo Leopardi,* in *Les Grands Ecrivains étrangers,* Paris, 1913.

Juliusburger, Klaus. *L'antichità in ispecie ellenica in Giacomo Leopardi.* Bern, 1949.

Levi, Giulio Augusto. *Storia del pensiero di G. Leopardi.* Turin, 1911.

Maurois, André. "Giacomo Leopardi," *The Art of Writing,* trans. Gerard Hopkins. New York, 1960.

Mazzatinti, G., and M. Menghini. *Bibliografia leopardiana, Parte I, fino 1898; Parte II, 1898-1930; Parte III, 1931-51.* 3 vols. Florence, 1931-53.

Moroncini, Francesco. *Studio sul Leopardi filologo.* Naples, 1891.

Muscetta, Carlo. "L'ultimo canto di Saffo," *La rassegna della letteratura italiana.* LXVIII (1959), 194-218.

Oldfather, W. A. "Leopardi and Epictetus," *Italica,* XIV (1937), 44-53.

Origo, Iris. *Leopardi: A Biography.* New York, 1935.

—————— *Leopardi: A Study in Solitude.* London, 1953.

Peruzzi, Emilio. "Il primo monumento del canto *A Silvia,*" *Italica,* XXXIV (1957), 92-97.

Scheel, Hans Ludwig. *Leopardi und die Antike.* München, 1959.

Setti, Giovanni. *La Grecia letteraria nei "Pensieri" di Giacomo Leopardi.* Livorno, 1906.

Singh, G. *Leopardi and the Theory of Poetry.* Lexington, Kentucky, 1964.

Tanga, Igino. *La teoria della lingua nel Leopardi.* Rome, 1959.

Timpanaro, Sebastiano. *La filologia di Giacomo Leopardi.* Florence, 1955.

Toffanin, Giuseppe. *Prolegomeni alla lettura del Leopardi.* Naples, 1952.

Tortoreto, Alessandro. *Bibliografia analitica leopardiana (1952-1960).* Florence, 1963.

Van Horne, John. "Studies on Leopardi," *Bulletin of the State University of Iowa: Humanistic Studies,* I, no. 4 (1916), 1-13.

Vossler, Karl. *Leopardi,* translated into Italian by Thomas Gnoli. Naples, 1925.

Vossler, Karl, and Riccardo Bacchelli. *Nel centenario di Giacomo Leopardi.* Padua, 1937.

Whitfield, John H. *Giacomo Leopardi.* Oxford, 1954.

Woodbridge, B. M. "The Role of Illusion in Leopardi's Pessimism," *Italica,* XXIII (1945), 196-204.

Zumbini, Bonaventura. *Studi sul Leopardi.* 2 vols. Florence, 1902-4.

GENERAL BIBLIOGRAPHY

Aeschylus, ed. Gilbert Murray. Oxford, 1957.

Ancilla to the Pre-Socratic Philosophers, a complete translation of the fragments in Diels, *Fragmente der Vorsokratiker,* by Kathleen Freeman. Cambridge, Mass., 1952.

Apollonius Rhodius. *The Argonautica,* trans. R. C. Seaton. Loeb Classical Library. London, 1912.

Aristophanes. *Five Comedies of Aristophanes,* trans. Benjamin Bickley Rogers, ed. Andrew Chiappe. Garden City, 1955.

Aristotle. *The Basic Works of Aristotle,* ed. Richard McKeon. New York, 1941.

Brunck, Richard Franz Philipp, ed. *Analecta veterum poetarum Graecorum.* 3 vols. Argentorati, 1772-76.

Callimachus, trans. C. A. Trypanis. Loeb Classical Library. Cambridge, Mass., 1958.

Cicero. *Selected Works,* trans. Michael Grant. Baltimore, 1962.

The Complete Greek Tragedies, ed. David Grene and Richmond Lattimore. *Aeschylus,* 2 vols. *Sophocles,* 2 vols. *Euripides,* 5 vols. Chicago, 1963.

Elegy and Iambus, with the Anacreontea, trans. J. M. Edmonds. 2 vols. Loeb Classical Library. Cambridge, Mass., 1961.

Epictetus. *The Enchiridion,* trans. Thomas W. Higginson. New York, 1950.

Essential Works of Stoicism, ed. Moses Hadas. New York, 1961.

Euripides, trans. Arthur S. Way. 4 vols. Loeb Classical Library. London, 1925.

The Greek Anthology, trans. W. R. Paton. 5 vols. Loeb Classical Library. Cambridge, Mass., 1960.

Greek Bucolic Poets, trans. J. M. Edmonds. Loeb Classical Library. Cambridge, Mass., 1950.

The Greek Bucolic Poets, trans. A. S. F. Gow. Cambridge, 1953.

Herodotus. *The Persian Wars,* trans. George Rawlinson. New York, 1942.

Hesiod, trans. Richmond Lattimore. Ann Arbor, 1959.

Hesiodi Carmina, ed. F. S. Lehrs. Paris, 1878.

Hesiod, the Homeric Hymns, and Homerica, trans. Hugh G. Evelyn-White. Loeb Classical Library. Cambridge, Mass., 1943.

Homer. *The Iliad of Homer,* trans. Richmond Lattimore. Chicago, 1963.

_____ *The Iliad,* trans. A. T. Murray. 2 vols. Loeb Classical Library. Cambridge, Mass., 1957-60.

_____ *The Odyssey,* trans. A. T. Murray. 2 vols. Loeb Classical Library. Cambridge, Mass., 1960.

——————— *The Odyssey,* trans. E. V. Rieu. Baltimore, 1962.

Horace. *The Odes and Epodes of Horace,* ed. Clement Lawrence Smith. Washington, D. C., 1952.

Livy, trans. B. O. Foster. 13 vols. Loeb Classical Library. Cambridge, Mass., 1939.

Lucian, trans. A. M. Harmon. 8 vols. Loeb Classical Library. Cambridge, Mass., 1953.

Lyra Graeca, trans. J. M. Edmonds. 3 vols. Loeb Classical Library. Cambridge, Mass., 1958.

Ovid. *Heroides and Amores,* trans. Grant Showerman. Loeb Classical Library. Cambridge, Mass., 1958.

——————— *Metamorphoses,* trans. Frank Justus Miller. 2 vols. Loeb Classical Library. Cambridge, Mass., 1951.

Pausanias. *Description of Greece,* trans. W. H. S. Jones. 4 vols. Loeb Classical Library. Cambridge, Mass., 1959.

Pindar. *The Odes of Pindar,* trans. Sir John Sandys. Loeb Classical Library. Cambridge, Mass., 1961.

Plato. *Platonis Opera Omnia,* ed. Gottfried Stallbaum. Leipzig, 1850.

——————— *The Dialogues of Plato,* trans. B. Jowett. 2 vols. New York, 1937.

——————— *Il Fedone,* ed. Riccardo Rubrichi. Milan, 1953.

——————— *Plato I: Euthyphro, Apology, Crito, Phaedo, Phaedrus,* trans. Harold North Fowler. Loeb Classical Library. Cambridge, Mass., 1953.

——————— *Plato IV: Laches, Protagoras, Meno, Euthydemus,* trans. W. R. M. Lamb. Loeb Classical Library. London, 1924.

——————— *Plato V: Lysis, Symposium, Gorgias,* trans. W. R. M. Lamb. Loeb Classical Library. Cambridge, Mass., 1961.

——————— *The Republic,* trans. Paul Shorey. 2 vols. Loeb Classical Library. London, 1930-35.

Plotinus. *Plotini Enneades: Praemisso Porphyrii de vita Plotini deque ordine librorum eius libello,* ed. Richard Volkmann. 2 vols. Leipzig, 1883-84.

——————— *The Six Enneads,* trans. Stephen MacKenna and B. S. Page. Chicago, 1952.

Properce. *Elégies,* texte établi et traduit par D. Paganelli. Paris, 1947.

Sophocles, trans. F. Storr. 2 vols. Loeb Classical Library. New York, 1924.

Sophocles. *The Antigone of Sophocles,* abriged from the large edition of Sir Richard C. Jebb by E. S. Shuckburg. Cambridge, 1929.

Taylor, Thomas, trans. *An Essay on the Beautiful (from the Greek of Plotinus).* London, 1917.

——————— *Five Books of Plotinus.* London, 1794.

——————— *The Timaeus and Critias, the Thomas Taylor Translation,* foreword by R. C. Taliaferro. New York, 1944.

——————— *The Works of Plato.* 5 vols. London, 1804.

Thucydides. *The Complete Writings of Thucydides: The Peloponnesian War*, the unabridged Crawley translation with an introduction by John H. Finley, Jr. New York, 1951.
Tibulle et les auteurs du corpus tibullianum, trans. Max Ponchont. Paris, 1950.
Virgil, trans. H. Rushton Fairclough. 2 vols. Loeb Classical Library. Cambridge, Mass., 1960.
Virgil's Works: The Aeneid, Eclogues, Georgics, trans. J. W. Mackail. New York, 1950.
Xenophon. *Recollections of Socrates and Socrates' Defense before the Jury*, trans. Anna S. Benjamin. Indianapolis, 1965.

M. H. Abrams. *The Mirror and the Lamp: Romantic Theory and the Critical Tradition.* New York, 1958.
Anthology of Romanticism, ed. Ernest Bernbaum. New York, 1948.
Antologia della letteratura italiana, ed. Attilio Momigliano. 3 vols. Milan, 1958.
Arnold, Matthew. *Essays in Criticism: Second Series.* New York, 1930.
Babbitt, Irving. *The New Laokoon: An Essay on the Confusion of the Arts.* Boston, 1910.
Barthélemy, Jean-Jacques. *The Travels of Anacharsis the Younger, in Greece, during the Middle of the Fourth Century before the Christian Era*, abridged from the original work of the Abbé Barthélemy, trans. William Beaumont. London, 1825.
————— *Voyage du jeune Anacharsis en Grèce dans le milieu du quatrième siècle avant l'ère vulgaire.* 3 vols. Paris, 1893.
Bate, Walter Jackson. *From Classic to Romantic: Premises of Taste in Eighteenth-Century England.* Cambridge, Mass., 1946.
—————, ed. *Criticism: The Major Texts.* New York, 1952.
Bédier, Joseph, and Paul Hazard. *Histoire de la littérature française illustrée.* Paris, 1924.
Benet, William Rose. *Reader's Encyclopedia.* New York, 1948.
Bowra, C. M. *The Greek Experience.* London, 1957.
Brion, Marcel. *Pompeii and Herculaneum: The Glory and the Grief*, trans. John Rosenberg, photographs by Edwin Smith. New York, 1960.
Brumbaugh, R. S. *Plato on the One.* New Haven, 1961.
Buffon, George-Louis Leclerc, comte de. *Oeuvres philosophiques de Buffon*, ed. Jean Piveteau, *Corpus général des philosophes français*, vol. 41. Paris, 1954.
Bury, John Bagnell. *A History of Greece to the Death of Alexander the Great.* London, 1913.
Bush, Douglas. *Mythology and the Romantic Tradition in English Poetry.* New York, 1957.
Butler, E. M. *The Tyranny of Greece over Germany: A Study of the*

Influence Exercised by Greek Art and Poetry over the Great German Writers of the Eighteenth, Nineteenth and Twentieth Centuries. Cambridge, 1935.

The Cambridge History of English Literature, ed. Sir A. W. Ward and A. R. Waller. 14 vols. New York and Cambridge, 1916.

Caro, Annibal. *L'Eneide di Virgilio,* vol. 8, *Opere del commendatore Annibal Caro.* 8 vols. Milano, 1812.

Cassirer, Ernst. *An Essay on Man: An Introduction to a Philosophy of Human Culture.* New Haven, 1944.

Ciprotti, Pio. *Conoscere Pompei.* Rome, 1959.

Classical Literary Criticism, trans. T. S. Dorsch. Baltimore, 1965.

A Collection of English Poems, 1660-1800, ed. Ronald S. Crane. New York, 1932.

Condillac, Etienne Bonnot de. *Oeuvres philosophiques de Condillac,* ed. George Le Roy. 3 vols. *Corpus général des philosophes francais,* vol. 33. Paris, 1947-51.

Croiset, Alfred. *La Poésie de Pindare et les lois du lyrisme grec.* Paris, 1886.

Croiset, Maurice, and Alfred Croiset. *An Abridged History of Greek Literature,* trans. G. F. Heffelbower. New York, 1904.

Cumont, Franz Valéry Marie. *Recherches sur le symbolisme funéraire des romains,* vol. 35, *Bibliothèque archéologique et historique.* Paris, 1942.

Curtius, Ernst Robert. *European Literature and the Latin Middle Ages,* trans. Willard R. Trask. Bollingen Series, XXXVI. New York, 1953.

Des Places, Edouard, S. J. *Pindare et Platon.* Paris, 1949.

De Witt, Norman Wentworth. *Epicurus and His Philosophy.* Minneapolis, 1954.

Diderot, Denis. *Oeuvres complètes de Diderot,* ed. J. Assézat. 20 vols. Paris, 1875-77.

——————— *Oeuvres esthétiques,* ed. Paul Vernière. Paris, 1959.

Eliade, Mircea. *Cosmos and History: The Myth of the Eternal Return,* trans. Willard R. Trask. New York, 1959.

Fanger, D. L. "Romanticism and Comparative Literature," *Comparative Literature,* XIV (1962), 153-66.

Farrell, R. B. "Classicism," in Vol. 1 of *Periods in German Literature,* ed. J. Ritchie. 2 vols. Great Britain, 1967.

Foscolo, Ugo. *Opere,* edizione critica di M. Fubini. 19 vols. Firenze, 1933-67.

French Literature and Thought since the Revolution, ed. Ramon Guthrie and George E. Diller. New York, 1942.

Gay, Peter. *The Enlightenment: An Interpretation. The Rise of Modern Paganism.* New York, 1966.

Godwin, William. *Enquiry Concerning Political Justice and Its Influence on Morals and Happiness,* ed. F. E. L. Priestley. 2 vols. Toronto, 1946.

Greg, Walter W. *Pastoral Poetry and Pastoral Drama: A Literary Inquiry, with Special Reference to the Pre-Restoration Stage in England.* New York, 1959.

Guthrie, W. K. C. *The Greeks and Their Gods.* Boston, 1951.

——————— *A History of Greek Philosophy.* Cambridge, 1962.

Hadas, Moses. *Hellenistic Culture: Fusion and Diffusion.* New York, 1959.

Hazard, Paul. *La Pensée européenne au XVIIIe siècle, de Montesquieu à Lessing.* 2 vols. Paris, 1946.

Highet, Gilbert. *The Classical Tradition.* New York, 1957.

Hume, David. *The Philosophical Works,* ed. Thomas Hill Green and Thomas Hodge Grose. 4 vols. Aalen, 1964.

Jaeger, Werner. *Paideia: The Ideals of Greek Culture,* trans. Gilbert Highet. 3 vols. New York, 1960.

——————— *The Theology of the Early Greek Philosophers,* trans. Edward S. Robinson. Oxford, 1947.

Jasinski, René. *Histoire de la littérature française.* 2 vols. Paris, 1947.

Jones, Richard Foster. *Ancients and Moderns, a Study of the Background of the Battle of the Books.* St. Louis, 1936.

Kerenyi, Carl. *Prometheus: Archetypal Image of Human Existence,* trans. Ralph Manheim. Bollingen Series, LXV. New York, 1963.

Kermode, Frank. *English Pastoral Poetry from the Beginnings to Marvell.* New York, 1952.

——————— *Romantic Image.* New York, 1964.

Kitto, H. D. F. *Greek Tragedy: A Literary Study.* Garden City, 1954.

Lessing, Gotthold Ephraim. *Laocoon: An Essay upon the Limits of Painting and Poetry,* trans. Ellen Frothingham. New York, 1961.

Lough, John. *An Introduction to Eighteenth-Century France.* London, 1960.

Luck, Georg. *The Latin Love Elegy.* London, 1959.

Manuel, Frank E. *The Eighteenth Century Confronts the Gods.* Cambridge, Mass., 1959.

More, Paul Elmer. *Hellenistic Philosophies,* vol. 2 in *The Greek Tradition from the Death of Socrates to the Council of Chalcedon (399 B.C. to A.D. 451).* Princeton, 1923.

——————— *Platonism,* vol. 1 in *The Greek Tradition from the Death of Socrates to the Council of Chalcedon (399 B.C. to A.D. 451).* Princeton, 1926.

Mornet, Daniel. *La Pensée française au XVIIIe siècle.* Paris, 1926.

Murray, Gilbert. *Aeschylus, the Creator of Tragedy.* Oxford, 1951.

——————— *A History of Ancient Greek Literature.* New York, 1897.

"Myth and Myth-Making," *Daedalus, Journal of the American Academy of Arts and Sciences,* LXXXVIII, No. 2 (1959).

Nairn, J. A. *Classical Hand-List,* ed. B. H. Blackwell. Oxford, 1953.

Nietzsche, Friedrich. *The Birth of Tragedy* and *The Genealogy of Morals,* trans. Francis Golffing. Garden City, 1959.

Nine Classic French Plays, ed. Joseph Secondo and Henri Peyre. Boston, 1936.

Nitze, William A. and Preston Dargan. *A History of French Literature: From the Earliest Times to the Great War.* New York, 1922.

Norwood, Gilbert. *Pindar.* Berkeley and Los Angeles, 1945.

Pater, Walter. *The Renaissance: Studies in Art and Poetry.* London, 1919.

Peacock, Thomas Love. *The Works of Thomas Love Peacock,* ed. H. F. B. Brett-Smith and C. E. Jones. 10 vols. Halliford Edition. London, 1934.

Perry, B. E. "The Early Greek Capacity for Viewing Things Separately," *Transactions and Proceedings of the American Philological Association,* LXVIII (1937), 403-27.

Peyre, Henri. *Bibliographie critique de l'hellénisme en France de 1843 à 1870.* Vol. 6 in *Yale Romantic Studies.* New Haven, 1932.

————— *Le Classicisme français.* New York, 1942.

Pierce, Frederick E. "The Hellenic Current in English Nineteenth-Century Poetry," *The Journal of English and Germanic Philology,* XVI (1917), 103-35.

Poetry of the English Renaissance, 1509-1660, ed. J. William Hebel and Hoyt H. Hudson. New York, 1929.

Poggioli, Renato. "The Oaten Flute," *Harvard Library Bulletin,* XI (1957), 147-84.

————— "Pastoral of the Self," *Daedalus, Journal of the American Academy of Arts and Sciences,* LXXXVIII (1959), 686-99.

Potter, John. *Archaeologia Graeca.* 2 vols. London, 1715.

Prendergast, Guy Lushington. *A Complete Concordance to the Iliad of Homer.* London, 1875.

Robertson, J. G. *A History of German Literature.* Edinburgh and London, 1953.

————— *Studies in the Genesis of Romantic Theories in the Eighteenth Century.* Cambridge, 1923.

Rose, H. J. *A Handbook of Greek Literature from Homer to the Age of Lucian.* London, 1950.

————— *Handbook of Greek Mythology.* New York, 1959.

Rousseau, Jean-Jacques. *Les Confessions: Les reveries du promeneur solitaire,* ed. Pierre Grosclaude. Paris, 1954.

Sarton, George. *A History of Science: Ancient Science through the Golden Age of Greece.* New York, 1964.

Shaftsbury, Anthony Ashley Cooper, Earl of. *Characteristics of Men, Manners, Opinions, Times, etc.* London, 1900.

Shorey, Paul. *Platonism, Ancient and Modern.* Berkeley, 1938.

Stewart, Zeph. "Song of Silenus," *Harvard Studies in Classical Philology,* LXIV (1959), 179-205.

Taylor, Alfred Edward. *A Commentary on Plato's Timaeus.* Oxford, 1928.

—————— *Plato*. New York, n. d.

Thomson, George. *Aeschylus and Athens*. London, 1941.

Thomson, J. A. K. *The Art of the Logos*. London, 1935.

Toffanin, Giuseppe. *La fine del logos*, vol. 3 in *Storia dell'umanesimo*. 3 vols. Bologna, 1959.

Trilling, Lionel. *The Opposing Self: Nine Essays in Criticism*. New York, 1955.

Trousson, Raymond. *Le Thème de Prométhée dans la littérature européenne*. 2 vols. Geneva, 1964.

Vico, Giambattista. *The New Science of Giambattista Vico*, trans. from 3rd ed., 1744, by Thomas Goddard Bergin and Max Harold Fisch. Ithaca, 1948.

Whitman, Cedric. *Homer and the Heroic Tradition*. Cambridge, Mass., 1958.

—————— *Sophocles: A Study of Heroic Humanism*. Cambridge, Mass., 1951.

Willey, Basil. *The Eighteenth Century Background: Studies on the Idea of Nature in the Thought of the Period*. London, 1941.

Winckelmann, Johann Joachim. *The History of Ancient Art*, trans. Henry Lodge. 2 vols. Boston, 1880.

Wind, Edgar. *Pagan Mysteries in the Renaissance*. New Haven, 1958.

Wolf, Friedrich August. *Prolegomena ad Homerum: sive de operum homericorum prisca et genuina forma variisque mutationibus et probabili rationi et emendandi*, ed. Immanuel Bekker. Berlin, 1876.

Young, Edward. *Conjectures on Original Composition (in a Letter to Richardson) 1859*, ed. Edith Morley. Manchester, 1918.

—————— *Young's Night Thoughts*, ed. Rev. George Gilfillan. Edinburgh, 1853.

Index

231